MW01094613

AN
ENEMY
HATH
DONE
THIS

EZRA TAFT BENSON

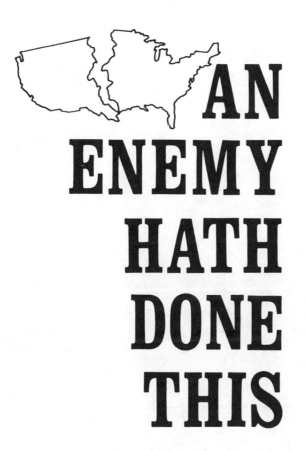

AN ENEMY HATH DONE THIS

by

EZRA TAFT BENSON

COMPILED BY

JERRELD L. NEWQUIST

PARLIAMENT PUBLISHERS
Salt Lake City, Utah
1969

. . . Sir, didst not thou sow good seed in thy field? from whence then hath it tares?

He said unto them, An enemy hath done this.

. . . .

—MATTHEW 13:27-28

"I apprehend no danger to our country from a foreign foe. . . . Our destruction, should it come at all, will be from another quarter. From the inattention of the people to the concerns of their government, from their carelessness and negligence, I must confess that I do apprehend some danger. I fear that they may place too implicit a confidence in their public servants, and fail properly to scrutinize their conduct; that in this way they may be made the dupes of designing men, and become the instruments of their own undoing. Make them intelligent, and they will be vigilant; give them the means of detecting the wrong, and they will apply the remedy." (Daniel Webster, June 1, 1837; *Works* 1:403)

FOREWORD

In this book the Honorable Ezra Taft Benson, former Secretary of Agriculture, forcefully and eloquently discusses the serious dangers which are threatening this nation, especially from within.

Mr. Benson emphasizes and warns against the grave perils that arise when government condones the breakdown of law and order, and he explains many of the forces which work against the proper functioning of law enforcement agencies and other proper responsibilities of the government of a free people.

One especially grievous commentary refers to a decline of U. S. morals and predicts the consequences of national complacence. It reads as follows:

"I do not believe that the greatest threat to our future is from bombs or guided missiles. I do not think our civilization will die that way. I think it will die when we no longer care — when the spiritual forces that make us wish to be right and noble die in the hearts of men, when we disregard the importance of law and order." (P. 6)

That explains and gives ample justification for the title of this most interesting and timely book, *An Enemy Hath Done This*. If we lose our freedom, if our nation is destroyed, it will be because of internal forces of fiscal irresponsibility, subversion, and lawlessness, rather than by conquest or assault from any enemy without. These internal forces are today challenging and weakening the vitality, stamina, and tenacity of our national will and resolve.

I believe there is in former Secretary Benson's commentary, contained in this book, an important message for every citizen in our nation, for we must remember that only by upholding and sustaining the moral principles upon which our Republic was founded can we expect our nation to remain strong and retain its position of world leadership. Unless we can preserve law and order and maintain a safe society, we cannot survive — our liberties will perish.

Another peril to our internal security lies in unsound and extravagant fiscal policies — the habit of deficit spending by the Federal Government. It is highly imperative for our future security and welfare that this nation return to and consistently pursue fiscal policies that are sound and sane. With regular annual programs of deficit spending, and with a continually unfavorable balance of payments that is shaking world confidence in the soundness of the dollar, our Government, in its fiscal policies, is traveling down a dangerous road — one that can easily lead to economic disaster.

I believe that Mr. Benson's book contains material which is both provocative and profound. I believe it should be read by every American citizen, and I hope that the central truth it conveys that Americans, by their lack of self-discipline, by their apathy and indifference, and by their lack of will and resolve can succeed in destroying America, is soon understood by all. The hour is growing late!

As I have written elsewhere, "I have a profound faith in America. I am confident that when the American people read from the record . . . and become fully cognizant of the extent of the crime and corruption which fester in our midst, they will demand action. . . . The principal and basic weapon that must be provided is a resurgence of old-fashioned morality in the nation. Apathy must go; it needs to be replaced by the outraged righteousness of a people who rose to greatness in this world through the spiritual values that their forefathers wrote into the Declaration of Independence and the Constitution of the United States. . . . We cannot, we must not, shirk our responsibility. . . . This challenge can be, and it must be, faced with resolute purpose and effort."[1]

John L. McClellan, United States Senator
Chairman, Government Operations Committee

---

[1]John L. McClellan, *Crime Without Punishment*, Popular Library Edition, 1963, pp. 7, 245-246.

INTRODUCTION

In his book, *Caesar and Christ*, Will Durant, in summarizing the causes of the destruction of the Roman Empire, stated: "A great civilization is not conquered from without until it has destroyed itself within. The essential causes of Rome's decline lay in her people, her morals, her class struggle, her failing trade, her bureaucratic despotism, her stifling taxes, her consuming wars. . . ."

This typifies an observation which has been made repeatedly by historians: There is a direct relationship between the moral decay of the people and the corruption and collapse of their government.

It is not true, of course, that a nation, upon finding itself on the road to national suicide, must plunge blindly on to the end. To avoid self-destruction, however, it is first necessary that the people recognize that extensive violation of moral law is the underlying cause of their approaching doom.

The first step is not easy, because it is extremely difficult for a people to discern moral truth who are not practitioners of moral truth. Fortunate indeed is that nation who, in its time of need, has men of national stature who possess that rare combination of incorruptible integrity, penetrating insight, and unflinching courage who will point the way. Such a man is Ezra Taft Benson, religious leader, writer, speaker and statesman, whose selfless devotion to the cause of freedom is known to millions.

In this book he draws from his long years of study, mature wisdom, and broad experience as he discusses and applies those principles of constitutional government which must be adhered to if individual liberty is to survive in the United States.

His position is clear: Government, whether state, local or national, is an agency for defending life, liberty and property and not a force for the redistribution of wealth or the conferring of economic favors.

There are those who seem to believe our Constitution is outmoded and who condemn a strict adherence to its principles. That position is untenable to the author of this book, who accepts without question the existence of inviolable moral law as the basis upon which our system of government rests. Man is as powerless to change moral law as he is to change physical law, and it is completely illogical to dilute eternal truth with error in the name of "moderation" or any other philosophy.

The Constitution originally granted to government the power to use force against the individual only for the purposes of defending the nation, punishing evil (crime), adjudicating and enforcing property rights, and compelling each citizen to bear his fair share of the burden of performing these functions. That is all!

The nature of these functions does not change and, therefore, as this book points out, it is a violation of the constitutional rights of the individual for government to tax him for any other purposes or to regiment him in his private and business affairs.

The message of this book is of the utmost importance, and if we the people fail to incorporate into the affairs of our government the principles of private morality which it teaches, we cannot hope to escape the fate of other nations who have gone to their destruction following the same path we are now taking.

Professor H. Verlan Andersen

Brigham Young University

PREFACE

When Ezra Taft Benson accepted the call in 1952 to serve as Secretary of Agriculture, he was assured that he would never be expected to support anything he didn't agree with. As was later reported, "His undeviating course . . . won from even his political critics an almost universal acclaim for his personal integrity and common sense so often lacking on the political scene."

On one occasion he was introduced by a prominent Senator from the opposing political party as a man who would go down in history as "one of our greatest Secretaries of Agriculture." From a leader of his own party came this declaration: "To my mind, the one American, above all others, who personifies our traditional spirit of initiative and personal incentive is Ezra Taft Benson . . . If there ever was a man who unfailingly put principles above partisan advantage or personal popularity, that man is Ezra Taft Benson."

As a true spokesman for liberty, he believes that "when a man stands for freedom he stands for God. And as long as he stands for freedom he stands with God. And were he to stand alone he would still stand with God. . . ."

He is a man who has never feared being controversial in defense of freedom and liberty. He believes — with Jefferson — that "He who fears criticism is hopeless. Only those who do things are criticized. To hesitate for fear of criticism is cowardly."

He has continued to speak out in opposition to the growth of the socialistic state and the evils of the godless international communist criminal conspiracy which "seeketh to overthrow the freedom of all lands, nations and countries . . . for it is built up by the devil, who is the father of all lies. . ." (Ether 8:25)

To those critics who have complained that a person who serves in a church capacity should not comment on such matters, Elder Benson's reply has been that "speaking out against immoral or unjust actions of political leaders has been the burden of prophets and disciples of God from time immemorial. It was for this very reason that many of them were persecuted. Some of them were stoned, some of them were burned, many were imprisoned. Nevertheless, it was their God-given task, as watchmen on the tower, to speak up." (Elder Benson is a member of the Council of the Twelve Apostles of The Church of Jesus Christ of Latter-day Saints.)

To those who have criticized him for defending unpopular patriotic organizations and individuals, his answer has been that he believed "it is always good strategy to stand up for the right, even when it is unpopular." He believes—with J. Edgar Hoover—that "In the battle for the life of our nation, to paraphrase one of our great presidents, we must look to those who enter the arena of active struggle; whose faces are stained by dust and sweat and blood; who strive valiantly to overcome temporary obstacles; who, supported by faith, enthusiasm and devotion, assault the enemy stronghold with the sword of patriotism." (June 16, 1959)

Because of the many requests from responsible individuals that he bring together some of his addresses and writings which have resulted from his vigorously raising a warning voice regarding the threatening dangers ahead, Elder Benson has authorized me to compile this material for publication. With his permission I have added appropriate footnotes taken from the writings of the founding fathers, as well as other prominent statesmen and economic thinkers and other authorities.

While Elder Benson is an apostle and one of the General Authorities of The Church of Jesus Christ of Latter-day Saints, neither the Church nor its leaders are in any way responsible for this book. The views expressed are those of Elder Benson, and he takes full responsibility for them. As he himself has written, "Obviously only one man, President David O. McKay, speaks for The Church of Jesus Christ of Latter-day Saints on matters of policy." (*Church News,* March 16, 1963)

The contents of the book are divided into three sections. Section I, "Stand Up For Freedom," and Section III, "Our

Immediate Responsibility," are made up from addresses given to various audiences throughout the land. Section II, "The Proper Role of Government," begins with an address by that title which discusses the principles involved in the proper role of government. In the other chapters application is made of those principles in discussions of various aspects of foreign and domestic policy.

The chapters originally given as addresses are so marked. The others were specially prepared for inclusion in this book and have not previously been presented in speech or writing. Certain repetitions of thought or expression which would not be usual in a work authored specifically as a book have been retained in this compilation in order to preserve an argument intact or to maintain flow and continuity in an individual chapter. Certain other features of style or format are likewise attributable to the nature of this work. In general, the italicizations express emphasis made by the compiler.

In the words of John Adams, "These are not the vapors of a melancholy mind, nor the effusions of envy, disappointed ambition, nor of a spirit of opposition to government, but the emanations of a heart that burns for its country's welfare. No one of any feeling, born and educated in this once happy country, can consider the numerous distresses, the gross indignities, the barbarous ignorance, the haughty usurpations, that we have reason to fear are meditating for ourselves, our children, our neighbors, in short, for all our countrymen and all their posterity, without the utmost agonies of heart and many tears." (*A Dissertation on the Canon and Feudal Law*)

The questions raised by the title of the book, *An Enemy Hath Done This,* will be made clear by the reader himself as he proceeds through the book. "Yes," recently wrote General Curtis E. LeMay, "America is in grave danger. . . . The point of no return is almost upon us. The danger is real. It is pressing." (*America Is In Danger*)

As compiler, I wish to express sincere appreciation: First, to Ezra Taft Benson for the privilege and opportunity which has been mine to work with him in the preparation of this compilation of his most timely messages. It is my conviction that he truly is one of the great patriots and sound political thinkers of this generation, as well as one of the most dedicated and inspirational spiritual leaders of his time.

Next, to John L. McClellan, United States Senator from Arkansas, Chairman of the Government Operations Committee, courageous leader in America's war on vice and crime, for his most appropriate Foreword.

To H. Verlan Andersen, Professor of Accounting at Brigham Young University, author of the excellent small book, *Many Are Called But Few Are Chosen,* for his timely Introduction.

And to Parliament Publishers, Salt Lake City, Utah, for the publication of this volume.

This constitutes the seventh volume authored by Ezra Taft Benson. His other volumes were *Farmers At The Crossroads* (Devin-Adair, 1956), *So Shall Ye Reap* (Deseret Book Co., 1960), *Freedom To Farm* (Doubleday, 1960), *The Red Carpet* (Bookcraft, 1962), *Crossfire: The Eight Years With Eisenhower* (Doubleday, 1962) and *Title of Liberty* (Deseret Book Co., 1964). Also, many excerpts from his speeches and writings were included in the compilation, *Prophets, Principles and National Survival* (Publishers Press, 1964), which is quoted from rather extensively in this present volume.

It is hoped that the words of this book will be read and contemplated by many Americans and other lovers of liberty, for — in the words of Elder Benson — "There is no excuse that can compensate for the loss of liberty." He could also add these words of the great General Douglas MacArthur:

"I do not stand here as advocate for any partisan cause, for the issues are fundamental and quite beyond the realm of partisan consideration. They must be resolved on the highest plane of national interest if our course is to prove sound and

our future protected. I trust, therefore, that you will do me
the justice of receiving that which I have to say as solely ex-
pressing the considered viewpoint of a fellow American. I
address you with neither rancor nor bitterness . . . with but
one purpose in mind — to serve my country." (*A Soldier
Speaks,* pp. 243-244)

Jerreld L. Newquist
Compiler

CONTENTS

SECTION III: OUR IMMEDIATE
RESPONSIBILITY

Section I

STAND UP FOR FREEDOM

"The honor and safety of our bleeding country, and every other motive that can influence the brave and heroic patriot, call loudly upon us, to acquit ourselves with spirit. In short, *we must now determine to be enslaved or free.* If we make freedom our choice, we must obtain it by the blessing of Heaven on our united and vigorous efforts." (George Washington, August 8, 1776; *Writings* 4:331)

CHAPTER I

AMERICANS ARE DESTROYING AMERICA[1]

"I tell you that freedom does not mean the freedom to exploit law in order to destroy it. It is not freedom which permits the Trojan Horse to be wheeled within the gates, and those within it to be heard in the name of tolerating a different point of view! He who is not for Rome and Roman law and Roman liberty is against Rome. He who espouses tyranny and oppression and the old despotisms is against Rome. He who plots against established authority and incites the populace to violence is against Rome. He cannot ride two horses at the same time; He cannot be for lawful ordinances and for an alien conspiracy at one and the same moment! One is a Roman or not a Roman!" (Cicero, 106-43 BC, quoted by Taylor Caldwell, *A Pillar of Iron*, p. 511)

We live in a time of crisis. *Never since the period of the Civil War has this nation faced such critical days. Americans are destroying America.*[2]

Members of The Church of Jesus Christ of Latter-day Saints—the Mormon Church—believe that:

. . . governments were instituted of God for the benefit of man; and that he holds men accountable for their acts in relation

---

[1]An address given on April 6, 1968, at the General Conference of The Church of Jesus Christ of Latter-day Saints, Salt Lake City, Utah. It was entered in the *Congressional Record* on April 22, 1968, pp. S4351-3, by Senator John L. McClellan of Arkansas. It was also printed in the May 29, 1968, issue of *Review of the News,* and was reprinted in pamphlet form by Americans For Constitutional Government.

[2]*"It is proper to take alarm at the first experiment on our liberties.* We hold this prudent jealousy to be the first duty of citizens, and one of the noblest characteristics of the late Revoluion. The freemen of America did not wait till usurped power had strengthened itself by exercise, and entangled the question in precedents. They saw all the consequences in the principle, and they avoided the consequences by denying the principle." (James Madison, "A Memorial and Remonstrance," 1785; *Works* 1:163)

to them, both in making laws and administering them, for the good and safety of society.

. . . that no government can exist in peace, except such laws are framed and held inviolate as will secure to each individual the free exercise of conscience, the right and control of property,[3] and the protection of life.

. . . that all governments necessarily require civil officers and magistrates to enforce the laws of the same; and that such as will administer the law in equity and justice should be sought for and upheld by the voice of the people.

. . . that all men are bound to sustain and uphold the respective governments in which they reside, while protected in their inherent and inalienable rights by the laws of such governments; and that *sedition and rebellion* are unbecoming every citizen thus protected, and *should be punished accordingly; . . .* (D&C 134:1-3, 5)

No people can maintain freedom unless their political institutions are founded upon faith in God and belief in the existence of moral law.[4] God has endowed men with certain unalienable rights and no legislature and no majority, however great, may morally limit or destroy these. *The function of government is to protect life, liberty and property and anything more or less than this is usurpation and oppression.*

The Constitution of the United States was prepared and adopted by courageous men acting under inspiration from the Almighty.[5] It is a solemn contract between the peoples of the states of this nation which all officers of government are under duty to obey. The eternal moral laws expressed therein must be adhered to or individual liberty will perish. It is the respon-

---

[3]"The moment the idea is admitted into society that property is not as sacred as the laws of God, and that there is not a force of law and public justice to protect it, anarchy and tyranny commence." (John Adams, *Works* 6:9)

[4]"True law is right reason in agreement with nature; it is of universal application, unchanging and everlasting; . . . It is a sin to try to alter this law, nor is it allowable to attempt to repeal any part of it, and it is impossible to abolish it entirely. We cannot be freed from its obligations by senate or people, and . . . one eternal and unchangeable law will be valid for all nations and all times, and there will be one master and ruler, that is God, over us all, for he is the author of this law, its promulgator, and its enforcing judge." (Cicero, *The Republic* III, 33)

[5]"I have always regarded that Constitution as the most remarkable work known to men in modern times to have been produced by the human intellect, at a single stroke (so to speak), in its application to political affairs." (William Gladstone, July 20, 1887; John Bartlett, *Familiar Quotations,* Eleventh Edition, p. 450)

sibility of government to punish crime and provide for the administration of justice and to protect the right and control of property.

But today these basic principles and concepts are being flaunted, disregarded and challenged, even by men in high places. Through the exercise of political expediency the government is condoning the breakdown of law and order.

Law enforcement in America is at the point of crisis. A recent Life Line broadcast warned that:

> In Chicago, 64 men quit the police force in one month. Baltimore has 360 police vacancies. Washington, D.C., is 230 men short of its authorized complement. And cities all over the country are desperately seeking recruits.
>
> Police aren't striking; they're quitting, and it is understandable. They're being demoralized by the hostile attitudes of the politically-minded Supreme Court. They're being demoralized by a weird penal system which frees hardened criminals almost as fast as they're arrested. . . . Policemen are demoralized by slanted news reporting, distorted facts which show police activities from the criminal's side. And they're being demoralized by an avalanche of new laws which are making it even harder to convict the guilty. San Diego Police Chief Wesley B. Sharp warns that "If there isn't a change, the increase in crime will lead to anarchy and criminals will control the nation." (*Life Line Freedom Talk* No. 53, February 22, 1968)

Edmund Burke, the great English statesman, explained that:

> Men are qualified for civil liberty in exact proportion to their disposition to put moral chains upon their own appetites, — in proportion as their love of justice is above their rapacity — in proportion as their soundness and sobriety and understanding is above their vanity and presumption — in proportion as they are more disposed to listen to the counsels of the wise and good, in preference to the flattery of knaves. Society cannot exist, unless a controlling power upon will and appetite be placed somewhere; and the less of it there is within, the more there must be without. *It is ordained in the eternal constitution of things, that men of intemperate minds cannot be free.* Their passions forge their fetters. (*Works* 4:51-2; *P.P.N.S.,*[6] p. 33)

---

[6]*Prophets, Principles and National Survival,* compiled by Jerreld L. Newquist. Publishers Press, Salt Lake City, Utah.

I do not believe the greatest threat to our future is from bombs or guided missiles. I do not think our civilization will die that way. I think it will die when we no longer care — when the spiritual forces that make us wish to be right and noble die in the hearts of men, when we disregard the importance of law and order.[7]

If American freedom is lost — if America is destroyed — if our blood-bought freedom is surrendered — it will be because of Americans. What's more, it will probably not be only the work of subversive and criminal Americans. The Benedict Arnolds will not be the only ones to forfeit our freedom.

"At what point then is the approach of danger to be expected?" asked Abraham Lincoln, and answered, "If it ever reaches us, it must spring up amongst us. It cannot come from abroad. If destruction be our lot, we must ourselves be its author and finisher. As a nation of freemen we must live through all time, or die by suicide." (Springfield, Ill., January 27, 1838; *P.P.N.S.*, p. 62)

If America is destroyed, it may be by Americans who salute the flag, sing the national anthem, march in patriotic parades, cheer Fourth of July speakers — normally good Americans, but Americans who fail to comprehend what is required to keep our country strong and free, Americans who have been lulled away into a false security.

Great nations are never conquered from outside unless they are rotten inside. Our greatest national problem today is erosion, not the erosion of the soil but erosion of the national morality — erosion of traditional enforcement of law and order.

Theodore Roosevelt said: "The things that will destroy America are prosperity-at-any-price, peace-at-any-price, safety-first instead of duty-first, the love of soft living and the get-rich-quick theory of life." (Ezra Taft Benson, *The Red Carpet,* p. 315)

---

[7]"Liberty lies in the hearts of men and women; when it dies there, no constitution, no law, no court can save it. No constitution, no law, no court can do much to help it." (Judge Learned Hand, quoted in *The Instructor,* 1962, p. 303)

In this blessed land we have exalted security, comfort and ease above freedom. If we dwelled at length on the many things that are disturbing in the life of America today, we might well become discouraged. I mention only a few of the reported startling evidences of national illness — our moral erosion.

—There is a decline of U.S. morals and moral fibre, a turning to pleasure and away from hard work and high standards of the past.

—There is a growing worry in our universities over cheating in examinations.

—Nation-wide juvenile delinquencies show an eight-fold increase since 1950.

—There is a 500-million dollar smut industry in this country causing youngsters to wrestle with standards of value.

—America is the biggest market for narcotics.

—Although we consider ourselves a people who believe in law and order, we have seen much evidence of the passion of the mob.

—Riots have occurred in 137 different cities and towns in 33 months resulting in 120 deaths, including 12 police officers slain; 3,623 other persons injured; 28,932 arrested and hundreds of millions of dollars property damage.

—Crime in U.S. is up 88 per cent in seven years — rising nearly nine times faster than population — up 16 per cent per year according to the FBI. Crime costs some $20 billion a year and less than 21 per cent of reported crimes result in arrests and less than one-third of those in convictions.

—In the midst of a cold war and preparation for a possible shooting war of survival, we have faced 651 strikes at missile bases in six years.

—The U.S. Government has racked up a shameful record of 31 Treasury deficits in the past 35 years.

—The sky-rocketing cost of the welfare state increased in eight years from 6.9 billion to 20.3 billion dollars in 1961 and stood at 87 billion 578 million in 1966.

—There are over 7,700,000 on relief in federal, state, and local programs.

—During the past 33 years our budget has increased 20 times over, and our national debt has increased from $16 billion to an admitted $324 billion. Adding accrued liabilities payable in the future our real indebtedness exceeds $1 trillion, or an average indebtedness of $5,200 for every man, woman and child in the United States.

—Our present federal debt is equal to a first mortgage of $10,000 on all owned homes in the country and is reported to exceed the combined debt of all countries of the world. Annual interest on the soaring national debt is over $15 billion — only defense and welfare expenditures are higher.

—American currencies are weaker than those of Germany and Japan who were defeated in World War II.

—Inflation has struck a serious blow to the value of the American dollar.

—We continue to move in the direction of more federal intervention, more concentration of power, more spending, more taxing, more paternalism, more state-ism. (*U.S. News and World Report,* February 5, 1968; An Address by Dr. Ernest L. Wilkinson, BYU, April 21, 1966; *Whither America,* Senator Everett Dirksen, December 15, 1967; Dr. James C. Dolley, University of Texas).

The present shocking situation was summed up succinctly by J. Edgar Hoover in the April 1967 *F.B.I. Law Enforcement Bulletin* in these words:

> Morality, integrity, *law and order,* and other cherished principles of our great heritage are battling for survival in many communities today. They are under constant attack from degrading and corrupting influences which, if not halted, will sweep away every vestige of decency and order remaining in our society.

A recent issue of the well-known and highly respected, *Babson's Washington Forecast Letter,* carried a four-page Special Supplement which concluded as follows:

Whom are we to indict for sparking this chaos in America? Are the prime defendants the Stokely Carmichaels, the H. Rapp Browns, the hippies, the draft-card burners, the peaceniks, the juvenile delinquents, the rabble rousers, the Commies who have gained respectability as 'honest dissenters'? Certainly, most of these could be brought before the bar of justice to answer charges of law violations . . . and they should be.

However, there is a stronger, truer bill of indictment which may be drawn against those who have invited the bloody blackmail of America by permitting, even encouraging, mounting civil disobedience. . . .

And then the article names men of national prominence and continues,

These men of power, prestige, and great influence in the political structure of America have permitted the concept of "freedom of speech" to be expanded to include subversion, intimidation, sedition, and incitement to riot; they have condoned the distortion of "academic freedom" to encompass the adulteration of young minds with Communist doctrine and the disintegration of a well-disciplined educational system; they have allowed "freedom of assembly" to mushroom into disruption of peaceful activity, mob rule, riot and insurrection.

Unless those in authority in the United States can be influenced to abandon the suicidal course on which they have embarked — or unless they can be replaced by men who will — we cannot hope to restore in our nation the kind of domestic peace and order which has made our many generations proud to be Americans . . . living in a land of freedom, security, opportunity, and justice under law.

The crisis we now face is the most serious, the most dangerous, in the history of our country. Each of us must diligently employ our influence and our effort — in speech, letters, and at the ballot box — to help set straight the way.

The facts are clear. *Our problem centers in Washington, D.C.* And this applies to the administration of both political parties. In the words of James Madison, "Since the general civilization of mankind, I believe there are more instances of the abridgement of freedom of the people by gradual and silent encroachments of those in power, than by violent and sudden usurpations." (*Elliot's Debates* 3:87; *P.P.N.S.*, p. 104)

If America is to withstand these influences and trends, there must be a renewal of the spirit of our forefathers, an appreciation of the American way of life, a strengthening of muscle and sinew and the character of the nation. *America needs guts as well as guns. National character is the core of national defense.*

Could many of our ills today have resulted from our failure to train a strong citizenry from the only source we have — the boys and girls of each community? Have they grown up to believe in . . .

> Politics without principle
>
> Pleasure without conscience
>
> Knowledge without effort
>
> Wealth without work
>
> Business without morality
>
> Science without humanity
>
> Worship without sacrifice

In recent months a nationwide survey of high school and college students has been conducted. The U.S. Junior Chamber of Commerce reveals that:

> —41 percent believe that freedom of the press should be canceled.
>
> —53 percent believe in government ownership of banks, railroads, and steel companies.
>
> —62 percent said that the government had the responsibility to provide jobs.
>
> —62 percent thought a worker should not produce all that he can.
>
> —61 percent rejected the profit incentive as necessary to the survival of free enterprise.
>
> —84 percent denied that patriotism is vital and plays an important part in our lives. (*Bookmailer News,* Vol. 10, November 1, 1965)

Letters which come to my desk from worried parents, deeply concerned by what is being taught to their children in the schools, are shocking to say the least.

We can never survive unless our young people understand and appreciate our American system which has given more of the good things of life than any other system in the world — unless they have a dedication that exceeds the dedication of the enemy. Character must become important in this country again. The old essentials of honesty, self-respect, loyalty, support for law and order, *must* be taught the younger generation.[8]

I appeal to people everywhere, young and old, to heed these words of Dean Alfange:

> I do not choose to be a common man. It is my right to be uncommon. I seek opportunity to develop whatever talents God gave me — not security. I do not wish to be a kept citizen, humbled and dulled by having the state look after me. I want to take the calculated risk; to dream and to build, to fail and to succeed. I refuse to barter incentive for a dole. I prefer the challenges of life to the guaranteed existence; the thrill of fulfillment to the stale calm of utopia. I will not trade freedom for beneficence nor my dignity for a handout. I will never cower before any earthly master nor bend to any threat. It is my heritage to stand erect, proud and unafraid; to think and act myself, enjoy the benefit of my creations and to face the world boldly and say— "This, with God's help, I have done." All this is what it means to be an American.

Those of us conscious of the seriousness of the situation must act and act now. It has been said that it takes something spectacular to get folks excited, like a burning house. NOBODY NOTICES ONE THAT IS SIMPLY DECAYING. But, in America today we not only have decaying but burning before our very eyes. How much we need hearts today who

[8]"Let every American, every lover of liberty, every well wisher to his posterity, swear by the blood of the Revolution, never to violate in the least particular, the laws of the country; and never to tolerate their violation by others. . . . Let reverence for the laws, be breathed by every American mother, to the lisping babe, that prattles on her lap—let it be taught in schools, in seminaries, and in colleges; —let it be preached from the pulpit, proclaimed in legislative halls, and enforced in courts of justice. And, in short, let it become the *political religion* of the nation. . . ." (Abraham Lincoln, January 27, 1838; *Collected Works* 1:112)

will respond to the inspiring words of the poet, John Green-
leaf Whittier:

>Where's the manly spirit
>Of the true-hearted and the unshackled gone?
>Sons of old freemen, do we but inherit their names alone?
>Is the old Pilgrim spirit quench'd within us?
>Stoops the proud manhood of our souls so low,
>That Mammon's lure or Party's wile can win us to
>   silence new?
>Now, when our land to ruin's brink is verging,
>In God's name let us speak while there is time;
>Now, when the padlocks for our lips is forging,
>Silence is a Crime. (*The Freeman*, July 1967, p. 413)

*Our priceless heritage is threatened today as never be-
fore in our lifetime* — from without by the forces of godless
communism and at home by our complacency and by the insidious forces of the socialist-communist conspiracy with the
help of those who would abandon the ancient landmarks set
by our fathers, and take us down the road to destruction. It
was Alexander Hamilton who warned that: "Nothing is more
common than for a free people, in times of heat and violence,
to gratify momentary passions, by letting into the government,
principles and precedents which afterwards prove fatal to themselves. (*Alexander Hamilton and the Founding of the Nation*,
p. 462; *P.P.N.S.*, p. 21)

Serious and concerned citizens everywhere are asking,
"Can we cope with these threatening realities?" Yes, we can. If
we would allow the local police to do their job, they could
handle the rioting and looting. *Yes, we can,* if we have the
courage and the wisdom to return to the basic concepts, to recall the spirit of the founding fathers and accept wholeheartedly these words of Thomas Paine whose writings helped so
much to stir people to action during the days of the American
Revolution, when he said:

>*These are the times that try men's souls.* The summer soldier
>and the sunshine patriot will in this crisis, shrink from the service
>of his country; but he that stands it NOW, deserves the love and
>thanks of man and woman. Tyranny, like hell, is not easily
>conquered; yet we have this consolation with us, that the harder

the conflict, the more glorious the triumph. What we obtain too cheap, we esteem too lightly; 'tis dearness only that gives everything its value. Heaven knows how to put a proper price upon its goods; and it would be strange indeed, if so celestial an article as FREEDOM should not be highly rated. (*The Political Works of Thomas Paine,* p. 55)

As American citizens who love freedom, we must return to a respect for national morality — respect for law and order. There is no other way of safety for us and our posterity. The hour is late, the time is short. We must begin now, in earnest, and invite God's blessings on our efforts.[9]

The United States should be a bastion of real freedom. We should not support the world's greatest evil, the Godless, socialist-communist conspiracy that seeks to destroy all we hold dear as a great Christian nation and to promote insidiously the breakdown of law and order and the erosion of our morality.

With God's help we must return to those basic concepts, those eternal verities, the rule of law and order upon which this nation was established[10] With an aroused citizenry and the help of Almighty God it can be accomplished. God grant it may be so, I humbly pray.

---

[9]"In this day of gathering storm, as the moral deterioration of political power spreads its growing infection, it is essential that every spiritual force be mobilized to defend and preserve the religious base upon which this nation was founded. For it is that base which has been the motivating impulse to our moral and national growth. History fails to record a single precedent in which nations subject to moral decay have not passed into political and economic decline. There has been either a spiritual reawakening to overcome the moral lapse, or a progressive deterioration leading to ultimate national disaster." (General Douglas MacArthur, December 12, 1951; *A Soldier Speaks*, pp. 285-286)

[10]" . . . Law is not a product of human thought, nor is it any enactment of peoples, but something eternal which rules the whole universe by its wisdom in command and prohibition. . . . Law is the primal and ultimate mind of God, whose reason directs all things. . . . " (Cicero, *Laws* II, 8)

CHAPTER 2

THE THREAT TO OUR FREEDOM[1]

"Freedom is the natural condition of the human race, in which the Almighty intended men to live. Those who fight the purposes of the Almighty will not succeed. They always have been, they always will be, beaten." (Abraham Lincoln, quoted by Lucius E. Chittenden, *Recollections of President Lincoln and His Administration,* p. 76)

Humbly and gratefully I stand before you today. This is a signal honor, a very great pleasure and a challenging responsibility.

I do not pose as an authority on the German economy. I have been here too often and too long to be an authority. An American authority on Germany is one who has just returned from a three-day visit — his first.

I came here first in December 1923. On that visit, my first German breakfast cost me six billion marks — then about fifteen cents in American money.

I was here for a year as a church official in 1946 on an emergency relief mission, distributing food, clothing, bedding, etc., to a nation flat on its back economically from long years of war.

During the period 1953 to 1961 I came here several times as a government official — U. S. Minister of Agriculture — to consult with government, business, industry, and farm leaders in the interest of the expansion of world trade.

This time I came here with my wife and youngest child, New Year's Day 1964, to live for an indefinite period to direct the work of The Church of Jesus Christ of Latter-day Saints

[1]An address given on May 12, 1964, at a luncheon of the American Chamber of Commerce in Germany at the Hotel Frankfurter Hof, Frankfurt, Germany.

(Mormon), in seven nations, with headquarters in this great city of Frankfurt, in a nation and with a people I love.

We are very happy here, and most grateful for the warm hospitality and friendship of people throughout the German Republic and other parts of northern Europe.

No, I will not talk about the German economy. I would like to talk about it if I felt more competent. As a trained economist and ex-government official I find much to praise.

I am not here to tickle your ears — to entertain you. I will talk to you frankly and honestly as one who loves his country. The message I bring is not a happy one, but it is the truth, and time is always on the side of truth. A great German once said, "Truth must be repeated again and again because error is constantly being preached round about us." (Goethe, 1749-1832, quoted in *The Freeman,* July, 1958)

Ralph Waldo Emerson said that every mind must make a choice between truth and repose.[2]

I speak to you today as a fellow citizen of the United States of America, deeply concerned with the welfare of our beloved country.

George Washington stated, "Truth will ultimately prevail, where there are pains taken to bring it to light."

Lincoln said, "If danger ever reaches us it must spring up amongst us. It cannot come from abroad. If destruction be our lot, we must ourselves be its author and finisher. As a nation of freemen, we must live through all time, or die by suicide." (January 27, 1838)

Today we are in the midst of continuing international crisis. The outlook for world peace and security is dark indeed.

---

[2]"God offers to every mind its choice between truth and repose. Take which you please,—you can never have both. Between these, as a pendulum, man oscillates. He in whom the love of repose predominates will accept the first creed, the first philosophy, the first political party he meets,—most likely his father's. He gets rest, commodity and reputation; but he shuts the door of truth. He in whom the love of truth predominates will . . . abstain from dogmatism, and recognize all the opposite negations between which, as walls, his being is swung. He submits to the inconvenience of suspense and imperfect opinion, but he is a candidate for truth, as the other is not, and respects the highest law of his being." (Ralph Waldo Emerson, Essay on *Intellect*)

The gravity of the world situation is increasing almost daily. The United Nations is unable to settle the troubles of the world. In truth we are faced with the hard fact that the United Nations seems to have largely failed in its efforts.[3]

The days ahead are sobering and challenging.

All over the world the light of freedom is being diminished. Across whole continents of the earth freedom is being totally obliterated. Never in recorded history has any movement spread itself so far and so fast as has socialistic-communism in the past few years. In less than half a century this evil system has gained control over one-third of mankind, and it is steadily pursuing its vicious goal of control over all the rest of the world. Since World War II, people have been brought under the communist yoke at the rate of 6,000 per hour, 144,000 per day, 52,000,000 per year.

Again I say, never in recorded history has any movement spread its power so far and so fast as has socialistic-communism in the last three decades. The facts are not pleasant to review. Communist leaders are jubilant with their success. They are driving freedom back on almost every front.

It is time, therefore, that every American become alerted and informed about the aims, tactics, and schemes of the world-wide conspiracy.

The fight against the godless conspiracy is a very real part of every man's duty. It is the fight against slavery, immorality, atheism, terrorism, cruelty, barbarism, deceit, and the destruction of human life through a kind of tyranny unsurpassed by anything in human history. Here is a struggle against the evil, satanical priestcraft of Lucifer.

Yes, the days ahead are sobering and challenging.

A few years ago a beloved spiritual leader delivered an inspiring prayer at the dedication of a temple near London, England. I quote a short paragraph from that memorable prayer by President David O. McKay:

> Next to life, we express gratitude for the gift of free agency. When thou didst create man, thou placed within him part of thine

---
[3]See chapter on the United Nations.

Omnipotence and bade him choose for himself. Liberty and conscience thus became a sacred part of human nature. Freedom not only to think, but to speak and act, is a God-given privilege.

Our heritage of freedom is as precious as life itself. It is truly a God-given gift to man. We are moral agents with freedom to choose between right and wrong.

Past material advances have been the fruit of our freedom — our free enterprise capitalistic system, our American way of life, our God-given freedom of choice. Progress of the future must stem from this same basic freedom.

Because our forefathers — yours and mine — fought for the ideal of freedom, because our fathers preserved that ideal through our free competitive enterprise system under our God-given free agency, because they were willing to make religion the vital force of daily living, all of us have climbed through the years to new heights of well-being and inner strengths.

But it is not only in the moral choice of right and wrong that man is free. Among the relentless quests of human history is the quest for political freedom. When the American patriot, Patrick Henry, shouted his immortal "Give me liberty or give me death," he did not speak idly. When at Philadelphia in 1776, the signers of the Declaration of Independence affixed their signatures to that sacred document, they, in a very real sense, were choosing liberty or death. Not one of them but knew full well that if the Revolution failed, if the fight for freedom should come to naught, they would be branded as rebels and hanged as traitors.

The inspired founding fathers formulated a system of government with checks and balances protecting the freedom of the people. But even this was not enough. The first order of the new congress was to draw up a Bill of Rights — ten amendments guaranteeing for all time the fundamental freedoms that the American people insist are theirs by the will of God, not by the will of government.

Yes, the founders of our country bequeathed to us a heritage of freedom and unity that is our most priceless political possession.

But to be enjoyed, freedom must be won continually. The major responsibility of government is to guard the lives and safeguard the freedom of its citizens. Yet even in the operation of government — especially big government — there are real dangers to our freedom.

Today the scope and variety of governmental operations have become amazingly wide. We are touched by government from before we are born until after we die. Government impinges on our lives every hour of the day and night.

Yet, while most of these governmental activities appear helpful in greater or lesser degree, we must face the central problem of just how much of our lives, of our freedom, of our economy, and of our society, we want to entrust to government. And we must face the further fact of just what division of functions we in the U.S. want to make between Washington and our state capitals. We must be aware of the price we pay when we place more and more of our lives in the hands of centralized government. We must realize what this trend, what these changes toward centralized power in government are doing to our free institutions.

Is there, indeed, any characteristic of the American people which is more abiding than a distaste for being run from Washington? Woodrow Wilson said: *"The history of liberty is a history of the limitations of governmental power, not the increase of it."* (May 9, 1912)

Before we embark on such programs of federal aid for an ever-widening range of social and economic services — assuming the services are needed and wanted — we should ask ourselves these questions:

1. Can the federal government perform these services more efficiently than private enterprise, or states, or local communities?

2. What would be the effect on our free institutions?

3. What would be the effect on the morale and character of our people? The supreme test of any policy is this: How will it effect the morale and character of the people?

If the honest and carefully considered answers to these questions point to the launching of federal programs, then these programs can be of great service.

If, however, these proposed programs contemplate a high degree of federal financing and decision-making; if they spring from collectivist thinking; if they expose themselves to partisan politics; if they weaken the morale and character of our people — then, on the basis of the record, their prospects are not good.

The historian Glover of Oxford University makes this cryptic comment: "It is better for the development of character and contentment to do certain things badly yourself than to have them done better for you by someone else."

It is high time we awakened to the dangers of excessive government in business, in education, in agriculture, and other segments of our economy. It is time we realized the perils of too great a centralization of power, and too much dependence on public agencies. We must stand up and be counted. I agree with Tom Anderson:

> As American businessmen you must stand up and be counted — else you'll be counted out. . . . *The middle of the road between the extremes of good and evil is evil.* When freedom is at stake, your silence is not golden, it's yellow. . . . Why change the American system which produced the greatest freedom for the greatest number of people in human history, along with the world's highest standard of living, for socialism. . . . Under any name Socialism has been a miserable failure for 1,000 years. . . . A government big enough to give you everything you want is big enough to take everything you've got.

We must not forget that nations may — and usually do — sow the seeds of their own destruction while enjoying unprecedented prosperity.

The socialistic-communist conspiracy to weaken the United States involves attacks on many fronts. To weaken the American free-enterprise economy which outproduced both its enemies and allies during World War II is a high-priority target of the communist leaders. Their press and other propaganda media are therefore constantly selling the principles of centralized or federal control of farms, railroads, electric power, schools, steel, maritime shipping, and many other aspects of the economy — but always in the name of public welfare.

Senator Strom Thurmond, one of the few patriot-statesmen in the U.S. Senate today — our more liberal body — sent me this personal statement May 8, 1964, which offers some hope:

> . . . People need to be reminded that most human beings labor for an incentive — usually either to gain a reward or to avoid the stick of punishment. Where the carrot of profit or gain is removed, then the stick of punishment for failure to produce must be applied to avoid economic collapse and starvation.
>
> Capitalism, or the free enterprise system, is in essence economic liberty, and it goes hand in hand with political liberty. It rests on the basic idea of human rights in property, for where there are no human rights to own property, then there are no other human rights and freedoms. Take away a man's right to own property and you take away his right to be independent, substituting serfdom in place of freedom. As former Supreme Court Justice Whittaker recently pointed out: "Private property rights are the soil in which our concepts of human rights grow and mature."
>
> Today, human rights in property are being restricted and threatened as never before. Much of this is being done in the name of "social justice" and "civil rights." What it all adds up to, however, is an attempt to level all men by government regulation and rule. This is so-called economic equality, better known as socialism. Socialism can be brought about by government regulation, taxation, and control of property almost as effectively as by outright state ownership of the means of production and distribution.
>
> The American capitalist system is superior by far to any economic system the world has ever known. Not only has it provided our people with a much higher level of production and wealth, but it also has provided a better distribution of all that has been produced so that more people enjoy more of our abundance than under any other system, including socialism and its blood brother, communism.
>
> This is evident by the much higher standard of living available to all Americans as opposed to any other people, especially those behind the Iron, Bamboo, and Cactus Curtains, where socialism prevails. . . .

We have seen in the past quarter century a tremendous shift from individual to governmental responsibility in many phases of economic and social life. We have seen a rapid shift of responsibility from the states to the federal government.

The magnitude of these changes is revealed by a few simple figures. Twenty-five years ago the federal government received one-fourth of all the taxes collected in the United States. Today, the federal government — in spite of the biggest tax cut in history of $5,400,000,000 (1.4 percent) in 1954 — collects not one-fourth, but 68 percent of all our taxes. Twenty-five years ago all taxes, federal, state and local, took 14 percent of our national income. Today, taxes take over 35 percent. Since 1932 federal spending has increased from around $4.7 billion to $98.8 billion a year — an increase of 2100 percent — and is still rising. (Byrd)

Our national debt has increased from $22 billion to over $315 billion. If to this be added the cost of goods already received and cost of services already rendered to the government (such as pensions), the federal debt now exceeds a trillion dollars, or $5300 for every man, woman and child in the United States.

The indebtedness of our country exceeds the combined indebtedness of all other countries.

The 1964 dollar is worth less than 40 cents compared to what it was in 1932 (Wilkinson).

Fighting first a prolonged depression and then a devastating war was used as an excuse to shift undue responsibility to the federal government. The shrinking of time and distance and the growing interdependence of our economic lives have been used as a guise to centralize more authority at the national capital. This has in it real danger.

Yet, deep in their hearts, the American people instinctively know that great concentration of power is an evil and a dangerous thing. They do not need to have it proved.

What lies behind this conviction? Basically, it is an intuitive knowledge that, sooner or later, the accumulation of power in a central government leads to a loss of freedom. Once power is concentrated, even for helpful purposes, it is all there, in one package, where it can be grabbed by those who may not be helpful in its use.

If power is diffused, this cannot happen. This is why the founders of our country carefully divided power between the state and federal levels. Nothing has happened in the meantime to call in question the validity of this arrangement.

Our traditional federal-state relationship, we must never forget, starts with a general presumption in favor of state and individual rights. Under the constitutional concept, powers not granted to the federal government are reserved to the states or to the people.

The framers of our Constitution knew that many forces work toward the concentration of power at the federal level. They knew it somehow seems easier to impose so-called "progress" on localities than to wait for them to bring it about themselves. Raids on the federal treasury can be all too rapidly accomplished by an organized few over the feeble protests of an apathetic majority. With more and more activity centered in the federal government, the relationship between the costs and the benefits of government programs becomes obscure. What follows is the voting of public money without having to accept direct local responsibility for higher taxes.

I know of no device of government which will lead more quickly to an increase in the number of federal programs than this. If this trend continues, the states may be left hollow shells, operating primarily as the field districts of federal departments and dependent upon the federal treasury for their support. . . .

The history of all mankind shows very clearly that if we would be free — and if we would stay free — we must stand eternal watch against the accumulation of too much power in government.[4]

---

[4]"When we resist . . . concentration of power, we are resisting the powers of death, because *concentration of power is what always precedes the destruction of human liberties.*" (Woodrow Wilson, May 9, 1912; George Saldes, *The Great Quotations,* Pocket Book Edition, p. 603)

There is hardly a single instance in all of history where the dictatorial centralization of power has been compatible with individual freedom — where it has not reduced the citizenry to the status of pawns and mere creatures of the state. God forbid that this should happen in America. Yet I am persuaded that the continuation of the trend of the past thirty years could make us pallbearers at the burial of the states as effective units of government.

The drift toward centralization of power is not inevitable. It can be slowed down, halted, reversed.

How? By state and local governments insisting that theirs is the responsibility for problems that are essentially local and state problems — insisting upon this, with the knowledge that responsibility and authority go hand in hand.

Inevitably, in centralized federal programs the money is not as wisely spent as if the states participated financially.

The people come to look to the federal government as the provider, at no cost to them, of whatever is needful.

The truth is that the federal government has no funds which it does not first, in some manner, take from the people. A dollar cannot make the round trip to Washington and back without shrinking in the process. As taxpayers we need to recognize these facts; programs which obscure them are contrary to the public interest.

The thought that the federal government is wealthy and the states poverty-stricken is a dangerous illusion. The federal debt in the United States is now sixteen times as great as the combined debt of the fifty states. It it difficult for the states to make a strong case for assistance from the federal government when anything the federal government spends must come from the states.

The states not only have rights, they also have responsibilities, and they have opportunities.

In the last analysis, we are not trying to protect one government entity from another. We are trying to protect the rights of individual people. If we ever forget this, the whole process of government is pointless.

George Washington said: "Government is not reason, it is not eloquence — it is force! Like fire, it is a dangerous servant and a fearful master!" "It is hardly lack of due process," said the Supreme Court, "for the government to regulate that which it subsidizes." We must ever remember that a planned and subsidized economy weakens initiative, discourages industry, destroys character, and demoralizes the people.

Our people must remain free. Our economy must remain free — free of excessive government paternalism, regimentation and control.

As a nation we are strong. With the freedom of economic enterprise that we possess, we are able to produce as much industrial goods as all the rest of the world combined — even though we are only seven percent of the world's people and possess only six percent of the world's land.

These abundant blessings have come to us through an economic system which rests largely on three pillars:

1. Free enterprise . . . the right to venture . . . the right to choose.
2. Private property . . . the right to own.
3. A market economy . . . the right to exchange.

Working together, we can maintain the strength of these pillars.

There are some in the U.S., nevertheless, who decry free enterprise, who would place business, agriculture, and labor in a government strait jacket.

Our economic order is not perfect, because it is operated by imperfect human beings, but it has given us more of the good things of life than any other system. The fundamental reason is that our economy is free. It must remain free. In that freedom ultimately lies our basic economic strength.

Let us admit the weaknesses that exist. Let us work aggressively to correct them. But never let us make the catastrophic blunder of putting chains on our basic economic freedom.

Yes, our phenomenal material advances have been the fruit of our freedom — our free enterprise capitalistic system, our American way of life, our God-given freedom of choice.

The progress of the future must stem from this same basic freedom.

Yet, these basic American beliefs, principles, and attitudes are threatened today as never before.

By whom are they threatened? These basic concepts are threatened by three groups:

1. *They are threatened by well-meaning but uninformed people who see the shortcomings of our economic system and believe they can legislate them out of existence.* They try to reach the promised land by passing laws. They do not understand our economic system and its limitations. They would load it down with burdens it was never intended to carry. As their schemes begin to break down, more and more controls must be supplied. Patch is placed upon patch, regulation is added to regulation and ultimately, by degree, freedom is lost — without our desiring to lose it and without our knowing why or how it was lost.

2. *Our heritage of freedom is threatened by another group — self-seeking men who see in government legislation a way to obtain special privileges for themselves or to restrain their competitors.* They use demagoguery as a smokescreen to deceive. These people have no love for freedom or enterprise. They would bargain away their birthright for a mess of pottage. They would learn the value of freedom only after it was gone.

3. *A third, still much smaller group is dedicated to the overthrow of the economic and social system that is our tradition.* Their philosophy does not stem from Jefferson, but is foreign to our shores. It is a total philosophy of life, atheistic, and utterly opposed to all that we hold dear as a great Christian nation. These men understand our system thoroughly — and they hate it thoroughly. They enlist innocent but willing followers from the uninformed and the unprincipled. Through rabble-rousing and demagoguery they play upon the economic reverses and hardships of the unsuspecting. They promise the impossible, and call black white, and mislead with fallacies masqueraded as truth.

If we lose our freedom, it will be to this strange and unlike coalition of the well-intentioned, the slothful, and the subversives.

It will be because we did not care enough — because we were not alert enough — because we were too apathetic to take note while the precious waters of our God-given freedom slipped — drop by drop — down the drain.

Heaven forbid that this should come to pass!

Let us remember that we are a prosperous people today because of a free enterprise system founded on spiritual, not material values alone. It is founded on freedom of choice — free agency — an eternal God-given principle.

The founding fathers, inspired though they were, did not invent the priceless blessing of individual freedom and respect for the dignity of man. No, that priceless gift to mankind sprang from the God of heaven and not from government. Yes, the founding fathers welded together the safeguards as best they could, but freedom must be continually won to be enjoyed. We must never forget these facts.

America has been called the land of opportunity — a land choice above all other lands! Let us keep it so!

We, in the choice land of America, as Theodore Roosevelt said a half century ago, "hold in our hands the hope of the world, the fate of the coming years, and shame and disgrace will be ours if in our eyes the light of high resolve is dimmed, if we trail in the dust the golden hopes of men."

With God's help the light of high resolve in the eyes of the American people must never be dimmed! Our freedom must — and will — be preserved.

My own political and economic creed is a simple one. I commend it to you:

I am for freedom and against slavery.

I am for social progress and against socialism.

I am for a dynamic economy and against waste.

I am for the private competitive market and against unnecessary government intervention.

I am for private ownership and against governmental ownership and control of the means of production and distribution.

I am for national security and against appeasement and capitulation to an obvious enemy.

> Today, as never before (says J. Edgar Hoover), America has need for men and women who possess the moral strength and courage of our fore-fathers — modern day patriots, with pride in our country and faith in freedom, unafraid to declare to anyone in the world, "I believe in liberty. I believe in justice. I will fight, if need be, to defend the dignity of man."
>
> Too often in recent years, patriotic symbols have been shunted aside. Our national heroes have been maligned, our history distorted. Has it become a disgrace to pledge allegiance to our flag — or to sign a loyalty oath, or pay tribute to our national anthem? Is it shameful to encourage our children to memorize the stirring words of the men of '76? Is it becoming opprobrious to state "In God we trust" when proclaiming our love of country?
>
> What we desperately need today is patriotism founded on a real understanding of the American ideal — a dedicated belief in our principles of freedom, and a determination to perpetuate America's heritage. (Feb. 22, 1962)

This contest in which we are engaged is as old as man and as young as hope. This issue is over the God-given eternal principle of freedom — free agency, the right of choice. In this struggle it is not enough to be right — we must put strength and action back of that which is right.

In the conflict with socialistic-communism we must have patience, courage and wisdom. We must also have friends. Russia has hostages; we have friends — millions of them in temporary slavery back of the iron curtain, and millions more to be mobilized throughout the free world. In Russia people are unable to challenge the despotic Godless dogmas forced on the people. We must take greater risks for freedom. We must dramatize "American might and Soviet myth."

Yes . . . America is a choice land — choice above all others. Blessed by the Almighty, our forebears have made and kept it so. It will continue to be a land of freedom and liberty so long as we are able to advance in the light of sound and enduring principles of right. To sacrifice such principles for momentary expediency — often selfishly motivated — is to endanger our noble heritage and is unworthy of our great American people.

With all my heart I love our great nation. I have lived and traveled abroad just enough to make me appreciate rather fully what we have in America. To me the U.S. is not just another nation. It is not just one of a family of nations. The U.S. is a nation with a great mission to perform for the benefit and blessing of liberty-loving people everywhere.[5] It is my firm conviction that the Constitution of the U.S. was established by men whom the God of heaven raised up unto this very purpose.[6] This is part of my religious faith.

The days ahead are sobering and challenging and will demand the faith, prayers, and loyalty of every American.

I share the hope of David Lawrence, expressed April 20, 1964, in what I consider to be America's best news magazine, *U.S. News & World Report,* that

> The America of our forefathers . . . will some day see through the guilt of phony liberalism and cynical disdain for patriotism and love of fatherland.
>
> This America that General MacArthur aroused is not the America of petty politics and tricky manipulation of public power. It is not an America of "double talk" which denounces yet embraces appeasement. It is not an America of cowardice. It is an America of resoluteness and courage and sacrifice. It is an America that applauds the man of honest convictions.

---

[5]"America is another name for opportunity. Our whole history appears like a last effort of divine Providence in behalf of the human race." (Ralph Waldo Emerson, quoted in *Freedoms Handbook,* Freedoms Foundation At Valley Forge)

[6]"We say that the Constitution of the United States is a glorious standard; it is founded in the wisdom of God. It is a heavenly banner; it is to all those who are privileged with the sweets of its liberty, like the cooling shades and refreshing waters of a great rock in a thirsty land. It is like a great tree under whose branches men from every clime can be shielded from the burning rays of the sun." (Joseph Smith, March 25, 1839; *History of the Church* 3:304)

May God give us the wisdom to recognize the threat to our freedom and the strength to meet this danger courageously.[7]

Our challenge is to keep America strong and free — strong socially, strong economically, and above all, strong spiritually, if our way of life is to endure. There is no other way. Only in this course is there safety for our nation.

God grant that we may resolutely follow this course in humility and faith, I humbly pray.

---

[7]"If ye love wealth better than liberty, the tranquility of servitude better than the animating contest of freedom, go home from us in peace. We ask not your counsels or arms. Crouch down and lick the hands which feed you. May your chains set lightly upon you, and may posterity forget that ye were our country-men." (Samuel Adams, 1776; *Great Quotations*, p. 808)

CHAPTER 3

STAND UP FOR FREEDOM[1]

"Many free countries have lost their liberty, and ours may lose hers; but if she shall, be it my proudest plume, not that I was last to desert, but that I never deserted her. . . .

"The probability that we may fall in that struggle ought not to deter us from the support of a course we believe to be just. It shall not deter me." (Abraham Lincoln, December 26, 1839; *Collected Works* 1:178)

Humbly and gratefully I stand before you — grateful for patriots such as you, humbled by the magnitude of the task before us. . . .

"And ye shall know the truth, and the truth shall make you free." (John 8:32)

Returning recently from two years abroad has caused me to reflect seriously on recent trends and present conditions in our beloved country. I am shocked and saddened at what I find. I am sorry to say that all is not well in so-called prosperous, wealthy and powerful America.

We have moved a long way — and are now moving further and more rapidly down the soul-destroying road of socialism. The evidence is clear — shockingly clear — for all to see.

With our national prestige at an embarrassingly all-time low, we continue to weaken our domestic economy by unsound fiscal, economic and foreign aid policies which corrupt our national currency. Ever-increasing centralization of power

---

[1]An address first given on February 11, 1966, at The Utah Forum for the American Idea in the Assembly Hall, Temple Square, Salt Lake City, Utah. It was filmed by The Utah Forum and distributed widely, having been shown to many groups assembled and to many TV audiences. The address was also reprinted in pamphlet form by American Opinion.

in the federal government in Washington, D.C., is reducing our local and state governments to virtual federal field offices while weakening individual initiative, enterprise and character.[2]

With the crass unconstitutional usurpation of powers by the Executive branch of the federal government, anti-spiritual decisions of the Supreme Court — all apparently approved by a weakly submissive rubber-stamp Congress — the days ahead are ominously frightening.

Surely — certainly — it behooves patriotic citizens — such as you — to meet together to seriously consider present conditions in our beloved nation. It is imperative that American citizens become alerted and informed regarding the threat to our welfare, happiness and freedom.

No American is worthy of citizenship in this great land who refuses to take an active interest in these matters.

All we hold dear as a great Christian nation is at stake.

In leaving for Europe two years ago, I could not help but feel a very deep sense of anxiety for this great land of America which had just passed through a terrible crisis. To have the President of the United States suddenly torn from his high office by the violent hand of an assassin was an insidious and dastardly act which struck at the very foundation of our Republic.

All of us felt the impact of it. All of us caught the ominous spirit of tragedy and sorrow which accompanied it. Each of us sensed in a very personal way the heart-break which had come to the Kennedy family.

But after the services and burial were over, we also realized something else. There was the cold, stark reality that the assassin's murder of President Kennedy was just one more

---

[2]"There are two measures which if not taken, we are undone. First, to check these unconstitutional invasions of State rights by the Federal judiciary. How? Not by impeachment, in the first instance, but by a strong protestation of both houses of Congress that such and such doctrines, advanced by the Supreme Court, are contrary to the Constitution; and if afterwards they relapse into the same heresies, impeach and set the whole adrift. For what was the government divided into three branches, but that each should watch over the others and oppose their usurpations?" (Thomas Jefferson, To Nathaniel Macon, August 19, 1821)

monstrous treachery in the long list of crimes against humanity which have been inspired down through the years by the godless philosophy of communism.

It was communism that sowed the seeds of treason in the mind of President Kennedy's assassin. This is something which must not be forgotten.

Now, two years and one month later, I am appalled at the shortness of our memories. When the events surrounding President Kennedy's assassination were remembered last December, practically no mention was made of Oswald's communist affiliations nor the present communist threat to our society. Have we so soon forgotten that communism sowed the seeds of hate that destroyed our President and that communism continually seeks to subvert and destroy our complete way of life?

The assassination of President Kennedy, the daily slaughter of our boys in Vietnam, the communist control of the Berkeley riots and communist-inspired demonstrations from coast to coast should serve as a shock therapy to that segment of our population who like to call themselves "liberals." America is big enough to make room for many different kinds of thinking, but many liberals have claimed to see virtues in socialism and communism which I, for one, have not been able to find. To promote their ideas, American liberals have become a highly organized, hard-core establishment in the United States, and they have been excusing their appeasement and coddling of communism on the ground that they were being "tolerant," "broadminded," and "working for peace."

But the assassination of President Kennedy should have jolted them into a realization that they have been pampering, protecting and promoting the very nest of serpents which produced Lee Harvey Oswald. The diabolical spirit of murder and violence which struck down the President is that same spirit of communist violence which has been allowed to spread its terror into the heart of every continent on the face of the earth. Perhaps those who have been apologists for this conquering Marxist socialist-communist movement might now agree to reconsider the fatal decision they have been following.

Two additional things happened in connection with this tragedy which are worthy of comment.

First was the speed with which the communist leaders spread the word that the slaying of the President must have been the work of American conservatives. Moscow has conducted a five-year propaganda campaign to make American conservatives look like hysterical fanatics. It has called them "rightists," "extremists," and even "fascists." Within an hour after the assassination and before Oswald was captured, Moscow was assuring the world that this crime was a product of the "rightist" movement in the United States.

The second thing that happened was the amazing rapidity with which American liberals took up the Moscow line. They too were quick to fix the blame, even though there hadn't been the slightest hint as to who had committed the crime. I wonder what would have happened if Oswald had not been captured and identified as an active communist who was in direct contact with Party headquarters in New York City? Undoubtedly the liberal element would be blaming this tragedy on conservative Americans to this day.

And even after Oswald was captured and identified as a Moscow-associated communist there were those who insisted that any who had opposed the President during his term of high office was guilty of that same "spirit of hate" as that which led to the President's death. This line of thinking was expressed by a number of prominent persons through the press, radio and TV. To me it was incomprehensible.

To equate Oswald's hate and homicidal bitterness with patriotic Americans who happened to oppose some of the policies of the President's administration was the height of distorted and fallacious thinking. The American people can respect their President, pray for their President, even have a strong affection for him, and still have an honest difference of opinion as to the merits of some of his programs.

Another recent development has been the call for national unity. I believe there needs to be a unity in our land. But it must not be blind, senseless, irresponsible unity. It should not be unity just for the sake of unity. It needs to be a unity built on sound principles.

We Americans have strayed far from sound principles — morally, constitutionally, and historically. It has been getting us into a quagmire of trouble all over the world, and especially here at home.

Americans at the grass roots level have sensed that their way of life is being threatened. During the last several years there has been a rising tide of resistance to the prevailing political trend. Compromises with communism abroad and flirtations with socialism at home have stirred up opposition in both political parties. If this has led to disunity then by all means let us return to a program of sound constitutional principles on which we can unite.

There would be no virtue in calling for unity to support certain legislation if the majority of Americans are opposed to it. And the fact that both Democrats and Republicans in Congress have at times resisted certain legislation shows that the executive branch of the government may get out of step with the people.

I believe the American people know what they want. It would appear that the people want their civil rights but not a destruction of states' rights.

The farmers want opportunity for reasonable income security but not agricultural "dictatorship" security.

Parents want better schools for their children but not a federal subsidy leading to control of the teachings and textbooks as well as the ideologies of the children.

People want sound pay-as-you-go spending with a balanced budget, not reckless spending and tax cuts with an unbalanced budget.

If there is a need for urban renewal, people want it under local direction, not under the red tape of Washington bureaus armed with confiscatory powers over property.

People want the development of power dams but not the strangulation of privately owned power companies which have proven far more efficient and economical than utilities run by the government.

In other words, there are some legitimate functions and services which the federal government can and should provide, but those who want the federal power to exceed the authority delegated to it by the Constitution will be resisted both by Democrats and Republicans.[3] This is what is happening in some limited areas today.

And anyone who tries to equate this love of constitutional principles as meaning hatred of our national leaders is using Goebbels-styled deception. History has already demonstrated that conservative opposition to national leaders was not "hate" but an attempt to do them a favor.

Let me give you some examples:

Was it "hate" when General Albert C. Wedemeyer pleaded with General Marshall and President Truman to reverse their policy before they lost China?

Was it "hate" when Whittaker Chambers tried to warn President Roosevelt in 1939 that Alger Hiss had been giving the Soviet Union more espionage data than any other member of the Washington spy network?

Was it "hate" when J. Edgar Hoover tried to warn President Truman that Harry Dexter White was a member of the Soviet spy apparatus and was doing great danger to the nation as Assistant Secretary of the Treasury?

Was it "hate" when I went to the Secretary of State under President Eisenhower and pleaded with him not to support the communist, Fidel Castro?

Was it "hate" when I urged the President of the United States to go to the aid of the brave freedom fighters in Hungary?

Was it "hate" when the Democratic Senator from Connecticut, Thomas Dodd, pleaded for two years with the Presi-

---

[3]"What country can preserve its liberties, if its rulers are not warned from time to time, that this people preserve the spirit of resistance?" (Thomas Jefferson, To Colonel Smith, November 13, 1787; *Works* 2:318)

dent not to support the United Nations bloodbath against the free people of Katanga?

Is it "hate" when distinguished military leaders advise that an all-out effort could end the Vietnam struggle overnight?

This list of acts by well-meaning citizens who want and wanted to prevent their Presidents from making serious mistakes could be extended at length. But they would all illustrate the same point. History will show that many terrible mistakes occurred because the advice of these well-informed and well-meaning citizens was not heeded.

Therefore, I repeat, this kind of resistance to a national leader is rooted in love and respect, not hate.[4] Regardless of which political party is in power, you do not want to see your President make a serious blunder. You don't want him to lose China. You don't want him to allow the enemy agents to make fools of us. You don't want him to lose Cuba. You don't want him to suffer the humiliation of a "Bay of Pigs disaster" or allow a Soviet Gibraltar to be built ninety miles from our shores.

Every one of these events which have been so disastrous and which have destroyed freedom for hundreds of millions of our allies, could have been prevented. And the voices of those who tried to warn Washington of what was coming cannot be attributed to hate. It has been out of the love for our country and respect for our leaders that the voice of warning has been raised.

What causes one to wonder is why these warnings were not carefully considered and acted upon. Why is it that men in high places in government, regardless of party, have been deceived? I am convinced that a major part of the cause can be justly laid at the door of the socialist-communist conspiracy which is led by masters of deceit who deceive the very elect. J. Edgar Hoover put it well when he said,

> I would have no fears if more Americans possessed the zeal, the fervor, the persistence, and the industry to learn about

---

[4]"Liberty has never come from government. Liberty has always come from the subjects of government. The history of liberty is the history of resistance." (Woodrow Wilson, May 9, 1912; *The Great Quotations*, p. 603)

this menace of Red fascism. I do fear for the liberal and progressive who have been hoodwinked and duped into joining
hands with the communists. (*Menace of Communism*, p. 11)

Therefore, *let those who call for unity and the elimination
of hate be sure they are not merely trying to silence the friends
of freedom.* These are they who respect their leaders and resist
them only when it is felt they are headed for a catastrophe.
What patriotic American would wish to stand silent if he saw
his President verging on a blunder because of bad advice or a
mistaken judgment of the facts?

I believe one of the most serious mistakes a President
could make would be to weaken the Constitution.

From the time I was a small boy I was taught that the
American Constitution is an inspired document. I was also
taught that the day will come when the Constitution will be
endangered and hang as it were by a single thread. I was
taught that we should study the Constitution, preserve its principles, and defend it against any who would destroy it. To the
best of my ability I have always tried to do this. I expect to
continue my efforts to help protect and safeguard our inspired
Constitution.[5]

Some two years ago, however, a critic from Washington
claimed that a person who serves in a church capacity should
not comment on such matters. He charged that the separation
of church and state requires that church officials restrict their
attention to the affairs of the church.

I, of course, also believe that the institutions of church
and state should be separated, but *I also do not agree that
spiritual leaders cannot comment on basic issues which involve
the very foundation of American liberty.*

---

[5]*"I consider it as nothing less than a question of freedom or slavery;* and in
proportion to the magnitude of the subject ought to be the freedom of the debate.
It is only in this way that we can hope to arrive at truth, and fulfill the great
responsibility which we hold to God and our country. Should I keep back my
opinions at such a time, through fear of giving offense, I should consider myself
as guilty of treason towards my country, and of an act of disloyalty towards the
majesty of heaven, which I revere above all earthly kings." (Patrick Henry,
March 23, 1775; *P.P.N.S.,* p. 516)

In fact, if this were true, we would have to throw away a substantial part of the Bible. *Speaking out against immoral or unjust actions of political leaders has been the burden of prophets and disciples of God from time immemorial.* It was for this very reason that many of them were persecuted. Some of them were burned, many were imprisoned. Nevertheless, it was their God-given task, as watchmen on the towers, to speak up.

It is certainly no different today.

To Moses God said: " . . . Proclaim liberty throughout all the land unto all the inhabitants thereof . . . " (Leviticus 25:10)

For God knows full well that the gospel — his plan for the blessing of his children — can prosper only in an atmosphere of freedom.

To modern men God has said: the Constitution "should be maintained for the rights and protection of all flesh. . . . " (Doctrine and Covenants 101:77)

Is the Constitution being maintained or is it in jeopardy? Senator J. William Fulbright of Arkansas says the American Constitution is nothing more than a product of the eighteenth century agrarian society. It is now obsolete, he claims. Senator Joseph S. Clark of Pennsylvania says the separation of powers with its checks and balances must be curtailed because they keep the President from making quick and decisive decisions. Gus Hall, head of the Communist Party USA, agrees with these two Senators and demands that there should be a new federal charter eliminating states' rights. America's national sovereignty should be abandoned according to Walt Rostow, chairman of the State Department Policy Planning Board. He has boldly demanded "an end of nationhood as it has been historically defined." (Quoted in the extension of remarks by Senator Strom Thurmond, Congressional Record, June 6, 1963, pp. A3662-3)

These are some of the same men who see great virtue in a collectivized, socialized society. They want vast powers concentrated in Washington. Samuel Adams of the Founding

Fathers said this was the very thing constitutional government was designed to prevent.

Arthur M. Schlesinger, Jr., is another powerful influence in Washington and a former presidential advisor. He not only advocates socialism for the United States but believes that we could eventually form a permanent alliance with communism. He says this would be achieved by having America move to the left while the communists move to the right. We would then meet at the vital center of the socialist-left. The American Constitution, of course, would automatically be discarded.

Arthur Schlesinger and his associates are also opposed to the liberation of the captive nations, even if these nations do it by themselves. These men do not look upon communism as an enemy. They consider communist leaders to be over-zealous allies who will mellow. Therefore, they believe in containing communism, but otherwise supporting it, not thwarting it. They further recommend that wherever communist or social- ist regimes are collapsing, we should prop them up . . . feed them, trade with them, grant them loans on long term credits.

From reading the daily paper you will know that the ideas of these men have, unfortunately, already been adopted by Washington as the official policy of the United States.

Now, I would say that in a great free country like ours, *if these men advocate these suicidal and often apparently trea- sonable doctrines, shouldn't every patriotic American be free to speak out against them?*[6]

At this particular moment in history the United States Constitution is definitely threatened and every citizen should know about it. The warning of this hour should resound through the corridors of every American institution — schools, churches, the halls of Congress, press, radio and TV and so far as I am concerned it will resound — with God's help.

---

[6]"We hold that our loyalty is due solely to the American Republic, and to all our public servants exactly in proportion as they efficiently serve the Republic. . . . Every man who parrots the cry of 'stand by the President' without adding the proviso 'so far as he serves the Republic' takes an attitude as essentially unmanly as that of any Stuart royalist who championed the doctrine that the king could do no wrong. No self-respecting and intelligent freeman could take such an atti- tude." (Theodore Roosevelt, 1918; *Works*, Mem. Ed., XXI, p. 321)

Our Republic and Constitution are being destroyed while enemies of freedom are being aided.[7] How? In ten ways:

1. By diplomatic recognition and aid, and trade and negotiations with the communists.

2. By disarmament of our military defenses.

3. By destruction of our security laws and the promotion of atheism by decisions of the Supreme Court.

4. By loss of sovereignty and solvency through international commitments and membership in world organizations.

5. By undermining of local law enforcement agencies and Congressional investigating committees.

6. By usurpations by the executive and judicial branches of our federal government.

7. By lawlessness in the name of civil rights.

8. By a staggering national debt with inflation and a corruption of the currency.

9. By a multiplicity of executive orders and federal programs which greatly weaken local and state governments.

10. By the sacrifice of American manhood by engaging in wars we apparently have no intention of winning.

Wherever possible I have tried to speak out. It is for this very reason that certain people in Washington have bitterly criticized me.[8] They don't want people to hear the message. It embarrasses them. The things that are destroying the Constitution are the things they have been voting for. They are afraid of their political careers if these facts are pointed out.

---

[7]"The military aspects of the Communist threat represent just one phase of *the most insidious and gigantic plot in history.* There are the economic, technological, political, ideological and other phases, all designed for one objective only, and that is the accomplishment of the ultimate Communist goal of total world domination. What is worse, *some of our own people, ranging from subversives to supposedly intelligent and patriotic citizens, seem anxious to have us destroy ourselves,* thus making the job that much easier for the Soviets." (General Thomas S. Power, *Design For Survival,* Pocket Book Edition, p. 36)

[8]"If I were to try to read, much less answer, all the attacks made on me, this shop might as well be closed for any other business. I do the very best I know how — the very best I can; and I mean to keep doing so until the end. If the end brings me out all right, what is said against me won't amount to anything. If the end brings me out wrong, ten angels swearing I was right would make no difference." (Abraham Lincoln, *Familiar Quotations,* p. 458)

They therefore try to silence any who carry the message — anyone who will stand up and be counted.[9]

But these liberal politicians are not the only ones who are trying to silence the warning voice of American patriots. Moscow is equally alarmed.

It was in 1960 when the communist leaders first decided to do something drastic about the rising tide of patriotism in the United States. The loss of Cuba to the Soviet Union had alerted Americans. Citizens were holding study groups, seminars and freedom schools. The more they studied the more they realized how fast communism was advancing on all fronts. They also learned to their amazement that Washington politicians were doing practically nothing about it. In fact in many cases they were doing things to promote communism. So the protests began to pour into the national capitol from every state in the union. All over America there was an awakening.

The Soviet leaders knew this trend could create a crisis for communism, not only in the United States but elsewhere.

Therefore, they called together communist delegates from eighty-one countries and held a meeting in Moscow.

In December, 1960, just five years ago, this communist convention issued an edict that the rising tide of patriotism and anti-communism must be smashed — especially in the United States. All the tricks of the hate propaganda and smear tactics were to be unleashed on the heads of American patriots.

Now, if the communists had been forced to do this job themselves, it would have been an utter failure. Americans would have simply closed ranks and united. But what mixes up so many people was the fact that the attack on patriotism and the smear of the anti-communist movement did not come

---

[9]"The simple fact is that when I took up my little sling and aimed at Communism, I also hit something else. What I hit was the forces of that great socialist revolution, which, in the name of liberalism, spasmodically, incompletely, somewhat formlessly, but always in the same direction, has been inching its ice cap over the nation for two decades. . . . No one could have been more dismayed than I at what I had hit, for though I knew it existed, I still had no adequate idea of its extent, the depth of its penetration or the fierce vindictiveness of its revolutionary temper, which is a reflex of its struggle to keep and advance its political power." (Whittaker Chambers, ex-Communist; *Witness,* pp. 741-742)

in the name of Moscow. It came in the name of influential Americans who espoused the socialist-communist line.

This was a minority bloc of American liberals who formed a propaganda coalition with the communists. Their strategy was ingenious. Almost overnight they drew the line of fire away from the communist conspiracy and focused the heat of attack on the patriots.

How did they do it? They did it by saying that THEY were against the communists but ALSO against the anti-communists. They said one was as bad as the other.

Now what kind of logic was this? What if we had taken this approach in the fight against Nazism? Informed patriots recognized it as confusion compounded by delusion. In any event, this deceptive line of propaganda had its impact. These liberal voices would denounce communism and then turn around and parrot the communist line. They claimed they were anti-communist, but spent most of their time fighting those who were really effective anti-communists.

As I asked some of them at the time, "Are you fighting the communists or not? You claim to be fighting the fire, but you spend nearly all of your time fighting the firemen!"

By 1962 these American liberals had almost completely neutralized the resurgence of American patriotism. They had frightened uninformed citizens away from study groups and patriotic rallies. They had made it popular to call patriotism a "controversial" subject which should not be discussed in school assemblies or churches.

From Washington, D.C., the FCC (Federal Communications Commission) issued an edict to radio and television stations that if they allowed the controversial subjects of "Americanism," "anti-communism," or "states' rights" to be discussed on their stations they would be required to give equal time, free of charge, to anyone wishing to present an opposite view.

Can you imagine this happening in a free country? I said to my family, "It is fantastic that anything like this could have happened in America."

We should all be opposed to socialistic-communism, for it is our mortal and spiritual enemy — the greatest evil in the world today. But the reason many liberals don't want the American people to form study groups to really understand and then fight socialistic-communism is that once the American people get the facts, they will begin to realize that much of what these liberals advocate is actually helping the enemy.

The liberals hope you'll believe them when they tell you how anti-communist they are. But they become alarmed if you really inform yourself on the subject of socialistic-communism. For after you inform yourself you might begin to study the liberal voting record. And this study would show you how much the liberals are giving aid and comfort to the enemy and how much the liberals are actually leading America toward socialism itself.

For *communism is just another form of socialism, as is fascism.* So now you can see the picture. These liberals want you to know how much they are doing for you — with your tax money, of course. But they don't want you to realize that the path they are pursuing is socialistic and that socialism is the same as communism in its ultimate effect on our liberties. When you point this out they want to shut you up; they accuse you of maligning them, of casting aspersions, of being political. No matter whether they label their bottle as liberalism, progressivism, or social reform, I know the contents of the bottle is poison to this Republic and I'm going to call it poison.

We do not need to question the motive of these liberals. They could be most sincere. But sincerity or supposed benevolence or even cleverness is not the question. The question is: "Are we going to save this country from the hands of the enemy and the deceived?"

As J. Edgar Hoover said,

> A tragedy of the past generation in the United States is that so many persons, including high-ranking statesmen, public officials, educators, ministers of the Gospel, professional men, have been duped into helping Communism. Communist leaders

have proclaimed that Communism must be partly built with non-Communist hands, and this, to a large extent, is true. (*Masters of Deceit,* p. 93)

We cannot defeat Communism with socialism, nor with secularism, nor with pacifism, nor with appeasement or accommodation. We can only defeat Communism with true Americanism. (Address, October 9, 1962)

So from the very beginning of this Moscow campaign to stop the anti-communist movement in this country, it was an important part of the communist strategy to get their liberal American friends to carry out an attack against patriotic organizations. Of course, the communists have learned not to attack all patriotic groups at once. Their strategy is to focus on just one organization and make it so detestable and ugly in the public mind that they can hold it up as sort of a tar baby and then use it to smear all other individuals or groups in the same category. . . .

J. Edgar Hoover has warned that the cold war is a real war and that the threat is increasing. I agree, and unfortunately we're losing the war.

I think it is time for every patriotic American to join with neighbors to study the Constitution and the conspiracy. Subscribe to several good patriotic magazines such as *American Opinion,* buy a few basic books, such as *Masters of Deceit* and *A Study of Communism,* by J. Edgar Hoover; *The Naked Communist,* by Cleon Skousen, recommended by President David O. McKay, in the General Conference of the Church, October, 1959; *You Can Trust the Communists,* by Dr. Fred Schwarz, etc. And then prepare to do some independent thinking. And remember that the organized who have a plan and are dedicated, though they be few, will always defeat the many who are not organized and who lack plans and dedication. The communists know this and have proven it. Isn't it about time that most Americans realized it too?

One of our most serious problems is the inferiority complex which people feel when they are not informed and organized. They dare not make a decision on these vital issues.

They let other people think for them. They stumble around in the middle of the road to avoid being "controversial" and get hit by the traffic going both ways.[10]

To the patriots I say this: *Take that long eternal look. Stand up for freedom, no matter what the cost.*

It can help to save your soul — and maybe your country . . .

The days ahead are sobering and challenging and will demand the faith, prayers and loyalty of every American.

As the ancient apostle declared:

> The night is far spent, the day is at hand: let us therefore cast off the works of darkness, and let us put on the armour of light. (Romans 13:12)

May God give us the wisdom to recognize the dangers of complacency, the threat to our freedom and the strength to meet this danger courageously. . . .

In this mighty struggle each of you has a part. Every person on the earth today chose the right side during the war in heaven. Be on the right side now. *Stand up and be counted.* If you get discouraged remember the words of Edward Everett Hale, when he said:

> I am only one, but still I am one.
> I cannot do everything, but still I can do something;
> And because I cannot do everything
> I will not refuse to do the something that I can do.
>
> *(Familiar Quotations,* p. 550)

And this is my prayer for you this day. May God bless all of you, each and every one.

---

[10]"Let us be diverted by none of those sophistical contrivances wherewith we are so industriously plied and belabored — contrivances such as groping for some middle ground between the right and the wrong." (Abraham Lincoln, February 27, 1860; *Collected Works* 3:550)

CHAPTER 4

STRENGTH FOR THE BATTLE[1]

"Neither let us be slandered from our duty by false accusations against us, nor frightened from it by menaces of destruction to the Government nor of dungeons to ourselves. *Let us have faith that right makes might, and in that faith, let us, to the end, dare to do our duty as we understand it.*" (Abraham Lincoln, February 27, 1860; *Collected Works* 3:550)

My fellow Americans: Humbly and gratefully I stand before you — grateful for patriots such as you, humbled by the magnitude of the task before us.

I am honored to be in your presence and grateful for those who wish to remember their God, their family and their country. Those who fail to cherish the noble deeds of their forefathers will never do much, for good, to be remembered by their posterity. I commend you for meeting together on Independence Day, both to honor the spirit and the men of '76. God bless you for it.

During this three-day rally you have been informed, inspired, and, I hope, moved to labor even more diligently for liberty. Now at the conclusion may I pass on a few points for patriots to ponder.

My heart is filled with gratitude as I contemplate the unselfish work being done by patriots such as you gathered here today. In spite of the seriousness of our times, it is hopeful when public-spirited citizens from far and near will assemble, with a recognition of the need for divine guidance, to consider two of our most basic institutions, family and country.

[1]An address first given on July 4, 1966, at the New England Rally for God, Family and Country, in the Statler Hilton Hotel, Boston, Massachusetts. It was reprinted in pamphlet form by Bookcraft.

If pride in family is a sin, I hope the good Lord will forgive me. We have just celebrated the marriage of our daughter Beth, the youngest of our six, choice children, all of whom are devoted to God, family and country. All of them, with their fine companions and our sixteen grandchildren, were together at our old-fashioned three-floor home.

As I officiated at the marriage of our children, but especially the last one in the Salt Lake Temple, tears of gratitude filled the eyes of all of us. Thank God for family, for country and for the knowledge I have that God lives, that he hears and answers prayer and that he loves his children everywhere and that he loves this great nation, America, established by men whom he inspired for that very purpose.

I introduce my subject today "Strength for the Battle" by quoting from a weekly newspaper, *News-Advertiser,* published in Hurricane, Utah, which serves Southern Utah, Northern Arizona and Eastern Nevada and whose publisher is a courageous, devoted patriot. He sent me a copy of the June 30th issue emphasizing Independence Day, just as I was leaving Salt Lake City for Boston.

After paying high tribute to a recent statement by President David O. McKay on communism, he then ends his column, "A Note From The Publisher," as follows:

"We conclude this note for the week by giving you 'Day of Decision' by Johnny Sea, which can be obtained on recording set to music, which may stir you out of your apathetic, sleep-like complacency if you will but take time to listen to it."

Now read this:

> The other day I heard someone say, "You know, *America is in real trouble.*" It's true. Old glory has never fallen so close to the earth. Our embassies are being stoned; our diplomats are often in fear for their lives, and we're involved in a half-dozen nameless, winless conflicts spilling American blood on foreign soil.
>
> Our young men are dying for ideals which don't seem to mean too much to Americans any more. The truth is, America's real trouble doesn't lie in the rice paddies in Vietnam, in the masses of Red China, or in the diabolical intrigues to the south of us.

The real trouble lies in the playgrounds of St. Louis, the hillside mansions of San Francisco and in the slums of Chicago — the disease which is slowly eating away the small Southern towns, the fishing villages of New England, and in the hot, dusty streets of the Midwest.

This is the age of the American cynic; the year of the unbeliever; the day of doubt. We've killed all the sacred cows and destroyed all the images and there's nothing left to respect.

Old fashioned love of God, country and family is passe, and we stare at our shoe laces when they play the National Anthem.

We wouldn't want to be seen at a political rally, or a town hall meeting, and we don't want to be caught with our eyes closed during public prayer. We've decided that the only way to get into public office is to buy it.

Our heroes are the fast guys who get away with things.

Patriotism, the old hand-over-the-heart, flag waving, singing patriotism has been condemned.

Think about this: Patriotism, when you tear away the fancy phrases and crepe paper, is plain and simple pride. It's a new car, prettier girls, bigger house sort of pride in country. Somewhere along the way we have lost that pride.

Our form of government is the same. We still say America stands for the same things, but next time you're at a party, ask someone to sing America and see what happens. The basic ideals and structure of America haven't changed — we have. You and me. Our enemies know it. They've seen the news reels of the discontented marching around the universities.

They've distorted and blown up our mistakes. They've been putting steel wedges in the cracks in our wall of solidarity. The new idea is, "Don't attack America, wear it down gradually. It will eventually fall under the weight of its own corruption." And did you know, it's working!

This sneering complacency, once stamped out by the bloody feet of the tattered Continental army in 1776, once drowned beneath the keel of the USS Arizona in Pearl Harbor Bay, has risen again.

This deadly "let George do it" attitude lights the Viet Cong in the swampy jungles of Vietnam. This "better Red than Dead" cancer is more feared by the American soldier than all the communist mortar shells. It kills the vitality and spirit of America.

Democracy is a frail and fragile instrument, made of hope, prayer, and Yankee ingenuity.

It's held together by Fourth of July flag waving patriotism and we've almost exhausted our supply of it.

Try this test: "Lift your eyes to a flag, then sing out as loud as you can that old, outworn, antiquated freedom hymn you learned so many years ago:

"For purple mountains majesty, above the fruited plains, America, America, God shed his grace on thee. . . . "

Now, if you feel a little pride swelling up inside of you, if you feel a little mist in your eye, thank God for you, mister, you're still an American.

And then the publisher ends his column:

Monday is July 4, 1966. This year is a great year of decision, it has been said. Let's make the right decision, folks, for it's you and your neighbor and friends involved.

And then on the back cover in a full-page box, sponsored by three companies in Hurricane, Utah, appears a reproduction of the Declaration of Independence, of a Minute Man and the Statue of Liberty and these words, "Is She Standing Alone?" " . . . Not if millions of Americans are willing to stand with her in defense of our God-given liberties. The time has come to show the courage and determination to resist all encroachments upon our freedom, whether from within or without. So, on this anniversary of our Independence — and on every other day — let us stand up with her and be counted . . . for freedom!"

J. Edgar Hoover, in his sobering report, *Communist Target — Youth,* warns us that,

The menace of communism is not a simple forthright threat. Instead, it is a conspiracy which can be controlled only through full understanding of the true nature of the conspiracy and the ability to separate truth from propaganda. Only our apathy and laxity in the face of threat, which communist infiltration efforts represent, can cause such a failure. It is the duty of all Americans to fully understand the true import of this threat to our heritage, to expose it, and to combat it with every weapon at our command. (pp. 10-11)

I agree with Mr. Hoover.

President David O. McKay, of the Mormon Church, has warned us time and time again that there is present in our own United States, "influences the avowed object of which is to sow discord and contention among men with a view of undermining, weakening, if not entirely destroying our Constitutional form of government. . . . It is the enemy from within," warns this great leader, "that is most menacing, especially when it threatens to disintegrate our established form of government." (*Statements on Communism and the Constitution*, p. 3)

Our complacency as a nation is shocking — yes, almost unbelievable!

We are a prosperous nation. Our people have high-paying jobs. Our incomes are high. Our standard of living is at an unprecedented level. We do not like to be disturbed as we enjoy our comfortable complacency. We live in the soft present and feel the future is secure. We do not worry about history. We seem oblivious to the causes of the rise and fall of nations. We are blind to the hard fact that nations usually sow the seeds of their own destruction while enjoying unprecedented prosperity.

For thirty years we have aided the cause of the atheistic-socialistic conspiracy by permitting socialists, communists, and fellow-travelers in high places in government; by giving away vital military secrets; by squandering much of our material resources; by recklessly spending ourselves to near bankruptcy; by weakening our free enterprise system through adoption of socialistic policies; by wastefully bungling our foreign affairs; by ever increasing confiscatory taxation and by permitting the insidious infiltration of socialistic communist agents and sympathizers into almost every segment of American life.

Lenin said, "The soundest strategy in war is to postpone operations until the moral disintegration of the enemy renders the moral blow possible and easy."

Commenting on Lenin's statement the *Indianapolis Star* adds:

> Where then does the real danger lie? It lies with us — the American people.

Other great civilizations have died by suicide. The first free people, the Greeks, died thus.

And why did Greece fall: "A slackness and softness finally came over them to their ruin. In the end more than they wanted freedom they wanted security, a comfortable life, and they lost all —security, comfort and freedom."

It is the same with Americans today. The danger that threatens us is an internal danger. . . .

It is our own ignorance — ignorance of our own history and our heritage of liberty that threatens us. . . . Our lack of faith in freedom and ourselves, our own lack of confidence in the greatness of America and all that she stands for morally and materially is what puts us in mortal danger.

Too many of us are afraid — afraid of atomic war, afraid of the disapproval of our allies or the neutrals, afraid of the threats and boasts of the bloated tyrants in the Kremlin, afraid to offend others by taking action to defend ourselves. . . .

There is no greater evidence today of American complacency than this sad record. Yes, we have been lulled away into a false security. We are busy making money, enjoying our abundance but oblivious to the gradual loss of our freedom which has made all of these blessings possible. As a nation we are affluent but foolish.

This nation needs a revival of patriotism, a return to basic concepts, an awakening to the most deadly peril ever to threaten our people. *I say to you with all my heart that the danger is real and can be deadly.* We must become alerted and informed.

With our national prestige at or near an all-time low, when will we act like men of courage? Why this continuing policy of softness toward communism? When will we begin to take positions based on what is right and then stand firm?[2] The language and action of firmness will be respected and is the only safe course for our great nation to pursue. When will our national leaders mention at least the Monroe Doctrine?

[2]"It has been said of the world's history hitherto that might makes right. It is for us and for our time to reverse the maxim, and say that right makes might." (Abraham Lincoln; quoted in Burton Stevenson's *Home Book of Quotations*)

Grassroots thinking in America cries for strong, courageous leadership. Some American people are at long last becoming aroused in their hearts. They are far ahead of most
Washington politicians. They oppose their leaders making
concessions to Russia. They do not want to be lulled to sleep.
These American people are convinced that a firm stand against
the communist masters is the best protection against war. They
want to know the truth without bluffing.

The American people are entitled to the facts.[3] Our people know in their hearts that the opposite of victory is defeat,
whether you call it "coexistence" or "compromise" with a godless tyranny.

We are at war, and we must win the war. It's time to go
on the offensive. *Let's stop helping the enemy.* Let's stop half-
measures such as were used in Cuba. Let's be sure we're right
and then mobilize sufficient strength to win. For a change let's
try victory.

I have great faith in the American people. When fully
informed they will make wise decisions. They will stand up
and be counted for what is right.

It is my conviction, confirmed by scripture sacred to me,
that this is a choice land. It is a nation with a prophetic history
—with a spiritual foundation—a nation with a great mission
to perform for liberty-loving people everywhere.

Nearly two thousand years ago a perfect Man walked
the earth—Jesus the Christ. He was the Son of a Heavenly
Father and an earthly mother. He is the God of this world,
under the Father. In his life, all the virtues were lived and
kept in perfect balance; he taught men truth—that they might
be free; his example and precepts provide the great standard—
the only sure way—for all mankind. Among us he became the
first and only one who had the power to reunite his body
with his spirit after death. By his power all men who have
died shall be resurrected. Before him one day we all must

---

[3]"I am a firm believer in the people. If given the truth, they can be depended
upon to meet any national crisis. The great point is to bring them the real facts."
(Abraham Lincoln, *Great Quotations*, p. 338)

stand to be judged by his laws. He lives today, and in the not too distant future shall return, in triumph, to subdue his enemies, to reward men according to their deeds, and to assume his right role to rule and reign in righteousness over the entire earth.

Nearly two hundred years ago some inspired men walked this land. Not perfect men — but men raised up by the perfect Man to perform great work. Foreordained were they to lay the foundation of this Republic. Blessed by the Almighty in their struggle for liberty and independence, the power of heaven rested on these Founders as they drafted that great document for governing men — The Constitution of the United States. Like the Ten Commandments, the truths on which the Constitution were based were timeless; and also as with the Decalogue — the hand of the Lord was in it. They filled their mission well. From them we were endowed with a legacy of liberty — a Constitutional Republic.[4]

But today the Christian constitutionalist mourns for his country. He sees the spiritual and political faith of his fathers betrayed by wolves in sheep's clothing. He sees the forces of evil increasing in strength and momentum under the leadership of Satan, the archenemy of freedom. He sees the wicked honored and the valiant abused. He senses that his own generation faces Gethsemanes and Valley Forges that may yet rival or surpass the trials of the early apostles and the men of '76. And this gives him cause to reflect on the most basic of fundamentals — the reason for our existence. Once we understand that fundamental, the purpose for mortality, we may more easily chart a correct course in the perilous seas that are engulfing our nation.

This life is a probation — a probation in which you and I prove our mettle. A probation that has eternal consequences for each of us. And now is our time and season — as every generation has had theirs — to learn our duties and to do them.

---

[4]"I always consider the settlement of America with reverence and wonder as the opening of a grand scene and design in Providence for the illumination of the ignorant and the emancipation of the slavish part of mankind all over the earth." (John Adams, 1765, *A Dissertation On the Canon and Feudal Law*)

The Lord has so arranged things in this life that men are free agents unto themselves — to do good or evil. *The Lord allows men to only go so far* — but the latitude is great enough to permit some men to promote great wickedness among their fellowmen and to allow other men to promote great righteousness.

> Know this, that every soul is free
> To choose his life and what he'll be,
> For this eternal truth is given
> That God will force no man to heav'n.
>
> He'll call, persuade, direct aright,
> And bless with wisdom, love, and light,
> In nameless ways be good and kind,
> But never force the human mind.
>
> Freedom and reason make us men;
> Take these away, what are we then?
> Mere animals, and just as well
> The beasts may think of heav'n or hell.

Clearly, there would be little trial of faith if we received our full reward immediately for every goodly deed, or immediate retribution for every sin. But that there will be an eventual reckoning for each, there is no question.

That the Lord is displeased with wickedness is true. That he desires that it not occur is also true. That he will help those who oppose it is true. But that he allows wickedness to occur at all through his children here in mortality is proof of his having given them their freedom to choose, while reserving for him a basis for their final judgment. And herein lies the hope of all Christian constitutionalists. Why?

Because *the fight for freedom is God's fight.* For free agency is an eternal principle. It existed before the world was formed — it will exist forever. Some men may succeed in denying some aspects of this God-given freedom to their fellowmen, but their success is temporary. For freedom is a law of God, a permanent law. And, like any of God's laws, men cannot really break it with impunity. They can only break themselves upon it. So *when a man stands for freedom he stands with God. And as long as he stands for freedom he stands with God. And were he to stand alone he would still stand with God* — the best company and the greatest power in or out of this world. Where the Spirit of the Lord is, there is liberty; and because truth is eternal, any man will be eternally vindicated and rewarded for his stand for freedom.

Now being assured that freedom is a God-given principle that will triumph finally and eternally, there yet remains the crucial question: Can freedom triumph now? But the answer to that hangs on the answer to a yet more crucial question: What are we doing to keep freedom alive? For the answer to that first question — Can freedom triumph now? — you see, is speculative. But the answer to the second question — What are we doing to keep freedom alive? — has riding on it matters which will have eternal consequence to every soul, no matter what the temporary outcome; for the Lord has so endowed this matter of freedom with such everlasting repercussions that it sifted the spirits of men before this world in the Great War in heaven. And it seems today to be the central issue that is sifting those who are left in the world.

Men receive blessings by obedience to God's law. And without obedience there is no blessing. Before the final triumphal return of the Lord, *the question as to whether we may save our Constitutional Republic is simply based on two factors — the number of patriots and the extent of their obedience.*

That the Lord desires to save this nation which he raised up there is no doubt. But that he leaves it up to us, with his help, is the awful reality.

There is a time and season for all righteous things, and many of life's failures arise when men neither take the time nor find the season to perform their eternal duties. What then in this time and season may best equip us to have our Christian constitutional legacy, while at the same time rescuing our own souls? May I humbly submit six suggestions:

1. SPIRITUALITY. In a book, sacred to me as scripture, the Lord states that America is a land choice above all others; and that it shall remain free as long as the inhabitants worship the God of the land — Jesus Christ.

Certainly spirituality is the foundation upon which any battle against tyranny must be waged. And because this is basically the struggle of the forces of Christ versus anti-Christ, it is imperative that our people be in tune with the supreme leader of freedom — the Lord our God. And men only stay in tune when their lives are in harmony with God. For apart from God we cannot succeed, but as a partner with God we cannot fail. We must be in the amoral and immoral world—but not of it. We must be able to drop off to sleep at night without having to first sing lullabies to our conscience.

2. BALANCE. We have many responsibilities and one cannot expect the full blessings of a kind providence if he neglects any major duty.

A man has duties to his Church, his home, his country and his profession or job.

Duty to Church—Each man, in communication with his God, must determine the place and extent of the duty he owes to his church. And in a day when many pulpits are being turned into pipelines of collectivist propaganda, this becomes a serious consideration. The least any Christian can do is to daily study the word of the Lord and seek divine aid through daily prayer.

Duty to Home—Fathers, you cannot delegate your duty as the head of the home. Mothers, train up your children in righteousness. Do not attempt to save the world and let your own fireside fall apart. An evening at home once a week, which I call a "Home Evening," where parents and children can all be together to discuss matters, exhibit their talents, enjoy inspiring reading and have some recreation, is a good protector against the breakdown of the family. For many years now our Church has encouraged parents to hold weekly family "Home Evenings." To this end the Church has published a home evening manual with helpful suggestions for each week's activities that include family recreation, character-building lessons, etc.

The home is the rock foundation — the cornerstone of civilization. This nation will never rise above its homes. The church, the school and even the nation stand helpless before weakened and degraded homes. *"No other success can compensate for failure in the home."* (President David O. McKay) The duty of parents is to be of help to each other and to their children, then comes their duty to their neighbors, community, nation and world — in that order.

Duty to Country — No one can delegate his duty to preserve his freedom, for the price of liberty is still eternal vigilance. There are now thousands of businessmen behind the iron curtain who, if they had their lives to live over, would balance their time more judiciously and give more devotion to their civil responsibilities. *An ounce of energy in the preservation of freedom is worth a ton of effort to get it back once it is lost.*

Duty to Job — Every man should earn sufficient to provide the necessities of food, clothing, and shelter for his family. As Paul wrote to Timothy:

> But if any provide not for his own, and specially for those of his own house, he hath denied the faith, and is worse than an infidel. (I Timothy 5:8)

Indolence rolls out the carpet for the benevolent straightjacket of the character-destroying welfare state.

But, a man pays too high a price for worldly success if in his climb to prominence he sacrifices his spiritual, home and civic responsibilities.

How a person should apportion his time among his several duties requires good judgment and is a matter over which each should invite divine assistance.

3. COURAGEOUS ACTION. I have always felt that, while we should ask the Lord's blessings on all our doings and should never do anything upon which we cannot ask his blessings, *we also should not expect the Lord to do for us what we can do for ourselves.* I believe in faith and works, and that the Lord will bless more fully the man who works for what he prays for than he will the man who only prays.

Today *you cannot effectively fight for freedom and not be attacked* — and those who think they can are deceiving themselves. While I do not believe in stepping out of the path of duty to pick up a cross I don't need, a man is a coward who refuses to pick up a cross that clearly lies within his path. No cross — no crown, no gall — no glory, no thorns — no throne.[5]

Years ago a ballplayer started his prayer like this: "Dear Lord: Help me to be a sport in this little game of life. I don't ask for an easy place in the lineup. Play me anywhere you need me. I only ask that I might give you one-hundred percent of all I've got. If all the hard drives seem to come my way — I thank you for the compliment. Help me to realize that you won't let anything come my way that you and I can't handle together. . . . "

A man must not only stand for the right principles, but he must fight for them. And let me at this time salute those valiant patriots who have banded together in well-structured organizations with an intelligent program, and who are courageously acting to preserve and to restore and safeguard our inspired Constitution. They can be proud of the friends they've gained and the enemies they've earned.[6]

4. EDUCATION. We must each of us do our homework. "My people are destroyed," said Hosea, "for lack of knowledge." (Hosea 4:6) We must be wise as serpents; for as the Apostle Paul said, "We wrestle against the rulers of darkness, against spiritual wickedness in high places." (Ephesians 6:12)

We are going through what J. Reuben Clark once termed the greatest propaganda campaign of all time. We cannot believe all we read, and what we can believe is not all of the same value. We must sift. We must learn by study and prayer.

---

[5]"We should never incur the imputation of cowardice by fleeing from danger, while we should avoid the other extreme of rushing into danger, which is the height of folly. . . . (. . . it is wrong to court danger, but right to face it boldly), especially if you have more to gain by decisive action than you would lose by remaining in suspense." (Cicero, *On Moral Duties,* I, 24)

[6]"It is our duty to respect those patriotic citizens who have proved their strength in great and noble works, and have loyally served their country, and to honour them as much as if they were invested with some public office or military command." (Cicero, *On Moral Duties,* I, 41)

Study the scriptures and study the mortals who have been most consistently accurate about the most important things. When your freedom is at stake, your information had best be accurate.

5. HEALTH. *To meet and beat the enemy will take clear heads and strong bodies.* Hearts and hands grow strong based on what they're fed. Let us take into our body or soul only those things that would make us more effective instruments. We need all the physical, mental and moral power we can get.

Righteous concern about conditions is commendable when it leads to constructive action. But undue worry is debilitating. When we have done what we can, then let's leave the rest to God — including the worrying.

Man needs beneficial recreation, a change of pace that refreshes him for heavy tasks ahead.

Man also must take time to meditate, to sweep the cobwebs from his mind so that he might get a more firm grip on the truth and spend less time chasing phantoms and dallying in projects of lesser worth.

Clean hearts and healthful food, exercise, early sleep and fresh air, wholesome recreation and meditation, combined with optimism that comes from fighting for the right and knowing you'll eventually win for keeps — this is the tonic every patriot needs and deserves.

6. Finally, BE PREPARED. *We have a duty to survive, not only spiritually but physically.* Not survival at the cost of principles — for this is the surest way to defeat — but a survival that comes from intelligent preparation. For we face days ahead which will test the moral and physical sinews of all of us.

In the Bible, the Lord tells the story of the five wise and five foolish virgins. While they all had noble aspirations, the wise were prepared and the foolish weren't. The wise couldn't supply the needs of the foolish in the limited time that was left for their missions without frustrating their own responsibilities. So the foolish virgins got about their duty — but too late. It is time for all of us to get our spiritual and temporal house in order.

A man should not only be prepared to protect himself physically, but he should have on hand sufficient supplies to sustain himself and his family in an emergency. For many years the leaders of the Mormon Church have recommended with instructions that every family have on hand a year's supply of basic food and clothing and provision for shelter. This has been most helpful to families suffering temporary reverses. It could be useful in many circumstances.

We also need to get out of financial bondage — to be debt-free.

Now these suggestions regarding SPIRITUALITY, BALANCE, COURAGEOUS ACTION, EDUCATION, HEALTH and PREPARATION, are given not only to help equip one for the freedom struggle, but to help equip one for eternal life.

Let us get about our business. For any Christian constitutionalist who retreats from this battle jeopardizes his life here and hereafter. Seldom has so much responsibility hung on so few, so heavily; but our numbers are increasing, and we who have been warned have a responsibility to warn our neighbor.

To his disciples, the Lord said that they should be of good cheer for he had overcome the world — and so he had. And so can we if we are allied with him. *For time is on the side of truth and the wave of the future is freedom.*[7] There is no question of the eventual, final, and lasting triumph of righteousness. The major question for each of us is what part will we play in helping to bring it to pass.

There are some people who hesitate to get into this fight for freedom because it is controversial, or they're not sure if we're going to win.

---

[7]"We will make converts day by day; we will grow strong by the violence and injustice of our adversaries. And, unless truth be a mockery and justice a hollow lie, we will be in the majority after a while. . . . The battle of freedom is to be fought out in principle." (Abraham Lincoln, May 19, 1856; *Great Quotations*, p. 377)

Such people have two blind spots.

First, they fail to realize that *life's decisions should be based on principles — not on Gallup polls.*

There were men at Valley Forge who weren't sure how the Revolution would end, but they were in a much better position to save their own souls and their country than those timid men whose concern was deciding which side was going to win, or how to avoid controversy.

After all, *the basic purpose of life is to prove ourselves — not to be with the majority when it is wrong.*

We must discharge responsibilities not only to our church, home and profession, but also to our country. Otherwise we do not merit the full blessings of a kind providence.

There are people today all over the world who in their own courageous and sometimes quiet way are working for freedom. In many cases we will never know until the next life all they sacrificed for liberty. These patriots are receiving heaven's applause for the role they are playing, and in the long run that applause will be louder and longer than any they could receive in this world.[8]

Which leads me to the second blind spot of those who hesitate to get into the fight. And that is their failure to realize that *we will win in the long run,* and for keeps, and that they pass up great blessings by not getting into the battle now when the odds are against us and the rewards are greatest.

The only questions, before the final victory, are first, "What stand will each of us take in this struggle?" and second, "How much tragedy can be avoided by doing something now?"

Time is on the side of truth — and truth is eternal.

Those who are fighting against freedom may feel confident now, but they are short-sighted.

This is still God's world. The forces of evil, working through some mortals, have made a mess of a good part of it.

---

[8]"All those who have preserved, aided, or enlarged their fatherland have a special place prepared for them in the heavens, where they may enjoy an eternal life of happiness. . . . The best tasks are those undertaken in defence of your native land." (Cicero, *The Republic,* VI, 13 and 29)

But, it is still God's world. *In due time when each of us has had a chance to prove ourselves — including whether or not we are going to stand up for freedom — then God will interject himself, and the final and eternal victory shall be for free agency.* And then shall those complacent people on the sidelines, and those who took the wrong but temporarily popular course, lament their decisions.

To the patriots I say this: *Take that long eternal look. Stand up for freedom, no matter what the cost. Stand up and be counted.*

It can help to save your soul — and maybe your country. . . .[9]

This is a glorious hour in which to live. Generations past and future will mark well our response to our awesome duty. There is a reason why we have been born in this day. Ours is the task to try to live and perpetuate the principles of the Christ and the Constitution in the face of tremendous odds. May we, with God's help, have strength for the battle and fill our mission in honor for God, family and country. That is my humble and constant prayer this day and always.

---

[9]"The result is not doubtful. We shall not fail—if we stand firm, we shall not fail. *Wise councils* may *accelerate* or *mistakes delay it,* but, sooner or later the victory is *sure* to come." (Abraham Lincoln, June 16, 1858; *Collected Works* 2:468-9)

CHAPTER 5

TRADE AND TREASON[1]

"A nation can survive its fools and even the ambitious. But it cannot survive treason from within. An enemy at the gates is less formidable, for he is known and he carries his banners openly against the city. But the traitor moves among those within the gates freely, his sly whispers rustling through all the alleys, heard in the very halls of government itself. For the traitor appears no traitor; he speaks in the accents familiar to his victims, and he wears their face and their garments, and he appeals to the baseness that lies deep in the hearts of all men. He rots the soul of a nation; he works secretly and unknown in the night to undermine the pillars of a city; he infects the body politic so that it can no longer resist. A murderer is less to be feared. The traitor is the carrier of the plague." (Cicero's remarks to the Roman Senate, as recorded by Sallust; quoted in *Pillar of Iron,* p. 556)

Humbly and gratefully I approach this solemn responsibility. Grateful for freedom to speak out — humbled by the magnitude of the task before us. I shall speak to you frankly and honestly. Because of the nature of the message I bring I have committed most of it to writing.

What I say may not be popular with everybody. *This is a time when unpleasant truths must be told,* "even though the telling may disturb the ease and quiet of luxurious error. . . . On such occasions, the criticism, slander and misrepresentation that one gets are of no consequence." (J. Reuben Clark, *P.P.N.S.,* pp. 46-47)

---

[1]An address first given on February 17, 1967, at the Portland Forum for Americanism in the Benson High School Auditorium, Portland, Oregon. It was entered in the *Congressional Record* on March 14, 1967, pp. S3694-5, by Senator Strom Thurmond of South Carolina. It was reprinted in pamphlet form by Jeffersonian Publications and Christian Crusade.

What I shall say are my personal convictions borne out of an active life which has taken me into forty-five nations and brought me close to the insidious forces that would destroy our way of life in this choice land. I express these convictions and warnings today because of my love for my fellow citizens, all humanity, and our beloved country.[2]

The message I bring is not a happy one, but it is the truth and time is always on the side of truth.

Once again, with all the solemnity of my soul, I sound a voice of warning.

Our announced "policy of bridge-building to the Soviet swamp" brought this recent comment from a long-time foreign student of world affairs:

> Yes, the storm signals are up. The Russians have decided to force the issue. Not to atomic war, but to everything short of it. They have Cuba fortified. They have the Near East a near prey. They have our natural NATO allies nearly all turned against us. So why not try it on? Wipe out Israel? How can we stop it? We are deeply engaged in Vietnam, and the Russians have just summoned our fleet to get out of the Mediterranean.
>
> I do not believe that all this is accidental. I think it is cleverly coordinated: the "No Win" War, the sleepy sentimentality over the Russians, the freedom guaranteed to Communists, our deadliest enemies, to operate against us as they wish and our general inability to see what is being done to us.
>
> You are on the firing line now [he concludes]. May you still have a few rounds left! (Human Events, June 5, 1967)

Consider the following shocking facts.

Since World War II the communists have brought under bondage — enslaved — on the average approximately 6,000 persons per hour, 144,000 per day, 52,000,000 per year — every hour of every day of every year since 1945.

---

[2]"It is hard to speak properly upon a subject where it is even difficult to convince your hearers that you are speaking the truth. On the one hand, the friend who is familiar with every fact of the story may think that some point has not been set forth with that fullness which he wishes and knows it to deserve; on the other, he who is a stranger to the matter may be led by envy to suspect exaggeration if he hears anything above his own nature." (Pericles, 5th Cent. B. C.; quoted by Thucydides, *The History of the Peloponnesian War*, Chapter VI, 35)

Since 1945 the communists have murdered in one country alone enough people to wipe out the entire population of over fifteen of our states.

J. Edgar Hoover, the best-informed man in government on the socialist-communist conspiracy, stated:

> . . . we must now face the harsh truth that the objectives of communism are being steadily advanced because many of us do not readily recognize the means used to advance them. . . . No one who truly understands what it really is can be taken in by it. Yet the individual is handicapped by coming face to face with a conspiracy so monstrous he cannot believe it exists. The American mind simply has not come to a realization of the evil which has been introduced into our midst. (*P.P.N.S.*, p. 273)

I have personally witnessed the heart-rending results of the loss of freedom. I have seen it with my own eyes. I have been close to the godless evil of the socialist-communist conspiracy on both sides of the iron curtain, particularly during my years as European Mission President for my Church at the close of the war and today and also during my eight years in the Cabinet.

It may shock you to learn that the first communist cell in our government, so far as we know, was organized in the U.S. Department of Agriculture in the early 1930's. John Abt was there. It was John Abt whom Oswald, the accused assassin of President Kennedy, requested for his attorney. Harry Dexter White was there. Lee Pressman was there. And Communist Agent Alger Hiss, who was a principal architect of the godless United Nations and Secretary-General of the United Nations organizing conference, was there also.[3]

I stood in Czechoslovakia in 1946 and witnessed the ebbing away of freedom resulting in the total loss of liberty.

---

[3]"In the persons of Alger Hiss and Harry Dexter White, the Soviet Military Intelligence sat close to the heart of the United States Government. . . . Hiss became Director of the State Department's Office of Special Political Affairs and White became an Assistant Secretary of the Treasury. In a situation with few parallels in history, the agents of an enemy power were in a position to do much more than purloin documents. They were in a position to influence the nation's foreign policy in the interests of the nation's chief enemy, and not only on exceptional occasions, like Yalta . . . but in what must have been the staggering sum of day-to-day decisions." (Whittaker Chambers, ex-communist; *Witness*, p. 427)

I visited among the liberty-loving Polish people and talked with their leaders as the insidious freedom-destroying conspiracy moved in, imposing the chains of bondage on a Christian nation.

Wherever communism has come to power, it has destroyed the indispensable conditions for the intellectual and moral existence of man. Communism is totalitarianism that encompasses every manifestation of man's moral, political, and economic life.

Too many Americans do not fully comprehend the true meaning of communism. They are thinking of a competing system of political and economic order that has won acceptance and loyalty with other civilized nations.

This opinion reflects our inability or unwillingness to comprehend the true nature of the conflict between communism and us.[4] The antagonism is no old-fashioned diplomatic power struggle in which both sides maneuver for territorial possessions and spheres of influence. It is *a collision of two irreconcilable systems*: one that endeavors to preserve man's civilization and one that aims to destroy it. It is a war waged on many fronts over the moral, intellectual and economic conditions of human existence in the world.[5]

Communism is totalitarianism in which government control has been extended to practically every phase of human

---

[4]"It is natural to man to indulge in the illusions of hope. We are apt to shut our eyes against a painful truth, and listen to the song of that siren, till she transforms us into beasts. Is this the part of wise men, engaged in a great and arduous struggle for liberty? Are we disposed to be of the number of those who, having eyes, see not, and having ears, hear not, the things which so nearly concern their temporal salvation? For my part, whatever anguish of spirit it may cost, I am willing to know the whole truth; to know the worst and to provide for it." (Patrick Henry, March 23, 1775; *P.P.N.S.* p. 516)

[5]"*That is the real issue. . . . It is the eternal struggle between these two principles—right and wrong—throughout the world.* They are the two principles that have stood face to face from the beginning of time; and will ever continue to struggle. The one is the common right of humanity and the other the divine right of kings. It is the same principle in whatever shape it develops itself. It is the same spirit that says, 'You work and toil and earn bread, and I'll eat it.' No matter in what shape it comes, whether from the mouth of a king who seeks to bestride the people of his own nation and live by the fruit of their labor, or from one race of men as an apology for enslaving another race, it is the same tyrannical principle." (Abraham Lincoln, October 15, 1858; *Collected Works* 3:315)

life, subjugating man's conscience and sacrificing to the State his faith in all that is right and humane. It is fervent atheism that derides the human soul.

Totalitarianism means the total politicalization of life without exception. The state encompasses society in all its spheres. There is no corner where man can hide from the State, no place without regimentation.

The world has had an opportunity to observe and reflect on the true meaning of totalitarianism. German Nazism, which was an affinitive offshoot from the communist prototype. was a truly revealing manifestation of totalitarianism. Nazism, which is the popular abbreviation of national socialism, imported from Soviet Russia the one-party system, the pre-eminence of the party, the position of secret police, the concentration camps for dissidents, the methods of propaganda. Hitler was an excellent disciple of Lenin and Stalin, a perfect product of totalitarianism. The heinous Nazi crimes were the outcome of a consistent application of totalitarian principles.

Our mental and moral confusion towards communism could easily be avoided if we were ever mindful of the affinities of the two systems. After all, the inhumanities of communism differ little from the Nazi crimes against humanity.

Communism, in fact, is incomparably more dangerous to man's civilization than German Nazism whose doctrine of Aryan superiority prevented its dissemination to all mankind. Without this narrow racial limitation communism is capable of subjugating all that is human.

Consider the following 12 questions:

1. Would you have been concerned if, during World War II, a Nazi had murdered our President right here in our own country?

Yet, a communist, Lee Harvey Oswald, who maintained contact with Party headquarters in New York, is accused of murdering President Kennedy.

2. Would it have bothered you, if, after the assassination of the President by a Nazi, a top Nazi newspaper had called for a special commission headed by a hero of the Nazis to investigate the crime, only to have the new President appoint exactly such a commission three days later?

Yet following President Kennedy's assassination, the communist newspaper, *The Worker,* recommended that President Johnson form a commission with Earl Warren at its head to make an investigation. Three days later, Johnson did exactly that and Earl Warren later selected as assistant counsel for the commission a man who had belonged to one of the most notorious communism fronts in the country. (The Warren Court and its decisions have been honored with victory rallies by the Communist party.)

3. Would you have been aroused if, in our life-and-death struggle with the Nazis during World War II, we had refused the assistance of an ally who, without any strings attached, wanted to come to our aid and provide a half-million trained and armed men to fight an enemy he had already fought before, on a terrain with which he was acquainted?

Yet our government refuses the help of Chiang Kai-shek and his trained and equipped army which knows how to fight the communists on Asian land.

4. What would you have said during World War II if our government had told us that Mussolini was a different sort of fascist than Hitler, and therefore could be won to our side if only we would give him foreign aid and help train his pilots and military officers?

Yet our government has sent billions of dollars to Tito, a communist, and trained his pilots and military officers in our country, on the grounds that he is "independent" of Moscow. Tito has stated that in an all-out war between Russia and the United States, he will be on the side of the Russians.

5. Would you have been shocked during World War II if a union headed by a man who joined the Nazis in the 1930's caused a twelve-day public transportation strike in our largest city, at a cost of over one billion dollars?

Yet New York City recently suffered such a strike, and the leader of the union causing it was Mike Quill, who joined the Communist party in 1934 and followed the communist line consistently thereafter.

6. Would you have sought the impeachment of the President if, during World War II, he had asked American mothers to sacrifice their sons to stop Hitler, and at the same time requested an increase in trade with the Nazis?

Yet in his State of the Union address, the President asked us to sacrifice American manhood in a war against the communists in South Vietnam, and in the same speech asked that we build more bridges to the East through increased trade with the communists.

7. Would it have startled you during World War II if our government had encouraged businessmen to sell Nazi goods in their stores and trade with the Nazis, hence enabling Hitler to have more finances with which to slaughter our sons?

Yet, just this last September, the State Department said it was against the national interest for people to oppose the sale of communist goods in American stores, or to oppose trade with the communists by American businessmen. Could this mean that the national interest of the present administration is to promote communism?

8. Would you have suspected something if, during World War II, a man who had made substantial contributions to the Nazi Party and had been declared a security risk was honored at a White House ceremony?

Yet President Johnson presented a $50,000 tax-free award and a gold medal at the White House to Dr. Julius Robert Oppenheimer, who made contributions to the Communist party and up to the time of his death was listed as a security risk.

9. Would you have taken the Nazi threat seriously if, during World War II, they had claimed credit for starting one of the worst riots in our country's history?

Yet a communist took credit for the Watts riot in California in 1965, with all its destruction, pillage and bloodshed, and boasted that his group had spent two years in Watts agitating for the uprising.

10. Would you have disagreed with our defense policies during World War II if the Secretary of Defense had said our objectives against the Nazis were limited and did not include the destruction of the Nazi regime in Berlin?

Yet Secretary McNamara asserted in October, 1966, that our objectives in Vietnam are limited, and do not include the destruction of the communist regime in North Vietnam.

11. Would you have been disturbed if, during World War II, the courts had permitted a Nazi to run for political office in one of our states, and the Nazi had then received the votes of thousands of Americans?

Yet, an open and avowed leader of the Communist party was allowed by the courts to run for a county office in one of our states recently and she received over 87,000 votes. (Dorothy Healey)

12. Would it have shocked you during World War II if a Nazi folksinger had received a U.S. Government service award and had a government building named in his honor?

Yet, the late Woody Guthrie, an identified Communist who had worked as a columnist for one communist publication and contributed to another, received the Interior Department's Conservation Service Award in 1965, and Secretary Udall announced that a Bonneville Power Administration substation in the Pacific Northwest would be named the Woodie Guthrie sub-station.

In our dealings with communism let us ever be mindful of past experience. A policy of appeasement, rapprochement, or even friendship towards communism is as offensive and suicidal as it was toward Nazi Germany. And the fellow travelers of communism are no less despicable than those of the Nazi tyrants. In fact, why should we not condemn more harshly the appeasers of communism and deem their blindness incomparably more inexcusable after we experienced the barbarism of the Nazi totalitarianism?

And yet, *our policies continue to be guided by intellectual confusion and moral lethargy*. We wheel and deal with communist agents and officials as if they represent their peoples. We launch diplomatic maneuvers and counter-maneuvers as if we were engaged in an old-fashioned power struggle. We make treaties and agreements, accept promises and declarations as if we were dealing with Victorian England. We embark upon cultural exchanges as if the communists were receptive to cultural values. We trade with communist governments as if we were exchanging goods and services with merchants in London. In fact, our officials fraternize with communist officials in political, economic, social, and cultural matters while at that very moment thousands of individuals linger in communist prisons and concentration camps, or risk death trying to escape their tyrants.

Since our military involvement in Vietnam, our dealing and wheeling with communist officials has assumed shameful and even treacherous proportions. While American soldiers are cut down by Russian arms and ammunition, U.S. Government officials, in fact, are encouraging trading with communist Russia and her allies. And yet, we continue to curry the economic favors of the Kremlin masters.[6]

How can the President of the United States claim, as reported by the Vice President, that the so-called Cold War is over and predict that Congress will lower trade barriers with communist countries? How could he request Congress to ratify the consular convention with the Soviets who are pledged to bury us and enslave the world?

---

[6]"Capitalists the world over and their governments, will, in their desire to win the Soviet market, shut their eyes to the above-mentioned activities (espionage and subversion) and will thus be turned into blind deaf-mutes. They will furnish credits, which will serve us as a means of supporting the Communist parties in their countries, and, by supplying us with materials and techniques which are not available to us, will rebuild our war industry, which is essentially for our future attacks on our suppliers. In other words, they will be laboring to prepare their own suicide." (Lenin, quoted in *Congressional Record*, March 1, 1967)

In recent months the official list of "non-strategic" items that may be sold to communist governments has lengthened continually. In 1966, for instance, the Soviet Union was encouraged to buy from American manufacturers airborne communications and navigation equipment and a tire cord factory. Licenses were issued permitting the Czechoslovakian government to purchase ball and roller bearings, petroleum products, and a hydrogen plant. Airborne radar equipment and automotive replacement parts were approved for Red Rumania; for the Bulgarian regime, pumps and compressors; for Poland, more radio communication parts and various generators; for Hungary, electronic navigational aids and railway equipment; for Yugoslavia, aircraft parts and petroleum products; for East Germany, boring and drilling machines.

It is important to understand that our trade with the communist countries constitutes no trade with the people of those countries, but merely with communist governments. An American merchant who sells navigation equipment to Russia must negotiate and deal exclusively with Kremlin agents. And for the Kremlin all goods are "strategic" for its military, psychological, or economic war on the West.

And yet, in his 1966 State of the Union message to Congress, reaffirmed by his 1967 message theme of "bridges to the East," the President urged an expansion of trade "between the United States and Eastern Europe and the Soviet Union." In September 1966, the State Department even published a pamphlet entitled *Private Boycotts versus the National Interest,* in which it openly denounced those Americans who criticize our trade with communist governments.

All these bridges have proved to be one-way bridges, for the communists' trade with the West is merely one more strategic instrument in their war against the West. We should stop this senseless one-way "bridge building."

Does not the President understand the characteristics of a totalitarian regime that politicalizes every transaction? Everything is made a political transaction that concerns the destruction of the free world. Is our President blind to the fact that trade with communist officials first of all is political, and not business as usual? Shall we ascribe the President's attitude to moral cowardice, an amoral attitude toward the peoples entrapped by communism, or something else?

This recognition also indicts gravely those American merchants and manufacturers who in the bureaus of the Kremlin seek profitable orders and favors from the communist tyrants. In fact, some businessmen who are either exceptionally unintelligent or extraordinarily unscrupulous are now proffering their merchandise and service to the Kremlin masters, who at this very moment are aiding and supporting our enemies in Vietnam. In the waiting rooms of the Kremlin, American businessmen dream of personal gains and profits while thousands of American boys in Vietnam are slain by communist bullets made in the U.S.S.R. A shameful spectacle that is indicative of our incredible confusion and moral decay!

American businessmen are lending their managerial ability and capital resources to the communist masters who are boasting of their economic achievements. This is their boastful slogan: "In 1970 we shall surpass the U.S." This is conceivable only if we accomplish it for them. If we build their factories, supply them with our resources and technical knowhow and if, at the same time, we cause our apparatus or production to deteriorate through confiscatory taxation and inflation, through bureaucratic controls and expropriations. Then, and only then, may the most unscrupulous regime surpass the other.

Dr. Werner Keller, author of the great book, *The Bible as History,* concluded his recent book entitled *East Minus West = Zero,* outlining Russia's debt to the West, with these words:

> All that the West stands for, all that it has achieved and is still achieving culturally, technically, and scientifically, has been done without a single important contribution from the Russians. If the Russians had never existed at all it would have made not an iota of difference to what the West has to offer all humanity.
>
> The present position of Russia, had she not been taught, helped and supported by the West, would be unthinkable. Even at this moment Russia can only keep up by the continuous theft and exploitation of every new development in the free world.

It is tragic indeed that our trade with communist governments is planned and promoted by our own officials who have made aid to the Soviet Union the official policy of the American Government. Wherever private businessmen still hesitate to proffer their aid and support, the U.S. Government itself backs up the Kremlin with special deals, credit guarantees and outright subsidies.

The 1963 wheat deal was an example. The Federal Government not only paved the way for the transaction but also guaranteed the Soviets credit and subsidized the communists to the tune of $42 million. In addition, concessions were made on freight rates. When private bankers refused to extend credit to the grain exporters, the President had the Export-Import Bank, which is a government agency, guarantee the transaction.

In many cases our economic aid to the enemy is channeled through the impotent, pro-communist United Nations Organization. We pay at least 32 percent of all U.N. operations which cost more than $500 million in 1966.

We contributed at least 40 percent of the expenses of the International Development Association and the Special United Nations Fund for Economic Development which, according to their own words, "provide systematic assistance in fields essential to technical, economic, and social development of less-developed countries." As all communist countries can be classified as "less-developed," a great deal of U.N. assistance is channeled towards communist governments. Through the Special Fund, for instance, we covered 40 percent of the costs of an agricultural experimental station in communist Cuba. And through the United Nations Economic and Social Council we subsidize the University of Havana, which every year is graduating thousands of young communists.

Our intellectual confusion and moral lethargy also shape our attitude and policy towards the communist satellites. Poland, for instance, has received no less than $548 million in U.S. aid, while Yugoslavia garnered some $2.4 billion.

The rationale of this aid springs from our hope to divide the communist camp and, in particular, achieve satellite independence from Moscow. But all available evidence indicates that our aid merely serves to consolidate and fortify the position of the Kremlin and its foreign henchmen. Communist Tito, with whom I have talked face to face, has stated repeatedly that he will stand firmly with Moscow in any rift with the United States. According to him, our military operations in Vietnam are "aggressive acts by reactionary forces," are "shameful" and "dangerous to world peace." This attitude is hardly suited to create confidence in our aid to communists. After all, communism is a barbaric system wherever it raises its ugly head, in Moscow and Peking, Warsaw and Belgrade, Prague and Havana. Aiding and supporting the communists is offensive and suicidal not only in Moscow, but anywhere in the world.

And *it is inexcusable no matter who does it*. Of course, we would hope that our government, whose example is so important in world affairs, would point the way out of this confusion and blindness. But unfortunately the New Frontier and Great Society administrations and the so-called New Republicanism not only shattered this hope, but, also, to our greatest dismay, often led the way into darkness. But this confusion of ours does not in the least clear from fault or blame other free world governments who are guilty of the same failure.

It is a new and strange chapter of history when the enemies of the United States receive aid and support from our allies. A British Government agency, for instance, has agreed to supply credit guarantees for the sale of a $28 million fertilizer factory to the Castro government. Two years ago socialist Britain sold 950 buses on credit to Castro. While the U.S. Government gives all-out support to the British effort to bring down the white-minority Government of Rhodesia, the British Labor Government supports Castro's Cuba with both credit and trade.

Red China's biggest trade partner is Japan. British Hong Kong is the biggest source of hard currency for Red China, and Canada sells her vast quantities of grain. Western Europe supplies chemical fertilizer. She gets steel from West Germany, France, Belgium and Japan; airplanes from Britain; ships from France and the Netherlands; diesel locomotives from France. These are our allies.

Even the North Vietnam Government does brisk business with allies of the U.S. Japan buys anthracite and sells industrial goods which are carried to North Vietnam on communist-flag freighters.

A dozen ships flying the flags of Britain, Cyprus and Malta deliver European goods to Haiphong, and ships from Hong Kong probably deliver American goods.

The economic significance of this aid to our enemies is overshadowed by far by its moral meaning. Our actions and policies towards communism reflect the extent of subversion within our own government, our incredible confusion, indecision, and even cowardice. We tremendously overrate the productivity of communism and lack faith in the values we defend. We are weak intellectually and morally. In our confusion we are betraying the intellectual and moral heritage of the West.

In a recent State of the Union address the President said:

> I ask and urge the Congress to help our foreign and commercial trade policies by passing an East-West Trade Bill and approving our consular convention with the Soviet Union.

Commenting on this, the weekly magazine, *Review of the News* said:

> The war in Vietnam is, for all practical purposes, a war between the United States and the Soviet bloc, for it is the Soviet bloc which contributes the vast amount of military equipment which makes it possible for the primitive economy of North Vietnam to wage this war against us. No amount of semantic trickery on the part of the President can change this fact of reality. That is why the war is costing us billions, and Lyndon Johnson knows it. There are others who know it also, policy makers like McNamara, Rusk, Rostow, and the rest of the clique. (*Review of the News,* Vol. 3, No. 4, p. 21)

There seems to be no limit to our follies — our essentially treasonable policies. On June 1, 1964, the present Administration and the Kremlin signed the Consular Convention which provides for the reciprocal establishment of consulates in all major cities of the U.S. and U.S.S.R. At present, Soviet diplomatic personnel are stationed only at their Washington embassy and with the U.N. in New York. In fact, there are no Soviet consulates anywhere in the Western Hemisphere. If the U.S. Government now sets the precedent by opening our country to additional Kremlin agents, how can our Latin-American neighbors resist similar Soviet demands?

A consul is a public officer who is authorized to protect the interests and to foster the commercial affairs of his country's subjects in a foreign country. As consuls have no representative character like ambassadors they cannot claim general immunity and extra-territoriality attached to diplomatic representatives. But, under the terms of the Johnson-Kremlin convention, consular officers and employees would be completely immune from criminal prosecution, even in the case of felonies.

And now the U.S. Senate has ratified the Consular Treaty with our enemy — the enemy of freedom and righteousness — the greatest evil in this world. And this, in spite of the Soviet's dismal record of treaty violations.

This unfortunate action by our Senate opens further the door to espionage, subversion and sabotage and is further aid to the enemy. It is treasonable.

Our "soft-on-communism" ratification of the Consular Treaty has left me stunned and sick at heart. Such weak-kneed, cowardly action does not represent the feelings of America at the grass-roots.

Our prestige as a nation is at an all-time low. When will we act like men of courage? When will we stand up to the godless leaders of the communist conspiracy — the greatest evil in this world? What has happened to our leadership — including the leadership of the Republican Party? There seems to be little moral courage and statesmanship left.

Have we lost interest in the freedom of God's children — in the basic concepts that have made this country?

The hour is late. God help us wake up and act before it is too late.

How blind can we be? We grant consular rights to the Kremlin communists, oppressors of their own nation. The communist agents then are "to foster the commercial affairs of their subjects," who are forbidden to trade abroad under the penalty of death. The communist agents are "to protect the interests of their citizens," who are prisoners. There are no emigrants from Soviet Russia, only refugees. When they manage to escape, risking death at the border, they are often haunted, blackmailed or even murdered by communist agents abroad. I have seen it at the shameful Berlin wall. And, finally, we offer diplomatic immunity to such agents!

How bent we are on our own destruction! We now promote "cultural exchange," supposedly in the interest of mutual understanding and peace to provide contact between the communist nations and us. We exchange athletes, scientists, singers, pianists, and other artists, supposedly, in order to mend the break in communications and thus end amicably the Cold War.

We readily admit that the Russian people are very much like the American people. But we are not confronted by the Russian people who themselves are extremely regimented and whose lives are totally dominated by the communist regime. We are confronted by a communist conspiracy that does not "exchange" in good faith, but uses every transaction for its sinister ends. American tourists who visit Russia are shown exactly what the communist agents want them to see. I know — I've been there. But Soviet nationals who visit the United States are either communist functionaries or individuals under their vigilant control with family hostages left behind the iron curtain. The communists make every professor, every dancer, pianist, and athlete their political agents. Every sporting match, artistic performance, and speech is made a political action. We are confronted by a monolithic totalitarianism that differs radically from our own system of individuality, the many-sided, libertarian, pluralistic nature of the West.

Again and again we are inclined to accept communist promises and declarations at Western face value. We ignore communist standards of morality that, according to Lenin, make deceit a duty and virtue. This is why disarmament agreements, treaties, and negotiations with the communists are surely suicidal.[7]

And yet we are eager to make such agreements, and have, in fact, taken a number of steps toward disarmament. In 1963 the Kennedy Administration entered the Moscow Treaty which was to stop testing nuclear explosives above ground and under water.

The treaty was hailed by the Administration as the first joint East-West move toward disarmament of any kind since World War II. It was signed five years after the negotiations had begun and two years after the Soviets had broken a voluntary accord against testing. The new agreement is so loose that it requires no international inspection and permits any of the three nations to repudiate it in time of danger. There is nothing to prevent clandestine tests but the honor and integrity of the participating parties. And yet, we are dealing with murderers who have neither honor nor integrity. They declare that, "treaties are like pie crust — made to be broken." How could we, leaders of the greatest nation in the world, make this deal with the devil through his emissaries?

To rely on truth, integrity, and honor in communism entails unbearable risks of our security and survival. The treaty prevents our full development of any new weapons requiring the use of nuclear warheads. It prevents us from testing our intercontinental ballistic missiles on which our strategic defenses greatly depend. It prevents us from developing an effective anti-missile defense system on which our survival may depend. And finally, it prevents us from developing tactical

---

[7]"Any pacts and agreements with the Soviets can be expected to be as meaningless and one-sided in the future as they have been in the past. Instruments of this kind are a favorite Soviet device to make their intended victims relax their guard and, therefore, tend to increase rather than decrease the threat of aggression. This applies, in particular, to proposed disarmament and similar agreements designed to weaken our deterrent posture." (General Thomas S. Power, *Design For War,* p. 28)

atomic weapons that would give us invincibility on the battle-field. In short, the Moscow Treaty neutralized our major military advantage over the communists and would subject us to Soviet conventional forces and their proficiency in subversion, guerrilla warfare and internal revolution. The war in Vietnam is a good example.

Hear the warning of the Senate Internal Security Sub-committee:

> Acceptance of any precipitate program of disarmament would constitute for the West a strategic defeat of enormous magnitude, leaving an irresolute Western world only the recourse of seeking accommodation with an aggressive movement which is dedicated to achieving mastery of the globe.

But our weakness is not primarily strategic and military, it is intellectual and moral. In a world of enormous tensions and conflicts have we lost our sense of direction and the will to survive?

We must ever remember that we are at war with a clever, ruthless, unprincipled enemy. *And we are losing the war.* Yes, and we will continue to lose unless we the American people become alerted and informed — unless we stand up to the enemy of all we hold dear.

Why do we bow and yield to their unreasonable and dangerous demands: When will we act like men of courage and faith? The language of courage is the only language they respect. *Let's be sure we're right and stand firm.*

Some timid souls speak fearfully of war. The communist economy would not support a major war. They can't even feed their own people.

It is time for the citizens of this nation to vigorously question and oppose programs and policies which threaten our very existence.

The record is obvious, that since World War II, we have dealt with, appeased, begged, pleaded, bought off and otherwise conducted business with communists only to see the threat grow greater and more menacing than ever.

Why does our President condemn in word communist aggression and then seek to bolster their economies through aid and trade "when the Moscow government is supplying MIG's to the North Vietnamese to kill American boys?" (David Lawrence)

Why fight the communists in Vietnam and help them everywhere else? Why does the Administration move so vigorously to increase trade with the enemy?

Why does the Administration send wheat to feed those who are making the guns and bullets to kill our American boys in Vietnam?

"Why," as a prominent agricultural publisher has asked, "is the main plan of our foreign policy predicated on friendship with Russia? Only one word can adequately answer that question. The word is treason. We —'our' State Department — made Russia. Ever since Roosevelt, we have exported factories, food, equipment, and American know-how to Russia and her satellites. Russia is the enemy. Treason is 'giving aid and comfort to the enemy.'[8]

"In 1967 let us resolve to win in Vietnam and in Cuba and China. In 1967 and every year let us dedicate ourselves to making the criminal communist conspiracy fail everywhere; and to freeing the enslaved of the world." (Tom Anderson) . . .

For two decades "our government has been paying the Soviet blackmailers with one concession after another." How long will we continue this dangerous and diabolical surrender of our legitimate rights?

---

[8]"The courts of the United States have stated the following acts to be treasonable: The use or attempted use of any force or violence against the Government of the United States, or its military or naval forces; *the acquisition, use or disposal of any property with knowledge that it is to be, or with intent that it shall be, of assistance to the enemy in their hostilities against the United States; the performance of any act or the publication of statements or information which will give or supply in any way, aid and comfort to the enemies of the United States;* the direction, aiding, counseling, or countenancing of any of the foregoing acts; *such acts are held to be treasonable whether committed within the United States or elsewhere;* whether committed by a citizen of the United States, or by an alien domiciled, or residing, in the United States, inasmuch as resident aliens, as well as citizens, owe allegiance to the United States and its laws." (Proclamation issued on April 16, 1917, by President Woodrow Wilson)

When will we proclaim the truth — as we did in 1776 — that we may be free? When will we stand up to the greatest evil in this world — the greatest enemy of our God-given freedom? *The hour is late.*

One of the greatest errors ever made by an American President occurred when Franklin D. Roosevelt extended diplomatic recognition to the godless Soviet conspiracy — after each of four American Presidents in succession had refused to do so.

Without this tragic action in 1933 by an American President, perhaps insensitive to the dangers of socialism and communism, Soviet communism would have collapsed in ruins. Why do we continue to keep this evil, freedom-destroying system alive by such indefensible action?

Statesman-patriot, Dean Clarence E. Manion, who has had a son in Vietnam, put it this way:

> The truth is that there is no such thing as a legitimate Communist government anywhere on earth. The truth is that what our State Department calls the "closed societies" of Communism are iron-ringed jails from which the inmates may attempt to escape only at the risk of their lives. (I know — I've been at the shameful Berlin wall.) The truth is that conditions in these Communist jails are so horrible that hundreds of people risk and often lose their lives in attempts to escape from them. The truth is that the hundreds of millions of helpless people who are held in this monstrous Red captivity are scandalized by the calloused indifference of our government to their cruel fate as expressed in a foreign policy which is deliberately calculated to "help stabilize tottering Communist regimes, as in East Germany."
>
> The truth is that without our positive and active help, all of these "tottering Communist regimes" would fall of their own weight within six months after our help was withdrawn.
>
> The truth is that if we withdrew our official prohibition against an invasion of the Red Chinese mainland by the Nationalist Chinese Army on Formosa, that invasion would take place immediately, and 90 per cent of the enslaved Chinese on the mainland would join the attack against their Red Chinese jailers.
>
> This would solve our problem in South Vietnam and Laos where the Red forces are being supplied and supervised by the Red Chinese government. The collapse of Communism in China

would start a chain reaction of anti-Communist revolution which would sweep across Europe to the eastern boundary of West Germany.

The consequences of an official proclamation of the truth about Communists and Communist governments by the government of the United States would open the door to the destruction of Communism by its own oppressed victims without international war and without the use of American military force.

The truth that made us free will restore our freedom now and lift the hearts and hopes of millions whom our present policy of retreat and surrender has doomed to perpetual slavery.

This will not be a signal for international nuclear war, but for successful anti-Communist revolution which will melt down the Iron Curtain from the inside. This is the high road of moral principal that leads to peace with freedom for America and for mankind. (*The Conservative American,* pp. 200-202)

M. Stanton Evans, brilliant young editor of the *Indianapolis News,* put it well in his new book, *The Politics of Surrender,* which every American should read, when he said:

If we seriously intend to resist Communist aggression, our first indicated move is to stop doing things which strengthen the adversary. We should stop giving aid, direct and indirect, to Moscow and other Iron Curtain countries; curtail the East-West trade which helps fuel the Bolshevik's creaking industrial machinery; enforce the Battle Act and other legislative measures seeking to forestall trade by U.S. aid recipients with Communist nations; stop cultural exchanges which make for improved Soviet espionage; stop Soviet scientists from touring our restricted installations; stop foreign aid and diplomatic aid to people like Sukarno and Nkrumah; stop paying the bills for Communist U.N. members, etc.

The aggression of atheistic communist countries supported by the treasonous policies of our own government and some misguided American businessmen, led to the killing of over five thousand American soldiers last year.

This is the result of the so-called "building bridges of friendship" by increasing trade with the communists who are supplying Asian hordes with the material to kill our boys in Vietnam.

The lead article in the June, 1967, *American Opinion* magazine began as follows: "More than 200 American soldiers are now being killed by the Communists each week in Vietnam" and another 200 maimed and wounded. The U.S. has suffered more than 60,000 casualties in this undeclared no-win war.

The Vietnam war is part of the communist's fight for world control. In this no-win war over 11,000 of the flower of our young men have been killed and tens of thousands maimed. A recent headline read, "2,092 killed, wounded or missing last week." Hundreds of billions of dollars are being drained from our economy — which is being bled white by this senselessly prolonged war. Every move which weakens this nation economically, morally or psychologically is a move that helps the world take-over by communism.

As Admiral James K. Davis has emphasized, "The cold war is not a brush-war, but a grim, dangerous part of a relentless fight 'for keeps,' the stages being our survival as a free nation, and Vietnam being but a step in the mounting progression of communist aggression toward winning the overall war for communist world domination." (*Titusville Herald,* December 2, 1966, Titusville, Pa.)

After six years of war we have nearly half a million troops supporting a no-win war which is costing the taxpayer more than $2 million per month, against a third-rate country of 17 million people, smaller than the state of Missouri.

My fellow citizens — normally, I am slow to anger. It is my nature to seek to find the good in what every man does and to give him the benefit of any reasonable doubt. I strive to follow the admonition to be forgiving. But it has become increasingly difficult for me the last while to restrain my wrath at what I consider to be not only a lack of support, but an ACTUAL BETRAYAL of our valiant fighting men and our allies. A betrayal of the suffering, loneliness and sacrifices of the mothers, wives, and children of our fighting men.

I refer to *what appears to be a deliberate and determined effort to provide our enemies with the means to kill our sons.*

It is perhaps not just anger that I feel at this betrayal of our fighting men, their families and this nation, by trading with the enemy. Deep within my soul is a feeling of sickness and revulsion at the seeming injustice of it all, of bitter disappointment in the attitude of a few of my fellow Americans.

Thomas Jefferson is quoted as follows:

> A departure from principle in one instance becomes a precedent for a second; that second for a third; and so on, till the bulk of the society is reduced to mere automatons of misery, to have no sensibilities left but for sin and suffering. (Thomas Jefferson, *Works* 7:14.)

As it is, ladies and gentlemen, I am not mollified — rather I am angered and hurt. Hurt that my nation, with a spiritual foundation, which I love so dearly, could act with such great dishonor in respect to its own fighting men.

A challenge would seem to be in order.

I challenge our youth everywhere to adopt as a part of their innermost feelings and desires the cry:

"Keep faith with our fighting men! No aid or comfort to the enemy."

I challenge with reverence, the mothers and wives of our servicemen — not to distract and concern their heroes by complaining to them — but to make their congressmen, senators and all government officials aware of our united concern. Let our plea, and our prayers be:

"Keep faith with our sons. Don't provide our enemy any means to destroy our boys. Stop all trade with the enemy. Let our valiant men return to us in honor having won an honorable victorious fight for freedom." The way to end the war in Vietnam is to win it.

I challenge the fathers and husbands of this nation. Gentlemen, who is to restore honor, honesty, virtue, integrity, and loyalty to our way of life? We, as fathers and husbands, are the real leaders of our civilization — of our nation. We are responsible if the blight on its glory is not removed. Gentlemen, let our cry be: "I shall become and remain a man of principle. I shall lead my family, my friends, my community and my nation also in the way of principle and not of expediency. I will defend my freedom and the freedom of my fellow men. I will raise my head high and look every man in the eye unashamed of my defense of that which is good. I shall be able to face every man returning from Vietnam knowing that I did not betray his faith."

I challenge us all to advocate, desire, teach and live God-fearing lives of righteousness. Truly American lives. *Let us stand up for freedom.*[9] Let us be true to God, family and country.

There is no other way of honor — no other way to save our great nation and the God-given liberty we cherish.

That we may heed the sacred call — before it is too late — is my humble prayer.

---

[9]*"To preserve the liberty of our country ought to be our only emulation,* and he will be the best soldier, and the best patriot, who contributes most to this glorious work, whatever his station, or from whatever part of the continent, he may come." (George Washington, General Orders, August 1, 1776)

CHAPTER 6

IT CAN HAPPEN HERE [1]

"Shall we gather strength by irresolution and inaction? Shall we acquire the means of effectual resistance, by lying supinely on our backs, and hugging the delusive phantom of hope, until our enemies shall have bound us hand and foot? Sir, we are not weak, if we make a proper use of the means which the God of nature hath placed in our power. . . . Besides, sir, we shall not fight our battles alone. There is a just God who presides over the destinies of nations; and who will raise up friends to fight our battles for us. *The battle, sir, is not to the strong alone; it is to the vigilant, the active, the brave. . . .* it is now too late to retire from the contest. There is no retreat, but in submission and slavery! Our chains are forged! Their clanking may be heard. . . . Why stand we here idle? . . . *Is life so dear, or peace so sweet, as to be purchased at the price of chains and slavery? Forbid it, Almighty God! I know not what course others may take; but as for me, give me liberty, or give me death!*" (Patrick Henry, March 23, 1775; *P.P.N.S.,* p. 517)

This is a signal honor, a very great pleasure and a challenging responsibility. My gratitude for this opportunity is increased by the realization that this is my second appearance at this great forum.

Because of the nature of the message I bring to you tonight, I have committed most of it to writing. I shall speak to you frankly and honestly. Some of you may not agree with everything I say. Thank God in this blessed land we can still

---

[1]An address given on February 28, 1966, at a meeting sponsored by the American Wake Up Committee, in St. Louis, Missouri.

speak our convictions. I pray it may ever be so. I have been in nations where this blessed privilege is no longer enjoyed.[2]

What I say are my personal convictions born out of an active life which has taken me into forty-five nations and brought me close to the insidious forces which would destroy our way of life. . . .

I speak then of *the greatest single evil in the world — a vicious, godless conspiracy.*

For a quarter of a century I have seen, at close range, on both sides of the iron curtain the insidious forward march of creeping socialism and its ruthless companion godless communism. It is a shocking record of bluff, bluster, deception, intrigue, bondage, and mass murder. Never in recorded history has any movement spread itself so far and so fast as has socialistic-communism in the past few years. The facts are not pleasant to review. Communist leaders are jubilant with their success. They are driving freedom back on almost every front. . . .

In less than half a century this evil system has gained control over one-third of mankind, and it is steadily pursuing its vicious goal of control over all the rest of the world, while we as Americans cry all is well in our passive complacency.

But the Communist party and its fellow travelers and sympathizers are "manifestly frightened by the possibility of the people of the U.S. becoming awakened. Communist success has always been achieved in an atmosphere of secrecy, deceit and confusion." (W. Cleon Skousen) Therefore, courageous organizations and individuals that are successful in awakening the American people are marked for annihilation.

---

[2]"It is an undertaking of some degree of delicacy to examine into the cause of public disorders. If a man happens not to succeed in such an inquiry, he will be thought weak and visionary; if he touches the true grievance, there is danger that he may come near to persons of weight and consequence, who will rather be exasperated at the discovery of their errors, than thankful for the occasion of correcting them. If he should be obliged to blame the favorites of the people, he will be considered as the tool of power; if he censures those in power, he will be looked on as an instrument of faction. But in all exertions of duty something is to be hazarded." (Edmund Burke, 1770; *Works* 1:435)

The smear seems to be the most widely used and effective tool of the conspiracy to discredit and weaken any effective anti-communist effort. The smear of any individual or organization by the communists, their dupes, and fellow travelers is evidence of effectiveness. If any of you are affiliated with patriotic organizations reportedly opposed to the communist conspiracy, which are not extensively smeared, you can rest assured your opposition is largely ineffective. You had best look for a more fruitful affiliation.[3]

It seems almost unbelievable that an average of 52 million liberty-loving people could be brought under communist bondage each and every year since World War II. Why this shocking record? How could this happen? How can men, many of them in high places, who seem to be so strong for Christian principles and basic American concepts be so effectively used to serve the communist conspiracy? How can our own people be lulled away into a false security crying, "All is well"?

I believe the answer is found in the fact that these godless communist conspirators and their gullible fellow travelers are masters of deceit — who deceive the very elect. Then, too, it has never happened here. We have always enjoyed freedom. Our liberty has never been seriously endangered in our lifetime. It can't happen here, we say. I say to you, it can happen here. It is happening here. In our comfortable complacency it is really happening here — now.

I quote that great American, J. Edgar Hoover:

> I confess to a real apprehension so long as communists are able to secure ministers of the gospel to promote their evil work and espouse a cause that is alien to the religion of Christ and Judaism. I do fear so long as school boards and parents tolerate conditions whereby communists and fellow travelers under the guise of academic freedom can teach our youth a way of life that eventually will destroy the sanctity of the home, that under-

---

[3]"One tried and proven weapon the Communists have used in the past has been the ruthless 'smear.' Congressional committees, patriotic organizations, the FBI and all those who attack subversion and defend American concepts are primary targets. . . . The best yardstick of the effectiveness of the fight against communism is the fury of the smear attacks against the fighter — launched and conducted by the Reds. . . . We may well be judged by the enemies we make." (J. Edgar Hoover, June 16, 1959)

mines faith in God, that causes them to scorn respect for con-
stituted authority and sabotage our revered Constitution. (*Menace of Communism,* p. 11)

*Our complacency as a nation is shocking — yes, almost
unbelievable!*[4]

We are a prosperous nation. Our people have high-paying
jobs. Our incomes are high. Our standard of living is at an
unprecedented level. We do not like to be disturbed as we enjoy our comfortable complacency. We live in the soft present
and feel the future is secure. We do not worry about history.
We seem oblivious to the causes of the rise and fall of nations.
We are blind to the hard fact that nations usually sow the seeds
of their own destruction while enjoying unprecedented
prosperity.

I say to you with all the fervor of my soul: *We are sow-
ing the seeds of our own destruction in America and much of
the free world today.* It is my sober warning to you today that
if the trends of the past thirty years — and especially the past
five years — continue, we will lose that which is as priceless as
life itself — our freedom — our liberty — our right to act as
free men. *It can happen here. It is happening here.*

*Our greatest need in America today is to be alerted and
informed.* When we have become alerted and informed, we
will soberly sense the need for a reversal of the present trends.
We will realize that the laws of economics are immutable. We
will be convinced that we must return to a spirit of humility,
faith in God and the basic concepts upon which this great
Christian nation has been established under the direction of
Divine Providence.

---

[4]"There is no greater tribute to the effectiveness of the Soviet fifth column
in this country than the obvious fact that it has befogged the American mind regarding its ruthless resolves to wipe out American independence. Nothing is so
clear-cut as its continual insistence within its own ranks that violent attack upon
the government here is highly essential. But so skilled are its propagandists—
disguised as non-Communists in the radio, newspaper and moving-picture world—
that they have made Americans believe every revelation of Red espionage is the
result of hysteria. They have done a fairly adequate job of making America
ashamed of defending its own freedom." (Louis F. Budenz, Ex-Communist; *Men
Without Faces,* pp. 7-8)

The sad and shocking story of what has happened in America in recent years must be told. Our people must have the facts. There is safety in an informed public.[5] There is real danger in a complacent, uninformed citizenry. This is our real danger today. Yes, the truth must be told even at the risk of destroying, in large measure, the influence of men who are widely respected and loved by the American people. The stakes are high. *Freedom and survival is the issue.*

Today we are at war. It is not enough to be against communism. We must shed our complacency and aggressively meet this challenge. . . . There can be no compromise with the communists. They are at war with us — with the entire cause of freedom — and the sooner every American faces this hard fact, the stronger our position will be. It is a real war. The lines are tightly drawn. The war is more insidious, more devious, more devastating, and more satanical than any war in our history. Moral principles, once universally recognized, are ignored. International law once respected is thrown to the wind.

The socialist-communist philosophy is devastatingly evil — destructive of all that is good, uplifting and beautiful. It strikes at the very foundation of all we hold dear. The communist "has convinced himself that nothing is evil which answers the call of expediency." This is a most damnable doctrine. People who truly accept such a philosophy have neither conscience nor honor. Force, trickery, lies, broken promises — to them such things are wholly justified.[6]

We believe in religion as a mode of life resulting from our faith in God. Communism contends that all religion must be overthrown because it inhibits the spirit of world revolution.

---

[5]"Enlighten the people generally, and tyranny and oppressions of body and mind will vanish like evil spirits at the dawn of day." (Thomas Jefferson, to M. Dupont De Nemours, April 24, 1816; *Works* 6:592)

[6]"Communism is not an evil thing only because it has been controlled by evil men since it first rose to power in 1917. It is organically evil. You must renounce 'bourgeois morality,' you must become an evil man before you can become a good communist. You must be a liar, a cheat, and probably a spy, before you can represent a communist nation in international diplomacy. You must have no more regard for honor when you sign an agreement on behalf of your country than a forger does when he puts a name on a check." (Senate Internal Security Subcommittee, *Soviet Political Agreements and Results,* p. vii)

Earl Browder, a long-time leader of the Communist party in the USA, said, ". . . we communists do not distinguish between good and bad religions, because we think they are all bad."

This atheistic, degrading, but militant philosophy is backed up with the strength and resources of a big country of 210 million people and a militaristic economy. In addition, communism has built an empire of 700 million more slaves. Besides this, it has agents in all free-world countries whose ultimate aim is to overthrow the existing social order and bring these countries under the red flag. And yet, in the face of all this, we gullibly sign treaties and accept promises of these godless murderers. When will we as a people awake to the awful threat which faces us? It must be soon or it will be too late. Already it is the eleventh hour.

The socialist-communist pattern and objective is being followed and achieved. The record is clear, especially the fantastic and terrifying communist advance and conquest of the past ten years. What will the world look like in another decade? Let us summarize the communist advance and strategy. . . .

Lenin died in 1924. But before he died, he had laid down for his followers the strategy for this conquest. It was, we should readily admit, brilliant, far-seeing, realistic, and majestically simple.[7] It has been paraphrased and summarized as follows:

> First, we will take Eastern Europe,
>
> Then the masses of Asia,
>
> Then we will encircle the United States, which will be the last bastion of capitalism.

---

[7]"The Communists have set forth their master plan of world conquest even more forthrightly than did Hitler in *Mein Kampf*. The Communist Manifesto said: 'The Communists disdain to conceal their views and aims.' Communists have never deviated from the theory enunciated by Marx and the strategy devised by Lenin. For those who want to understand communism, we prescribe, not a fifteen-day trip to Russia, but fifteen days in a library studying the Communist conspiracy." (Report of American Bar Association, Special Committee on Communist Tactics, Strategy, and Objectives)

We will not have to attack. It will fall like an overripe fruit into our hands.

As recent as twelve years ago most Americans, even some who were fairly well informed, did not know and would not believe that there was any such thing as a socialist-communist conspiracy. Today some of these same people will solemnly argue as to whether we have five years or maybe ten years before we too are living as slaves in a communist police state. They now realize it can happen here.

How did it all come about? Time will not permit details. However, the record of planned intrigue, deception and murder is available for all to see and read. The record is clear. Just a few highlights will suffice.

The *first* real great break for the communist conspiracy came in 1933. The United States formally recognized Stalin's godless, murderous regime. We extended diplomatic relations to atheistic Russia. I believed it to be a mistake then, and I am more convinced of it than ever today. Our recognition of Russia in 1933 tremendously increased their standing, prestige and credit, at home and with other nations. It saved them from financial collapse; and it enabled them greatly to increase their nests of spies and propaganda agents in this country and elsewhere in the world.[8]

And we've been bailing them out of their difficulties and bolstering their slave economy ever since. They have repudiated the hundreds of millions owed to the U.S. before World War II and have deceptively withheld even an expression of gratitude for more than eleven billion dollars' worth of food,

---

[8]"It is vital to American defense and to the integrity of American public opinion to know who are the Red agents of a foreign and hostile dictatorship. And yet, they are nowhere to be found — as Reds. . . . For instance, if I were permitted to, I could name more than four hundred concealed Reds functioning as editorial writers, actors, authors, educators, physicians and the like. I know them as members of the Communist conspiracy; I was acquainted with them and their records as builders of Communist fronts and undercover workers for Communist objectives. . . . If I were to mention these names before a court or commission, there would be such an uproar of criticism as to vitiate any good I might do to the nation's security." (Louis F. Budenz, Ex-Communist; *Men Without Faces*, pp. 233-4)

supplies, war materials, etc., under lend-lease. And we're still at it. Now it's wheat. Soft on communism, did someone say? No free nation has ever been more gullibly soft on this god-less conspiracy than our own beloved but foolhardy nation.

Their *second* great break came with the beginning of World War II, which was largely brought on through the world-wide diplomatic conniving of Stalin's agents, making Russia a wartime ally of the Western nations, thereby provid-ing the resulting opportunities for communism through the chaos of war.[9]

During the war and post-war periods communists kept the eyes and anger of the world focused on the crimes of Hitler. At the same time, Stalin, with his aim on Lenin's objectives, carried out conquest and crime, continuously and successfully, that far outdid even Hitler's dream. The record now began to be plain to see.

In August, 1939, Poland was betrayed and the eastern portion seized. In 1940 communism took over part of liberty-loving and America-loving Finland. Communism also swal-lowed up Estonia, Latvia, and Lithuania. Later, at the Tehe-ran Conference in 1943, with Alger Hiss as the principal ad-viser to President Franklin D. Roosevelt, it was made clear Stalin would be allowed to keep all and everything he had stolen.

Then a new series of conquests started. 1946: Albania, Hungary, Yugoslavia, Romania, and Bulgaria. 1947: the mock elections in Poland formally completed the two years of incredibly cruel subjugation of this traditional liberty-loving nation. Then in February, 1948, Czechoslovakia, created with

---

[9]"Since 1933 one of the main objectives in Soviet policy had been to maneu-ver America into war with Japan. Japan was a serious threat to Soviet desires in the Far East. If her power were broken, there would be no difficulty in realizing Soviet objectives in Asia. The Roosevelt Administration wittingly or unwittingly followed the Soviet line, and Harry Dexter White, an important and trusted official in the Administration, drafted a note to Japan that produced the war for which Roosevelt had been looking. . . . In other words, Harry Dexter White, a Soviet agent, helped in an important, even decisive, way to draft the ultimatum that pro-voked war between Japan and the United States. This was a primary Soviet aim in the Far East." (Anthony Kubek, *Communism At Pearl Harbor*, p. 20)

the help of our own President Woodrow Wilson, fell. In October, 1950, Stalin's agents formalized their puppet state of East Germany. This finished the job as planned by Lenin twenty-six years earlier. The ruthless communist conspiracy now had Eastern Europe entire, and the first step of their infamous three-step program was complete.

Step two was Asia. The record clearly indicates that while achieving step one in Eastern Europe, the communist masters were planning and working on step two to enslave Asia. The infiltration of China was already well advanced. Mao and the Chinese communists were already crushing their opposition. A prominent actor in this heart-rending drama was the great patriot, Chiang Kai-shek. General George Marshall also played a major but tragic role. His contribution was to help the communists. By 1950 the whole mainland of China was enslaved.

In 1951 Moscow's invaders seized Tibet. Then in the summer of 1953 came the shameful truce in Korea, so incredible in the light of past American history. Then in 1954 the better part of Indochina was taken over!

Then the blackout was temporarily slowed by Stalin's passing, but the conspiracy continued forward towards ultimate total victory. We also witnessed the effective use of the so-called neutralists of which Sukarno, like Cuba's Castro, is referred to by American leaders as the George Washington of Indochina.

And now Vietnam, Malaysia, Singapore and so on and on ahead of the diabolical schedule of the godless conspiracy.

It is frightening to note the extent to which the goals announced by the communist masters have been achieved and with American aid. Again I repeat their bold strategy:

First, we will take Eastern Europe, then, the masses of Asia. Then we will encircle the United States, which will be the last bastion of capitalism. We will not have to attack. It will fall like an overripe fruit into our hands.

Coming to the Western Hemisphere what do we find? The communist, Godless, insidious conspiracy is moving forward at a shocking pace. There are very few remaining really anti-communist governments in Latin America. The growing communist infiltration and influence right inside our own continental borders has become alarming. It is particularly alarming to those who know the extent of the problem. And to the great majority of the American people — uninformed as they are — it is not believed. Therein lies the real danger.

Who would have believed in 1953, for instance, that in just ten years Cuba would be a slave state in the communist empire — a military and political base for the continuing infiltration, subversion, and attack of all of Latin America? Or that certain officials in our own government would have helped so effectively to betray Cuba into communist hands by following almost exactly the same pattern as that which was used in the earlier betrayal of China? And, who would have believed ten years ago that the American people, only ninety miles away, would have been so conditioned by further years of pro-communist brainwashing that they would stand passively by, accepting these developments without demanding appropriate drastic action?

Who would have believed that State Department officials and Presidents of the United States would refuse to confirm the historic and inspired Monroe Doctrine — the center of our foreign policy for 140 years? Who would have believed our own State Department would refer to a Godless, blustering dictator as the "great liberator of the Cuban people"? Who would have believed that the American press would fall for the deceptive line of the communist conspiracy — even calling Castro the "George Washington of Cuba"?

And now our government has introduced the theme of "building bridges to the East." The sycophants in government and some servile press have dwelled upon this theme. The United States, according to them, has an obligation — in the interests of peace or trade or freedom — of building bridges of *understanding* with the Soviet Union and Rumania and Bulgaria and Czechoslovakia and Poland and Hungary and East Germany and Yugoslavia. How will this understanding come about? By resuming or extending trade relations, cultural exchanges, diplomatic relations, people-to-people programs, economic handouts, easy credits, and even scientific reciprocity. Forgotten is the welfare of the peoples in the Soviet Union and its satellites. The bridges of *understanding* are exclusively terminated at both ends by governmental leaders. Forgotten is the bloody history of the relationship between the communist leaders and the peoples in the captive nations. Neither President Johnson nor his public and private sycophants hold out conditions to the communist leaders: there are no demands in the name of humanity that political prisoners be released, that the doors of churches and seminaries and convents and schools be thrown open, that freely held elections be offered in the Soviet Union and its satellites, that natural rights to property be restored, that families be reunited in the sanctity of their homes, that travel restrictions be lifted so that people can freely cross and re-cross their own provincial and national boundaries.

The breast-beating, hand-wringing, pro-socialist-communist liberals of today cannot seem to remember the Katyn Forest Massacre; Stalin's purges and planned famines; the rape of Hungary, Poland, Lithuania, Latvia, Estonia, and Finland; the coup in Czechoslovakia; the concentration camps; the spies caught in the United Nations; the Warsaw Pact; the Soviet subversion in Africa, Asia, and Latin America; the Berlin airlift; the persecution and liquidation of Jews and Protestants and Catholics; the barbarism of Beria; the Hitler-Stalin pact; the Soviet support of Red China; and the vicious anti-American propaganda and demonstrations which have been and remain a routine affair throughout the communist world.

No rational person is against "understanding" *per se*. But there can be no understanding unless there is a common ground, a common premise on which to base understanding. What is there in common between the United States and any communist nation: Ours is a representative republic with a constitution in which is recognized the natural law and natural rights of man. It is a republic with a spiritual foundation characterized by freedom — freedom for the individual and for his society. It is a republic characterized by the dispersal and assignment of duties and responsibilities of the public servant and the private citizen. None of these are to be found in a communist state nor are they recognized as having value by communist leaders.

Where is the basis for "understanding"? There is none unless leaders of the United States wish to forsake all other values and join the communists in their worship at the altar of materialism.[10]

We are at war — apparently a no-win war — with communists in Vietnam — a war which will decide whether peoples in Southeast Asia will fall under the ruthless domination of communists or whether they shall be given the chance to pursue their happiness on earth in freedom and in an environment of decency. But the liberal, who still wrings his hands over the fate of six million Jews during World War II, is ready to consign millions more Asiatics to a fate of death or slavery.

At this very moment representatives of our soft-on-communism government are returning from a tour of the world talking "peace" with the very communists who blaspheme the Prince of Peace.

What is the key to these novel excursions into foreign policy? I honestly believe that much of this is traceable to the acceptability of pragmatism as the fundamental doctrine of U.S. foreign policy. This insidious doctrine which totally disregards all standards of right and wrong, good and evil, decency and indecency is heralded nowadays as a virtue. Be practical, be workable, be expedient, be pragmatic!

In his little book, *Realities of American Foreign Policy* (which I strongly suspect is and has been a State Department manual of action), George Kennan emphasized that the behavior of governments (i.e. governmental leaders, especially

---

[10]"Over a period of years, in its attempts toward accommodation and creation of a peaceful world, our government has gone a long way toward accepting the basic immorality of the Communist system. Americans might now ask their government if it had the moral right to agree to a world in which millions of people were kept in a condition of slavery, and to accept such condition through continued recognition of the Soviet Union as a legitimate government." (General Nathan F. Twining, *Neither Liberty Nor Safety*, p. 277)

diplomats) is and should be devoid of absolute standards of right and wrong. Under Kennan's logic, an individual acting on behalf of his government should acquire a separate code of ethics — or to phrase it more precisely, a code of non-ethics (which is, of course, synonymous with pragmatism).

Imbued with Kennanism, a diplomat can make yesterday's friend today's enemy. Kennanism allows a diplomat to forget history or remember history, whichever is convenient and expedient at the moment. Kennanism allows a diplomat to forget or remember facts, depending on their usefulness to justify behavior.

With this in mind we can understand how the pragmatist in the midst of war with North Vietnam can plan ahead for economic handouts to Southeast Asian countries, including North Vietnam. We can appreciate the American pragmatist being understanding of Canada and Australia selling wheat to Red China, since the pragmatist can conveniently forget why there is a wheat shortage in Red China.

We can appreciate the American pragmatist clamoring for negotiations with North Vietnam, but urging annihilation of Ian Smith's regime in Rhodesia.

It is pragmatism which makes the American diplomat amenable to the "inevitability of Red China's admission to the UN" or the "inevitability of the rise of the Democratic Left in Latin America" or the necessary suspension of freedoms in the "newly emerging nations." The pragmatist tolerates waste and graft and corruption and even idiocy in the dispensing of U.S. foreign aid.

These are not imaginary traits: they are very much real here, today in our beloved America.

Sovereignty for a nation is hard to come by and even more difficult to retain. It cannot be shared for then sovereignty becomes something else, and for want of a better word, when sovereignty is lessened the end-product is internationalism. Sovereignty is neither more nor less than self-government. And American self-government is blue-printed in the Constitution — a document which, together with the Declaration of Independence and the several state constitutions, is anything but pragmatic in letter and spirit. Such a government with its recognition of human rights — ordained by God — cannot help but be contaminated by an association with pragmatic governmental leaders, no matter what their country.

But the spirit of pragmatism is not confined to the conduct of foreign policy; it permeates domestic policy through the actions of the Executive, the Congress, and the Supreme Court. We have just witnessed a session of Congress in which more than eighty major bills were passed with the cooperation of the Congress. The emphasis on materialism in this legislation is nothing short of appalling. We are sharing the blessings of America with some of the most despicable tyrants in history through our foreign aid program. We have made large strides toward eliminating any and all semblances of personal and virtuous charity by a massive federal intrusion into the needs of the poor, the illiterate, the sick, and the elderly. The continuation of deficit spending furthers the destruction of property rights. It is no longer creeping but galloping socialism.

The Administration has established itself as supreme arbiter of what is right in schools at all levels, in the arts, in the aesthetic quality of highways, in city architecture, in employment policies, and even in the prices of commodities. The Executive branch, along with the Supreme Court, has literally completed the demolition of the 9th and 10th Amendments to the Constitution.

Today safety has been provided to communists in labor unions and to communists in their membership in the largest criminal conspiracy the world has ever known. Communists and fellow-travelers of the communists are regally received in the White House, as are degenerate artists and individuals who are a hair's breadth away from treasonable activities.

The streets of Washington and even the White House grounds are thronged with moral and physical cowards who cry "Surrender USA" — surrender to the diabolic wishes of communists. But the pragmatist in government "tolerates" the voices of "dissent" because "dialogue" is fashionable.

In the past two years the United States has gone a long way down the road to totalitarianism. The Executive, Congress and Supreme Court seem to have no substantive differences of opinion. They are one dynasty for all practical purposes. There is no longer a separation of powers — there is no more federalism — there is no more representative republic. The Constitution, torn to pieces, is simply ignored in favor of the whims and ukases of the Executive Branch and the freedom-destroying mental gymnastics of the Warren Court.

Ours is an era when socialism and social justice are confused; liberty is confused with license; morality is confused with pleasure; and constitutionality is confused with practicality.

Yes, we can take the liberals at their word: We are being led. Where are we being led? We are being led into the society of liberalism, socialism, soft-on-communism, and destruction of all we hold dear. Two examples will suffice:

1. *Education*: Buildings, faculties, students, books, laboratories, research centers, and "think factories" are being subsidized by the federal government. Pre-schoolers, kindergarteners, grade school and high school students are being subsidized by the federal government. School "drop-outs" and "drop-outs" from "drop-out" programs are being subsidized by the federal government.

College campuses under the bountiful federal government have become centers of radicalism; teach-ins, lecture-ins, sit-ins, demonstrations, "communist fronts" (not too dangerous, say the liberals, because they are not all oriented toward the Soviet Union — some are oriented toward Peking or Hanoi or Havana), non-student (sic) groups, and movements (Free Speech Movement, Filthy Speech Movement).

2. *Foreign Policy*: Our government has taken a giant step towards the surrender of United States sovereignty in the U.S. Canal Zone.

Our government has blithely allowed "allies' " vessels to carry on trade with North Vietnam and cooperated with these "allies" by resolutely refraining from the bombing of the major port facilities in North Vietnam.

The Executive Branch has yet to ask Congress to declare war on North Vietnam despite the fact that all branches of the armed services (Army, Navy, Air Force, Marines, Coast Guard) are at war against North Vietnam and despite the further fact that Americans have been involved in the war for more than ten years.

Our government intervened in the Rhodesian affair despite the fact that what had transpired there has absolutely nothing to do with the national security of the United States.

Our government has caused the traditional presidential proclamation on Captive Nations to become a totally innocuous document.

Our government has caused the forcible expulsion of General Wessin y Wessin from the Dominican Republic thereby removing the most prominent anti-communist leader from that communist-ridden nation.

Our government has remained almost totally silent on the matter of communist Cuba except to cooperate with Castro who is ready to unburden tens of thousands of unwanted Cubans upon the United States.

Our government supervised the sale of wheat to the Soviet Union. (Tens of billions of dollars are spent to defend the U.S. from its enemy, the Soviet Union, but we feed the enemy at cut-rate prices.)

Our government has remained virtually silent while, throughout the world, government-inspired demonstrations are conducted against U.S. embassies, legations, and U.S. diplomatic personnel, while U.S. Government-owned and privately owned property is destroyed. Not once has the government even threatened severance of diplomatic relations.

And what is happening here at home? Would anyone deny that scandalous stories of Walter Jenkins, Billie Sol Estes and Bobby Baker have been swept under a White House rug?

Would anyone deny that Otto Otepka has been sacrificed on the altar of national insecurity? Logic: a patriotic federal employee is obviously subversive.

Would anyone deny that the scandals revolving around the Job Corps are being blithely ignored by our government?

Would anyone deny that the appointment of Thurgood Marshall, former attorney for the NAACP, as Solicitor General is a study in hypocrisy?

Is there a better example of hypocrisy than the President's effusive endorsement of J. Edgar Hoover while the government promotes a U.S.-U.S.S.R. consular treaty and further U.S.-U.S.S.R. technical and scientific exchanges contrary to Hoover's unequivocal and exceptionally strong opposition to these items?

Would anyone deny that the President, the chief law enforcer in the United States, belies his position by playing gracious host to the late Martin L. King who has preached disobedience to laws which in his opinion are unjust?

What kind of leadership is conducting U.S. foreign policy when our Chief Executive can say:

> Today in both the open world of freedom and the curtained world of communism, men and their families are enjoying the comfort and contentment of a life none have ever known before.

Well, the leader of the so-called free world said it and we dare not guess the reaction of hundreds of millions of peasants on the Chinese mainland, in the Soviet Union, in East Germany, in Albania, Algeria, Cuba, North Korea, Czechoslovakia and North Vietnam. We dare not guess at the reaction of those whose families are bereft of members who pass the years away in prisons and slave-labor camps. . . .

Ten years ago the American people did not dream that the communist advance was getting so near home as to threaten the very take-over of Central and South America. Yet today you can count on the fingers of one hand all the countries, in the whole continent and sub-continent together, where the communists do not exercise dominant influences in the governments. Does this concern us as United States citizens? Again I say it can happen here. And apparently some American people are ready to accept what ten years ago they would not have considered even possible. Yes, it can — it is happening here.

Who would have believed a little over a decade ago that the Supreme Court of the United States would have willfully and disastrously punched large ragged holes in our God-inspired Constitution? Who would have believed the Court would have handed down so many decisions favorable to the communists and so weakening and destructive of our protection against them, that the communists themselves would openly declare certain of these decisions to be the greatest victory ever won by the communists in America?

Who would have believed ten years ago that a great patriot and beloved spiritual leader would warn us that recent decisions of our Supreme Court are leading this nation down the road to atheism?[11] (President David O. McKay)

Who would have believed ten years ago that the conference of Chief Justices of our state supreme courts would have been so disturbed by this usurpation of power by the Supreme Court as to say things about the Warren-led Supreme Court as harsh as anything that has been said by even the so-called "extreme rightists,"[12] who in reality are real patriots in the spirit of Patrick Henry and the founding fathers?

Who would have believed that Washington politicians would be openly and brazenly sending American wealth in quantities of many billions to aid avowed communists? Or that the United States would be discouraging Soviet satellites from

---

[11]"Recent rulings of the Supreme Court would have all reference to a Creator eliminated from our public schools and public offices. . . . Evidently the Supreme Court misinterprets the true meaning of the First Amendment, and is now leading a Christian nation down the road to atheism." (President David O. McKay, *Church News*, June 22, 1963)

[12]"It has long been an American boast that we have a government of laws and not of men. We believe that any study of recent decisions of the Supreme Court will raise at least considerable doubt as to the validity of that boast. . . . We think that the overall tendency of decisions of the Supreme Court over the last 25 years or more has been to press the extension of federal power and to press it rapidly." (Report of Conference of Chief Justices, August 23, 1958)

thinking of revolt and advising them to accept their status quo and make the best of their subservient relationship to Moscow without trying to change it?

Who would have believed ten years ago that the President of the U.S. would hold futile summit conferences with the murderous lords of the Kremlin, fraternizing with, and honoring as a guest of this nation, our arch enemy and one of the master murderers of all time, Nikita Khruschev?

And who would have imagined that within ten years another President of the United States would support, and get passed, legislation making it the official policy of the United States to turn over our own armed forces into the hands of the godless United Nations, already visibly controlled by the communists and their dependencies? Yet, that legislation has been on our statute books since September, 1961. The only question now is how fast the administration dares to implement it.

In view of all these and other facts one might well ask: America, what of the future?

And now, a President of the United States has been assassinated by a communist within the borders of the United States. Will a nation shocked with such dastardly action rededicate itself to the fight against the godless communist conspiracy? With cool heads and unwavering confidence and courage let us each do our part to become alerted and informed — to fight and defeat this godless conspiracy.

What will the next ten years bring? The Republic is now approaching its 200th anniversary. It has arrived at the threshold of the so-called Great Society. There are crimes in the streets and in the subways. And many of the criminals go unpunished but inconvenienced until the arresting officers are reprimanded and genial judges find loopholes and technicalities sufficient enough to turn the murderer, the rapist, and other felons loose upon society. There are marches against the government conducted by anarchists whose bearded faces, sandaled feet, and dirty clothes are so attractive that they are invited into the White House for a coffee break and a dialogue. Military-minded military officers are excoriated while conscientious cowards receive friendly television coverage. There are doctors, who are committed to save lives, who cry for more abortions and more mercy killings. Privately built, privately financed family homes are demolished to make room for publicly financed, public homes. We entertain lavishly a British Princess while her nation is trading with our enemy in Vietnam. We listen to cries of "police brutality" but ignore cries of "criminal brutality." We coddle communists and socialists and criminals and moral degenerates and pornographers with the battle-cry "freedom to dissent."

Has any nation ever recovered from such decadence except under catastrophic and revolutionary circumstances? We are in a headlong flight from decency in government and society.

What will the next ten years bring? Careful students of this problem, caused by the communist conspiracy, conclude that at the present rate of communist progress, the struggle will in ten years be over. Communist control, these authorities believe, will be visibly complete everywhere in the world except in North America and will actually be complete here in fact, if not in obvious form. Certainly, they say, within a decade, unless Americans become alerted, informed and take effective anti-communist action, the full scourge of brutal communistic tyranny will be in effect all over the country. This, they say, will include military occupation, concentration camps, tortures, terror and all that is required to enable about three percent of the population to rule the other ninety-seven percent as slaves. For achieving that "power and glory" throughout the world is, of course, the real purpose of communism. All else is mere pretense and deception on their part.

As, and if, we move toward that condition there will be gradual loss of our freedom, an increase of the inducements for the acceptance of communism, and a corresponding increase of the pressures to destroy or remove all opponents and all opposition to the communist advance.

There would be a further huge expansion of government and of its control over our economy, education, medical services, and every detail of our family and individual lives.

During such a period, it is reasonable to expect — unless sufficient brakes are put on the present stampede to the left, we will get exactly what the communist-socialist coalition is planning — the nationalization of insurance, transportation, communications, utilities, banks, farms, housing, hospitals, and schools. To take over our schools the educational system will first have been federalized and then prostituted entirely to serving the propaganda needs of the state planners with absolutely no regard for truth or scholarship or tradition. Already we have moved substantially in that direction.

Fantastic, you say?

Impossible? Not so long ago I personally heard the people of Czechoslovakia, Cuba and Poland express similar assurances, that the communist conspiracy would not take them over. But it did happen. Bondage did come. Freedom was lost.

No, I do not predict — nor do the experts — that all these tragic things must come to pass within ten years. I do say, however, that such is clearly indicated unless something is done to slow up, stop or reverse present communist progress in this hemisphere and particularly in the United States.

I expect to continue to pray, speak, and act with all my energy, and I hope you do also, to prevent the tragedy in America which has come to many other once-free lands. At present, unless we join with those small but determined and knowledgeable patriots, dedicated to preserve our freedom, a cold calculation would show that we will not be able to change the course of the present ominous and shocking trends in our beloved country.

As I return to the shores of this choice land, after two years abroad, it is my hope and prayer that the American people can be awakened sufficiently from their sleep of complacency — that they will become alerted and informed. It is also my hope and prayer that more will join forces with those who are opposing the conspiracy in an effective organization. Words will not stop the communists. We must be neither fatalists nor pessimists. We must be realists, of high character and deep spirituality.

Is has been carefully estimated that since August, 1945, the communists have averaged taking over about seven thousand newly enslaved subjects every hour. And please remember that these people, whether in Indonesia, Vietnam or Iraq or Korea, have the same love for their families, think of concentration camps with the same despairing horror, and feel the same pain under torture, as do you and I.[13]

So let me repeat that. Seven thousand more human beings just like you and me have been brought under the incredibly brutal rule of a communist police state, every hour, twenty-four hours of every day, 365 days of every year, for the past twenty years. And not only is that process not being interrupted in any way, today, the rate of conquest and enslavement is actually increasing. The number of slave labor camps increased under Khrushchev as compared to Stalin. Yet some gullible fuzzy heads are trying to tell us that the communists are changing — becoming more cooperative. They might change their strategy, but their objective is still to "bury us," to see that our children and grandchildren will live under communism. Their deadly conspiracy remains the same.

For decades our nation has been carried steadily down the road to communism by steps which were sold to the American people as means of fighting communism. And Vietnam can be the last big step in that blind and tragic march unless we can wake up and inform enough of our fellow citizens as to what is happening. America must become alerted and informed.

There are three possible methods by which the communists might take us over. One would be through a sufficient amount of infiltration and propaganda, to disguise communism as just another political party.

The second method would be by fomenting internal civil war in this country, and aiding the communists' side in that

---

[13]"Those who live under arbitrary power do . . . approve of liberty, and wish for it; they almost despair of recovering it. . . . Hence it is a common observation . . . that our cause is *the cause of mankind,* and that we are fighting for their liberty in defending our own. It is a glorious task assigned us by Providence; which has, I trust, given us spirit and virtue equal to it, and will at last crown it with success." (Benjamin Franklin, To Samuel Cooper, May 1, 1777; *Works* 8:214)

war with all necessary military might.

The third method would be by a slow insidious infiltration resulting in a take-over without the American people realizing it.

The Soviets would not attempt military conquest of so powerful and so extensive a country as the United States without availing themselves of a sufficiently strong fifth column in our midst, a fifth column which would provide the sabotage, the false leadership, and the sudden seizures of power and of means of communication, needed to convert the struggle, from the very beginning, into a civil war rather than clear-cut war with an external enemy.

We can foresee a possibility of the Kremlin taking this gamble in time. In fact, it is clear that the communists long-ago made plans to have this method available, in whole or in part, to whatever extent it might be useful. The trouble in our southern states has been fomented almost entirely by the communists for this purpose. It has been their plan, gradually carried out over a long period with meticulous cunning, to stir up such bitterness between the whites and blacks in the South that small flames of civil disorder would inevitably result. They could then fan and coalesce these little flames into one great conflagration of civil war, in time, if the need arose.

The whole slogan of "civil rights" as used to make trouble in the South today, is an exact parallel to the slogan of "agrarian reform" which they used in China. The new "civil rights" legislation is, I am convinced, about ten percent civil rights and about ninety percent a further extension of socialistic federal controls. It is a fraud. It is part of the pattern for the communist take-over of America. The whole "civil rights" program and slogan in America today is just as phony as were the "agrarian reform" program and slogan of the communists in China twenty years ago.[14]

---

[14]"The Communist Party, USA, has its orders direct from the Communist International in Moscow—fan the resentment of the American Negroes until it bursts into flame, next feed the flames until our nation is engulfed in horrible holocaust. Then the white American Communist will strike with full fury within, so that we shall be sore beset and wide open for attack from without. . . . I can only repeat that the Communist effort in this direction is unceasing." (Julia Brown, Negro Ex-F.B.I. Undercover Agent; *I Testify,* p. 179)

But the third method is far more in accordance with Lenin's long-range strategy. It is one which they are clearly relying on most heavily. And this is taking us over by a process so gradual and insidious that Soviet rule is slipped over so far on the American people, before they ever realize it is happening, that they can no longer resist the communist conspiracy as free citizens, but can resist the communist tyranny only by themselves becoming conspirators against established government.[15] The process in that direction is going on right now, gradually but surely and with ever-increasing spread and speed.

A part of that plan, of course, is to induce the gradual surrender of American sovereignty, piece by piece and step by step, to various international organizations.

Communism is not a political party, nor a military organization, nor an ideological crusade, nor a rebirth of Russian imperialist ambition, though it comprises and uses all these. Communism, in its unmistakable reality, is wholly a conspiracy, a gigantic conspiracy to enslave mankind, an increasingly successful conspiracy, controlled by determined, cunning and utterly ruthless gangsters, willing to use any means to achieve its end.

Today, as never before, America has need for men and women who possess the moral strength and courage of our forefathers — modern-day patriots, with pride in our country and faith in freedom.[16]

---

[15]"The tyrant overthrows the whole . . . constitution, not by seizing any new powers, but by his misuse of the powers he already possesses." (Cicero, *The Republic* II, 51) .

[16]"The true patriot will enquire into the causes of the *fears* and *jealousies* of his countrymen; and if he finds they are not *groundless,* he will be far from endeavoring to allay or stifle them: On the contrary . . . he will by all proper means in his power *foment* and *cherish* them: He will, as far as he is able, keep the attention of his fellow citizens awake to their grievances; and not suffer them to be at rest, till the causes of their just complaints are removed. — At such a time Philanthrop's Patriot (a King's man) [the apologist for government] may be 'very cautious of charging the want of *ability* or *integrity* to those with whom any of the powers of government are entrusted': But the *true* patriot, will constantly be jealous of those very men: Knowing that power, especially in times of corruption, makes men wanton; that it intoxicates the mind; and unless those with whom it is entrusted, are carefully watched, such is the weakness or the perverse-

"What we desperately need today," said Hoover of the FBI, "is patriotism founded on a real understanding of the American ideal — a dedicated belief in our principles of freedom and a determination to perpetuate America's heritage. . . . There must be in America a rebirth of the spirit of Valley Forge. . . . " (J. Edgar Hoover, February 22, 1962)

We are losing, rapidly losing, a cold war in which our freedom, our country, and our very existence are at stake. And while we do not seem to know we are losing this war, you can be sure the communists do. They realize it fully and they are jubilant with their success. There is just one thing — only one thing in the whole world — which the communists fear today. It is that, despite their tremendous influence in our government and over all of our means of mass communications — they fear that the American people will wake up too soon to what has really been happening and what is now happening right under their very noses.

The only thing which can possibly stop the communists is for the American people to learn the truth in time — to become alerted and informed, to join with neighbors in effective programs of exposure and opposition.[17] The one effective weapon is truth. It is the truth they fear. It is the truth that can defeat this godless conspiracy. That is the reason why the communists, their dupes and fellow-travelers smear, vilify and attack the one most effective organization in America in alert-

---

ness of human nature, they will be apt to *domineer* over the people, instead of governing them, according to the known laws of the state, to which *alone* they have submitted. If he finds, upon the best enquiry, the want of ability or integrity; that is, an ignorance of, or a disposition to depart from, the constitution, which is the measure and rule of government and submission, he will point them out, and *loudly proclaim them*: He will stir up the people, *incessantly* to complain of *such men*, till they are either reform'd, or remov'd from that sacred trust, which it is dangerous for them any longer to hold.—" (Emphasis per original) (Samuel Adams, 1771, Essay in *Boston Gazette;* quoted by Hamilton A. Long, *Your American Yardstick*, p. ix)

[17]"We can no more save our Republic from communism, merely by saying we are against communism, than parents can save their children from polio by fervently being against polio. To conquer any disease requires intelligent study to isolate the germ and discover the vaccine. As the number-one killer in the world today, communism is a disease which merits our *urgent study*." (Report of American Bar Association, Special Committee on Communist Tactics, Strategy, and Objectives)

ing and informing the American people. This patriotic, non-partisan, non-political organization has but one weapon — truth. The socialist-communist conspiracy cannot stand the light of truth. And so they direct their lying, venomous attacks at our most loyal and courageous patriots who are determined to spread the truth about the greatest evil in this world today. As Americans where do you stand?

There are some seven hundred million non-Russians, non-communists now living daily lives of virtual slavery behind the iron curtain, some forty million of them in the actual slave labor camps of Russia and Red China. These good people only a few years ago, enjoyed practically the same personal freedom as do you and I today. These people now say to each other, but above all to themselves: "If I had only known! If I had only believed! If I had only been alert and informed!"

As has been well said, *this is a world-wide battle, the first of its kind in history, between light and darkness; between freedom and slavery; between the spirit of Christianity and the spirit of anti-Christ for the souls and bodies of men.* Let's win the battle by alertness, by determination, by courage, by an energizing realization of the danger, if we can; but let's win it even with our lives, if the time comes when we must.

God grant that the United States of America may become alerted and informed and provide the courageous leadership so desperately needed in the world today. Then the enslaved people everywhere would start throwing off their shackles. And God grant that the restoration of freedom and honor and sanity to the conduct of human affairs will begin before the godless communist conspiracy destroys our civilization.

What a glorious day it would be to see America, a land choice above all other lands, exert her power and leadership. America, the greatest nation under heaven, is the hope of the free world, and the hope for the slaves of despotism. This nation can be the only effective deterrent to total communist slavery. *We can stop communism. We can restore and preserve freedom.*

Imagine the joy of mankind living in a free world once again, as brothers, as the God of heaven would have us do! That it may again be realized in our day, is my humble prayer.

CHAPTER 7

THE EROSION OF AMERICA[1]

"Liberty is the basis; and whoever would dare to sap the foundation, or overturn the structure, under whatever specious pretext he may attempt it, will merit the bitterest execration, and the severest punishment, which can be inflicted by his injured country." (George Washington, June 8, 1783; *Writings* 10:257)

What makes a nation great?

> Not serried ranks with flags unfurled,
> Not armoured ships that grind the world,
> Not hoarded wealth nor busy mills,
> Not cattle on a thousand hills,
> Not sages wise, nor schools or laws,
> Not boasted deeds in freedom's cause . . .
> All these may be, and yet the state
> In the eye of God be far from great.

> That land is great which knows the Lord,
> Whose songs are guided by His Word;
> Where justice rules 'twixt man and man,
> Where love controls in art and plan;
> Where, breathing in his native air,
> Each soul finds joy in praise and prayer . . .
> Thus may our country, good and great,
> Be God's delight . . . man's best estate.

This patriotic poem by Alexander Blackburn is a remarkable commentary on the twelfth verse of Psalm 33: "Blessed is the nation whose God is the Lord; and the people whom he hath chosen for his own inheritance." The United States of America has been — and still is — a great nation. *It has been great because it has been free.* It has been free because it has

---

[1]An address given on May 13, 1968, at the Annual Boy Scouts Banquet in Commerce, Texas.

trusted in God, and was founded upon the principles of freedom that are set forth in the Word of God. *This nation has a spiritual foundation.* To me, this land also has a prophetic history.

America is a great nation, and our beloved homeland. We join in chorus with . . .

> My country 'tis of thee,
> Sweet land of liberty . . .
> Land where our fathers died,
> Land of the Pilgrim's pride . . .

Yes, we sing of the land of the free and the home of the brave. We call this nation "America the Beautiful."

> O beautiful for spacious skies, for amber waves of grain
> For purple mountain majesties above the fruited plain.

Yes, America is beautiful. But is America safe?

Once China built a wall. She lived behind it. She laughed at her enemies. She felt secure. Soon an invader came from the North. Three times China found the enemy inside her gates. They did not storm the wall. They did not go around it. They simply bribed the gate-keeper.

It seems only yesterday that France built a wall — the Maginot Line. I have seen it before and after. Steel and stone. She felt secure behind it. She put her faith in it. Yet, France fell. Why? Something was missing. There was a gap through which the invader came. That gap was not only in the wall. It was in the spirit and morals of the people.

Today America builds a wall — a ring of steel — ships and planes — and guns and missiles. But is this enough? Does America have what China lacked? what France lacked? Does she have a total defense? She builds her wall. Does she build character? spirit? patriotic love of freedom? the will to sacrifice?

---

[2]"The prospect now before us in America ought . . . to engage the attention of every man of learning to matters of power and of right, that we may be neither led nor driven blindfolded to irretrievable destruction." (John Adams, 1765, *A Dissertation on the Canon and Feudal Law*)

It is sheer folly for Americans to think that military power and scientific knowledge alone provide the answer to the problems now confronting the nation. Military strength is only a component part. If the nation is to escape catastrophe, it must be armored with national character derived from moral and spiritual values. . . .

Let us not lose faith in God's ability to deal with tyrants today as He has in the past. As long as there is a remnant of people in a society who are capable of being instruments in the hands of God, who know how to intercede with God in prayer, mighty changes in the course of events can and will happen swiftly. (Gwynne W. Davidson, D.D., *The Red Carpet*, p. 289)

Before our very eyes the world changes. Nations collapse. Every edition of the press, every news commentator tell of another startling development.

Do you realize that a great republic, Greece, provided a great degree of freedom and a high standard of living, but it vanished. Rome came along with a great republic. Roman citizenship was cherished; yes, it was sought — it was bought. But Rome, falling into the throes of cheap politics, began to tax everything that could be taxed, and to regulate everything that could be regulated — even to the load that could be carried on an ass. And what was the result? Yes, they began to put names on the public payroll until a third of the citizens of Rome were on the national payroll, and that republic collapsed. A dictatorship followed until the fat accumulated during the days of the republic had been consumed, and then the Empire fell — and great was the fall thereof. It ushered in a period known as the Dark Ages, lasting a thousand years. Should our American private free enterprise system fall, what will be the result? Would this usher in a period again comparable only to the fall of Rome?

The late Edith Hamilton, world authority on Greek and Roman civilization, pinpointed the issue several years ago in these words:

Is it rational that now, when the young people may have to face problems harder than we faced . . . we are giving up the study of how the Greeks and Romans prevailed magnificently in a barbaric world; the study, too, of how that triumph ended, how a slackness and softness finally came over them to their ruin? In the end, more than they wanted freedom, they wanted security, a comfortable life, and they lost all — security and comfort and freedom. . . .

Are we not growing slack and soft in our political life? When the Athenians finally wanted not to give to the State, but the State to give to them, when the freedom they wished most for was freedom from responsibility, then Athens ceased to be free and was never free again. Is that not a challenge? (*The Freeman,* July, 1967, p. 400)

The prominent historian, Channing Pollock, observed that most democracies last for about 200 years. They are conceived and developed by simple, vigorous, idealistic, hard-working people who, unfortunately, with success become rich and decadent, learn to live without labor, depend more on the largess of big government, and end by trading domestic tyrants for foreign tyrants.

With the end of the second century of our republic a short eight years away, it appears very much in order to examine its political, social and economic structure to ascertain whether it contains a unique charter which makes it impervious to the lessons of history.

Are our people subject to the same frailties as the citizens of the nations that died in the past?

Can we overcome these weaknesses and remain the strongest and most blessed people on earth?

Are we willing to stand firmly with the basic American ideal that there can be no substitute for individual initiative and productivity?[3]

It has been pointed out many times, but generally ignored, that *what we have to fear is not force from without — but weakness from within.* No one is likely to destroy America but

---

[3]The principles of the so-called War On Poverty are quite a contrast to the attitude of the peoples of ancient Greece, as expressed by one of their leaders, Pericles: "Wealth we employ more for use than for show, and place the real disgrace of poverty not in owning to the fact but in declining the struggle against it." (Quoted by Thucydides, *The History of the Peloponnesian War,* VI, 40)

Americans. Our way of life could be destroyed without a shot being fired.[4]

In the year 1831, Alexis de Tocqueville, the famous French historian, came to our country to study our penal institutions. He came here at the request of the French Government. While in America, he also made a close study of our political and social institutions. In less than ten years de Tocqueville had become world-famous, as the result of the four-volume work which he wrote, entitled *Democracy In America*. Here is his own stirring explanation of the greatness of America:

> I sought for the greatness and genius of America in her commodious harbors and her ample rivers, and it was not there; in her fertile fields and boundless prairies, and it was not there; in her rich mines and her vast world commerce, and it was not there. Not until I went to the churches of America and heard her pulpits aflame with righteousness did I understand the secret of her genius and power. America is great because she is good, and if America ever ceases to be good, America will cease to be great. (*P.P.N.S., p.* 60.)

The history of nations shows that the cycle of the body politic slowly but surely undergoes change. It progresses —

> From bondage to spiritual faith
> From spiritual faith to courage
> From courage to freedom
> From freedom to abundance
> From abundance to selfishness
> From selfishness to complacency
> From complacency to apathy
> From apathy to fear
> From fear to dependency
> From dependency to bondage

---

[4]"The French historian, Francois Pierre Guillaume Guizot, while visiting in the United States, asked James Russell Lowell, 'How long will the American Republic endure?' Lowell's answer was: 'As long as the ideas of the men who founded it continue dominant.'

"And what were those ideas? Two fundamental principles were: Freedom from Dictatorship and Freedom of the Individual! This goes right back to our free agency, which is as precious as life itself." (President David O. McKay, 1964, *Statements On Communism and the Constitution*, p. 34)

Faith, courage, and freedom represent the life elements of growth — either in man or a nation. Spiritual faith and courage were the bone and sinew of the first freedom our people enjoyed on this continent. Then, as free hard-working Americans, our growth to abundance was only a matter of time. It is most significant that during this uphill struggle by Americans to create a civilization with an abundance for all, they gave no thought to the word "ease" as it might apply to their own way of life. People who are imbued with a strong spiritual faith which, in turn, endows them with the courage to fight and win their battles for freedom and abundance, would view with contempt any person seeking an easy way through life.

It was William Penn who said that "If we will not be governed by God, we must be governed by tyrants." (*Great Quotations,* p. 45.)

Do we dare ask ourselves if the United States, though cast in the role of a leader to preserve and strengthen world civilization, isn't itself tottering internally because too many of its citizens have abandoned the virtues that comprised the basic format of its own civilization? For instance, if spiritual faith, courage, and the willingness of our forbears to work hard were the sustaining virtues, and if, solely because of them, they were able to create our own civilization, can we now in the United States substitute for these virtues the human weaknesses of selfishness, complacency, apathy, and fear — and still hope to survive as a civilized nation?

. . . Moroni, an ancient American prophet, warned us with these words:

> Behold, this is a choice land, and whatsoever nation shall possess it shall be free from bondage, and from captivity, and from all other nations under heaven, if they will but serve the God of the land, who is Jesus Christ, who hath been manifested by the things which we have written. (Ether 2:12)

We stand and sing, "God Bless America, land that I love" and "I love thy rocks and rills, thy woods and templed hills." When we have opportunity to take a vacation, we go to the

mountains and see the beautiful views from the mountain peaks
. . . or to the seashore to observe the blue expanse of ocean
and rolling waves, and to other beauty spots of the nation.
And, of course, we are greatly impressed. But to appraise
America we must go further than this. We must see what is in
the hearts of the people. What is the in-look? We sing of our
great heritage and fly the flag. But we see the newspaper reports of crime, selfishness, and immorality. If the water in
the stream is foul, planting rose bushes on the banks will not
purify it.[5]

The late Calvin Coolidge pin-pointed the problem with
these words:

> We do not need more material development, we need more
> spiritual development. We do not need more intellectual power,
> we need more moral power. We do not need more knowledge, we
> need more character. We do not need more government, we need
> more culture. We do not need more law, we need more religion.
> We do not need more of the things that are seen, we need more
> of the things that are unseen. It is on that side of life that it is
> desirable to put the emphasis at the present time. If that side is
> strengthened, the other side will take care of itself. It is that side
> which is the foundation of all else. If the foundation be firm, the
> superstructure will stand. (*The Price of Freedom,* p. 390; *P.P.N.S.,*
> p. 35)

Philip Van Doren Stern said:

> The fight for freedom is an endless battle. Its victories are
> never final; its defeats never permanent. Each generation must
> defend its heritage, for each seeming conquest gives rise to new
> forces that will attempt to substitute fresh means of oppression for
> the old. There can be no peace in a world of life and growth.
> Every battle the fathers thought finished will have to be fought
> anew by their children if they wish to preserve and extend this
> freedom.

---

[5]"The daily spectacle of atrocious acts has stifled all feeling of pity in the
hearts of men. When every hour we see or hear of an act of dreadful cruelty we
lose all feeling of humanity. Crime no longer horrifies us. We smile at the enor-
mities of our youth. We condone passion, when we should understand that the
unrestrained emotions of man produce chaos. Once we were a nation of self-
control and austerity and had a reverence for life and justice. This is true no
longer. We prefer our politicians, particularly if they swagger with youth and are
accomplished jesters and liars. We love entertainment, even in law, even in government. Unless we reform, our terrible fate is inevitable." (Cicero, quoted in
A Pillar of Iron, p. 322)

In 1787 Edward Gibbon completed his noble work, *The Decline and Fall of the Roman Empire.* Here is the way he accounted for the fall:

1. The undermining of the dignity and sanctity of the home, which is the basis of human society.
2. Higher and higher taxes and the spending of public monies for free bread and circuses for the populace.
3. The mad craze for pleasure, sports becoming every year more and more exciting and more brutal.
4. The building of gigantic armaments when the real enemy was within the decadence of the people.
5. The decay of religion — faith fading into mere form, losing touch with life and becoming impotent to warn and guide the people.

Is there a parallel for us in America today? Could the same reasons that destroyed Rome destroy America?[6]

Nations are never conquered from outside unless they are rotten inside. "Our greatest national problem," wrote Tom Anderson, "is erosion. Not erosion of the soil, but erosion of the national morality." (*Straight Talk,* p. 73)

John Steinbeck said, "If I wanted to destroy a nation I would give it too much and I would have it on its knees, miserable, greedy and sick." He deplores the cynical immorality, the restlessness, the violence, and the ill temper of America. Having too much money and too little moral responsibility, we have become infected by a dangerous corruption which starts in the nursery and seeps into the highest offices of the land.[7]

Security can be exalted above freedom. "A nation can slip, bit by bit, to the point where the plain hard work required to recover is too much. Will diminishes and an old law of nature takes over — the strong survive and the weak per-

[6]"Those nations who ignore history are doomed to repeat its tragedies." (Cicero, quoted in *A Pillar of Iron,* p. xiii)

[7]"As Franklin emerged from the Constitutional Convention, a woman tugged on his sleeve and asked what system of government had been proposed for the American people. His famous reply remains timely after nearly two centuries: 'A Republic, if you can keep it.' Later amplifying his remarks, he predicted that the new nation would be well administered for a few years, 'but only end in despotism, as other forms have done before, when the people shall become so corrupted as to need despotic government, being incapable of any other'." (George C. Roche III, *The Freeman,* March 1967, p. 145)

ish." (Admiral Arleigh A. Burke, *U.S. News,* November 20, 1961)

Could it be that through the proper training of youth we are helping to serve America? Can we not contribute to America's stamina and survival? We can teach reverence to God, unselfishness, love of country, and the fundamental principles of righteous living. We can try to train youth through means of character. We must urge a religious life; we must encourage good education; we must promote patriotism; we must emphasize honesty, trustworthiness, loyalty, and many other fine attributes of good character. I won't go into all the details because of lack of time, but the opportunity is ours, and the need is great. One of the tasks is to re-discover and re-assert our faith in the spiritual, non-utilitarian values on which American life has rested from its beginning.

We might survive a nuclear attack — but we cannot survive (any better than Athens and Rome) moral degeneration and the abandonment of fundamental principles. For, as Daniel Webster said:

> Who shall reconstruct the fabric of demolished government? Who shall rear again the well-proportioned columns of constitutional liberty? Who shall frame together the skillful architecture which unites national sovereignty with State rights, individual security, and public prosperity? No, if these columns fall, they will be destined to a mournful, a melancholy immortality. Bitterer tears, however, will flow over them, than were ever shed over the monuments of Roman or Grecian art; for they will be the remnants of a more glorious edifice than Greece or Rome ever saw, the edifice of constitutional American liberty. (February 22, 1832; *P.P.N.S.,* p. 104)

We must make sure that freedom means more to our youth than just peace. We must make sure that freedom means more to our youth than just security. We must make sure that freedom means more to our youth than just selfish gain. We must emphasize the need of character in the citizens of America.

The power of America lies in every boy and girl back in the hinterlands of this great nation. The strength of America will be no greater than these young people as they grow in character and prepare themselves to step across the threshold of citizenship.

As citizens of our community, let's make sure we do our best in building the utmost in character and faith and judgment in these young people who, some day, will take our places. In closing, these words of Admiral Ben Moreell seem most appropriate:

> Is there a way ahead which will take us out of this morass? Is there a way to recover the sanity and balance which once marked our life? I am sure there is, if we are willing to pay the price. But it is not by resort to political legerdemain. It is by beating our way upstream, against the swift-running current, to those moral and spiritual values upon which this nation was built. We must be born again of the spirit!
>
> . . . if men are not right at the deeper level, in their understanding of the nature of the universe and man's position therein, they can tinker with economic and political problems from now until doomsday and still come up with the wrong answers.
>
> It is a case of putting first things first and the very first thing is a rehabilitation of our basic moral principles. Such an effort on our part will call forth the support of cosmic sanction, for God intended men to be free. "The God who gave us life gave us liberty at the same time," Jefferson observed. But we will need conviction, courage, tenacity, understanding, humility, compassion and above all, faith in our traditional American way of life, our inspired constitution and the Lord our God. (*The Freeman,* September 1966, p. 13)

Yes, this is a choice land — a land with a spiritual foundation and a prophetic history. America is not just another nation — not just one of a family of nations of the free world. This is a nation with a great mission to perform for liberty-loving people everywhere. It is my conviction that the constitution of this land was established by men whom the God of heaven raised up unto that very purpose. The U.S. is the last bastion of real freedom — the only effective protection against the world's greatest evil — the godless socialist-communist conspiracy that seeks to destroy all we hold dear as a great Christian nation.[8]

---

[8]"The preservation of the sacred fire of liberty, and the destiny of the republican model of government, are justly considered as *deeply,* perhaps as *finally,* staked on the experiment entrusted to the hands of the American people." (George Washington, First Inaugural Address, April 30, 1789; *Writings* 11:385)

Section II

THE PROPER ROLE OF GOVERNMENT

"Our legislators are not sufficiently apprized of the rightful limits of their powers; that their true office is to declare and enforce only our natural rights and duties, and to take none of them from us. No man has a natural right to commit aggression on the equal rights of another; and this is all from which the laws ought to restrain him; every man is under the natural duty of contributing to the necessities of the society; and this is all the laws should enforce on him; and, no man having a natural right to be the judge between himself and another, it is his natural duty to submit to the umpirage of an impartial third. When the laws have declared and enforced all this, they have fulfilled their functions, and *the idea is quite unfounded, that on entering into society we give up any natural right.* The trial of every law by one of these texts, would lessen much the labors of our legislators, and lighten equally our municipal codes." (Thomas Jefferson, To Francis W. Gilmer, June 7, 1816)

CHAPTER 8

THE PROPER ROLE OF GOVERNMENT[1]

"I have said, very many times, . . . that no man believed more than I in the principle of self-government; that it lies at the bottom of all my ideas of just government, from beginning to end. . . . I believe each individual is naturally entitled to do as he pleases with himself and the fruit of his labor, so far as it in no wise interferes with any other's rights — that each community, as a State, has a right to do exactly as it pleases with all the concerns within that State that interfere with the rights of no other State, and that the general government, upon principle, has no right to interfere with anything other than that general class of things that does concern the whole." (Abraham Lincoln, July 10, 1858; *Collected Works* 2:493)

My fellow Americans: I stand before you tonight humbly grateful to God for the blessings we all enjoy as citizens of these great United States of America. I am grateful for our founding fathers who were raised up with the courage to give their lives, with the unselfishness to give their fortunes, and the vision to pledge their sacred honor, in order to establish a new kind of government of their own choosing where men might be free. I am additionally grateful that these founding fathers had the faith and humility to accept the divine inspiration so necessary in setting forth a Constitution as the foundation for their new Republic.

---

[1]An address first delivered on February 29, 1968, before the Utah Forum for the American Idea, Salt Lake City, Utah. It was printed in full in the June 15, 1968 issue of *Vital Speeches of the Day*, pp. 514-520, and in pamphlet form by the American Opinion Bookstore, Salt Lake City, Utah, and Dr. W. S. McBirnie, Voice of Americanism, Glendale, California; and in abridged form by *Dan Smoot Report*, January 6, 1969. It was filmed for showing to assembled groups and TV audiences, and was used as the basis of a filmstrip (with Ezra Taft Benson as narrator) entitled "Man, Freedom and Government," produced by Publius and Associates, 9929 Las Tunas Drive, Temple City, California.

I am honored with the privilege of addressing you tonight on the vital subject of "The Proper Role of Government."

Men in the public spotlight constantly are asked to express an opinion on a myriad of government proposals and projects. "What do you think of TVA?" "What is your opinion of medicare?" "How do you feel about urban renewal?" The list is endless. All too often, answers to these questions seem to be based, not upon any solid principle, but upon the popularity of the specific government program in question. Seldom are men willing to oppose a popular program if they, themselves, wish to be popular — especially if they seek public office.

Such an approach to vital political questions of the day can only lead to public confusion and legislative chaos. Decisions of this nature should be based upon and measured against certain basic *principles* regarding the proper role of government. If principles are correct, then they can be applied to any specific proposal with confidence.

> Are there not, in reality, underlying universal principles with reference to which all issues must be resolved whether the society be simple or complex in its mechanical organization? It seems to me we could relieve ourselves of most of the bewilderment which so unsettles and distracts us by subjecting each situation to the simple test of right and wrong. Right and wrong as moral principles do not change. They are applicable and reliable determinants whether the situations with which we deal are simple or complicated. *There is always a right and wrong to every question which requires our solution.* (Albert E. Bowen; *P.P.N.S.,* pp. 21-22)

Unlike the political opportunist, the true statesman values principle above popularity, and works to create popularity for those political principles which are wise and just.[2]

---

[2]"Our statesmen will do well to remember these two precepts of Plato's. Forgetting personal interest they should aim at the public advantage and make that the object of all their efforts; again, they should care for the whole body politic and not abandon one part while protecting another. . . . Indifferent to influence and power he will give his undivided energies to the public service and will impartially promote the interests of every class and the good of the whole nation. He will never employ false charges to expose any man to hatred or unpopularity, but will cleave to justice and honour, and rather than abandon his principles will suffer the heaviest loss and brave even death itself." (Cicero, *On Moral Duties,* I, 25)

I should like to outline in clear, concise and straight-forward terms the political principles to which I subscribe. These are the guidelines which determine, now and in the future, my attitudes and actions toward all domestic proposals and projects of government. These are the principles which, in my opinion, proclaim the proper role of government in the domestic affairs of the nation.

[I] believe that governments were instituted of God for the benefit of man; and that he holds men accountable for their acts in relation to them, both in making laws and administering them, for the good and safety of society.

[I] believe that no government can exist in peace, except such laws are framed and held inviolate as will secure to each individual the free exercise of conscience, the right and control of property, and the protection of life.[3]

[I] believe that all men are bound to sustain and uphold the respective governments in which they reside, while protected in their inherent and inalienable rights by the laws of such governments;[4] and that sedition and rebellion are unbecoming every citizen thus protected, and should be punished accordingly; and that all governments have a right to enact such laws as in their own judgments are best calculated to secure the public interest; at the same time, however, holding sacred the freedom of conscience. (D&C 132:1-2, 5)

It is generally agreed that *the most important single function of government is to secure the rights and freedoms of individual citizens.* But, what are those rights? And what is their source? Until these questions are answered there is little likelihood that we can correctly determine *how* government can

---

[3]" . . . all men are by nature equally free and independent, and have certain inherent rights, of which, when they enter into a state of society, they cannot by any compact deprive or divest their posterity; namely, the enjoyment of life and liberty, with the means of acquiring and possessing property, and pursuing and obtaining happiness and safety." (George Mason, The Virginia Bill of Rights, June 12, 1776)

[4]"The obligation of subjects to the sovereign is understood to last as long, and no longer, than the power lasteth by which he is able to protect them. For *the right men have by nature to protect themselves, when none else can protect them, can by no covenant be relinquished.*" (Thomas Hobbes, 1651, *Leviathan* XXI)

best secure them.[5]   Thomas Paine, back in the days of the American Revolution, explained that:

> Rights are not gifts from one man to another, nor from one class of men to another. . . . It is impossible to discover any origin of rights otherwise than in the origin of man; it consequently follows that rights appertain to man in right of his existence, and must therefore be equal to every man. (*P.P.N.S.*, p. 134)

The great Thomas Jefferson asked:

> Can the liberties of a nation be thought secure when we have removed their only firm basis, a conviction in the minds of the people that these liberties are of the gift of God? That they are not to be violated but with his wrath? (Works 8:404; *P.P.N.S.*, p. 141)

Starting at the foundation of the pyramid, let us first consider the origin of those freedoms we have come to know as human rights. There are only two possible sources. Rights are either God-given as part of the Divine Plan, or they are granted by government as part of the political plan. Reason, necessity, tradition and religious convictions all lead me to accept the divine origin of these rights. If we accept the premise that human rights are granted by government, then we must be willing to accept the corollary that they can be denied by government. I, for one, shall never accept that premise. As the French political economist, Frederic Bastiat, phrased it so succinctly, "Life, liberty, and property do not exist because men have made laws. On the contrary, *it was the fact that life, liberty, and property existed beforehand that caused men to make laws in the first place.*" (*The Law*, p. 6)

I support the doctrine of separation of church and state as traditionally interpreted to prohibit the establishment of an official national religion. But I am opposed to the doctrines of separation of church and state as currently interpreted to divorce government from any formal recognition of God. The

---

[5]"The sacred rights of mankind are not to be rummaged for among old parchments or musty records. They are written as with a sunbeam in the whole volume of human nature by the hand of the Divinity itself, and can never be erased or obscured by mortal power." (Alexander Hamilton, 1775; *Alexander Hamilton and The Founding of the Nation*, p. 1)

current trend strikes a potentially fatal blow at the concept of the divine origin of our rights, and unlocks the door for an easy entry of future tyranny. If Americans should ever come to believe that their rights and freedom are instituted among men by politicians and bureaucrats, then they will no longer carry the proud inheritance of their forefathers, but will grovel before their masters seeking favors and dispensations — a throwback to the Feudal System of the Dark Ages. We must ever keep in mind the inspired words of Thomas Jefferson, as found in the Declaration of Independence:[6]

> We hold these truths to be self-evident, that all men are created equal, that they are endowed by their Creator with certain inalienable Rights, that among these are Life, Liberty and the pursuit of Happiness. That to secure these rights, Governments are instituted among Men, deriving their just powers from the consent of the governed. (*P.P.N.S.*, p. 519)

Since God created man with certain inalienable rights, and man, in turn, created government to help secure and safeguard those rights, it follows that man is superior to the creature which he created. *Man is superior to government and should remain master over it,* not the other way around. Even the nonbeliever can appreciate the logic of this relationship.[7]

Leaving aside, for a moment, the question of the divine origin of rights, it is obvious that a government is nothing more or less than a relatively small group of citizens who have been hired, in a sense, by the rest of us to perform certain functions and discharge responsibilities which have been authorized. It stands to reason that the government itself has no innate power or privilege to do anything. Its only source of

---

[6]"I have never had a feeling politically that did not spring from the sentiments embodied in the Declaration of Independence." (Abraham Lincoln, February 22, 1861; *Collected Works* 4:240)

[7]"All the powers of government, in free countries, emanate from the people: all organized and operative power exists by delegation from the people. Upon these two pillars is erected the whole fabric of our freedom. That all exercise of organized power should be for the benefit of the people is the first maxim of government; and in the delegation of power to the government, the problem to be solved is the most extensive possible grant of power to be exercised for the common good; with the most effective possible guard against its abuse to the injury of anyone." (John Quincy Adams, August 25, 1831; *Selected Writings of John and John Quincy Adams*, p. 374)

authority and power is from the people who have created it. This is made clear in the Preamble of the Constitution of the United States, which reads: "WE THE PEOPLE . . . do ordain and establish this Constitution for the United States of America."

The important thing to keep in mind is that the people who have created their government can give to that government only such powers as they, themselves, have in the first place. Obviously, they cannot give that which they do not possess. So, the question boils down to this. What powers properly belong to each and every person in the absence of and prior to the establishment of any organized governmental form? A hypothetical question? Yes, indeed! But, it is a question which is vital to an understanding of the principles which underlie the proper function of government.

Of course, as James Madison, sometimes called the Father of the Constitution, said, "If men were angels, no government would be necessary. If angels were to govern men, neither external nor internal controls on government would be necessary." (*The Federalist*, No. 51)

In a primitive state, there is no doubt that each man would be justified in using force, if necessary, to defend himself against physical harm, against theft of the fruits of his labor, and against enslavement of another. This principle was clearly explained by Bastiat:

> Each of us has a natural right — from God — to defend his person, his liberty, and his property. These are the three basic requirements of life, and the preservation of any one of them is completely dependent upon the preservation of the other two. For what are our faculties but the extension of our individuality? And what is property but an extension of our faculties? (*The Law*, p. 6)

So far so good. But now we come to the moment of truth. Suppose pioneer "A" wants another horse for his wagon. He doesn't have the money to buy one, but since pioneer "B" has an extra horse, he decides that he is entitled to share in his neighbor's good fortune. Is he entitled to take his neighbor's horse? Obviously not! If his neighbor wishes to give it or lend it, that is another question. But so long as pioneer "B" wishes to keep his property, pioneer "A" has no just claim to it.

If "A" has no power to take "B's" property, can he delegate any such power to the sheriff? No. Even if everyone in the community desires that "B" give his extra horse to "A," they have no right individually *or collectively* to force him to do it. They cannot delegate a power they themselves do not have. This important principle was clearly understood and explained by John Locke nearly 300 years ago:

> For nobody can transfer to another more power than he has in himself, and nobody has an absolute arbitrary power over himself, or over any other, to destroy his own life, or take away the life or property of another. (*Two Treatises of Civil Government,* II, 135; *P.P.N.S.,* p. 93)

This means, then, that *the proper function of government is limited only to those spheres of activity within which the individual citizen has the right to act.* By deriving its just powers from the governed, government becomes primarily a mechanism for defense against bodily harm, theft and involuntary servitude. It cannot claim the power to redistribute the wealth or force reluctant citizens to perform acts of charity against their will. *Government is created by man.*[8] No man possesses such power to delegate. The creature cannot exceed the creator.

In general terms, therefore, the proper role of government includes such defensive activities as maintaining national military and local police forces for protection against loss of life, loss of property, and loss of liberty at the hands of either foreign despots or domestic criminals. It also includes those powers necessarily incidental to the protective function such as:

(1) The maintenance of courts where those charged with crimes may be tried and where disputes between citizens may be impartially settled.

---

[8]"Governments, like clocks, go from the motions men give them, and as governments are made and moved by men, so by them are they ruined too. Wherefore, governments rather depend upon men than men upon governments." (William Penn, 1682; *Great Quotations,* p. 450)

(2) The establishment of a monetary system and a standard of weights and measures so that courts may render money judgments, taxing authorities may levy taxes, and citizens may have a uniform standard to use in their business dealings.[9]

My attitude toward government is succinctly expressed by the following provision taken from the Alabama Constitution:

> That the sole object and only legitimate end of government is to protect the citizen in the enjoyment of life, liberty, and property, and when the government assumes other functions it is usurpation and oppression. (Art. 1, Sec. 35)

An important test I use in passing judgment upon an act of government is this: If it were up to me as an individual to punish my neighbor for violating a given law, would it offend my conscience to do so? Since my conscience will never permit me to physically punish my fellowman unless he has done something evil, or unless he has failed to do something which I have a moral right to require of him to do, I will never knowingly authorize my agent, the government, to do this on my behalf.

I realize that when I give my consent to the adoption of a law, I specifically instruct the police — the government — to take either the life, liberty, or property of anyone who disobeys that law. Furthermore, I tell them if anyone resists the enforcement of the law, they are to use any means necessary — yes, even putting the law-breaker to death or putting him in jail — to overcome such resistance. These are extreme measures but unless laws are enforced, anarchy results.

As John Locke explained many years ago:

> The end of law is not to abolish or restrain, but to preserve and enlarge freedom. For in all the states of created beings, capable of laws, *where there is no law there is no freedom.* For liberty is to be free from restraint and violence from others, which cannot be where there is no law; and is not, as we are told, " a liberty for every man to do what he lists." For who could be free, when every other man's humour might domineer over him? But a liberty

---

[9] "Unless there is in the state [government] an even balance of rights, duties, and functions, so that the magistrates have enough power, the counsels of the eminent citizens enough influence, and the people enough liberty, this kind of government cannot be safe from revolution." (Cicero, *The Republic* II, 58)

to dispose and order freely as he lists his person, actions, possessions, and his whole property within the allowance of those laws
under which he is, and therein not to be subject to the arbitrary
will of another, but freely follow his own. (*Two Treatises of Civil
Government*, II, 57; *P.P.N.S.*, p. 101)

I believe we Americans should use extreme care before
lending our support to any proposed government program. We
should fully recognize that government is no plaything. As
George Washington warned, "Government is not reason, it is
not eloquence — it is force! Like fire, it is a dangerous servant
and a fearful master!" (*The Red Carpet*, p. 142) It is an instrument of force, and unless our conscience is clear that we
would not hesitate to put a man to death, put him in jail or forcibly deprive him of his property for failing to obey a given
law, we should oppose it.

Another standard I use in determining what law is good
and what is bad is the Constitution of the United States. I regard this inspired document as a solemn agreement between
the citizens of this nation which every officer of government is
under a sacred duty to obey. As Washington stated so clearly in
his immortal Farewell Address:

> The basis of our political systems is the right of the people
> to make and to alter their constitutions of government. — But the
> constitution which at any time exists, until changed by an explicit
> and authentic act of the whole people is sacredly obligatory upon
> all. The very idea of the power and the right of the people to es-
> tablish government presupposes the duty of every individual to
> obey the established government. (*P.P.N.S.*, p. 542)

I am especially mindful that the Constitution provides
that the great bulk of the legitimate activities of government
are to be carried out at the state or local level. This is the only
way in which the principle of "self-government" can be made
effective. As James Madison said, before the adoption of the
Constitution, "[We] rest all our political experiments on the
capacity of mankind for self-government." (*Federalist*, No. 39;
P.P.N.S., p. 125) Thomas Jefferson made this interesting observation: "Sometimes it is said that man cannot be trusted
with the government of himself. Can he, then, be trusted with

the government of others? Or have we found angels in the forms of kings to govern him? Let history answer this question." (*Works* 8:3; *P.P.N.S.*, p. 128)

It is a firm principle that the smallest or lowest level that can possibly undertake the task is the one that should do so. First, the community or the city. If the city cannot handle it, then the county. Next, the state; and only if no smaller unit can possibly do the job should the federal government be considered. This is merely the application to the field of politics of that wise and time-tested principle of never asking a larger group to do that which can be done by a smaller group. And so far as government is concerned, the smaller the unit and the closer it is to the people, the easier it is to guide it, to correct it, to keep it solvent and to keep our freedom. Thomas Jefferson understood this principle very well and explained it this way:

> The way to have good and safe government, is not to trust it all to one, but to divide it among the many, distributing to every one exactly the functions he is competent to. Let the national government be entrusted with the defense of the nation, and its foreign and federal relations; the State governments with the civil rights, law, police, and administration of what concern the State generally; the counties with the local concerns of the counties, and each ward direct the interests within itself. It is by dividing and subdividing these republics from the great national one down through all its subordinations, until it ends in the administration of every man's farm by himself; by placing under every one what his own eye may superintend, that all will be done for the best. *What has destroyed liberty and the rights of man in every government which has ever existed under the sun? The generalizing and concentrating all cares and powers into one body.* (*Works* 6:543; *P.P.N.S.*, p. 125)

It is well to remember that the people of the states of this republic created the federal government. The federal government did not create the states.[10]

---

[10]"*The people of the states* demanded a federal convention to form the constitution; the congress of the confederation, voting by states, authorized that federal convention; the federal convention, voting likewise by states, made the constitution; at the advice of the federal convention the federal congress referred that constitution severally to the people of each state; and by their united voice taken severally it was made the binding form of government. *The constitution . . . owes its life to the concurrent act of the people of the several states. . . .* " (George Bancroft, *History of the United States,* Last Revision, 6:450)

A category of government activity which, today, not only requires the closest scrutiny, but which also poses a grave danger to our continued freedom, is the activity *not* within the proper sphere of government. No one has the authority to grant such power as welfare programs, schemes for redistributing the wealth, and activities which coerce people into acting in accordance with a prescribed code of social planning. There is one simple test. Do I as an individual have a right to use force upon my neighbor to accomplish this goal? If I do have such a right, then I may delegate that power to my government to exercise on my behalf. If I do not have that right as an individual, then I cannot delegate it to government, and I cannot ask my government to perform the act for me.

To be sure, there are times when this principle of the proper role of government is most annoying and inconvenient. If I could only *force* the ignorant to provide for themselves, or the selfish to be generous with their wealth! But if we permit government to manufacture its own authority out of thin air, and to create self-proclaimed powers not delegated to it by the people, then the creature exceeds the creator and becomes master. Beyond that point, where shall the line be drawn? Who is to say "this far, but no farther"? What clear *principle* will stay the hand of government from reaching farther and yet farther into our daily lives? We shouldn't forget the wise words of President Grover Cleveland that " . . . *though the people support the Government the Government should not support the people.*" (*P.P.N.S.*, p. 345) We should also remember, as Frederic Bastiat reminded us, that "Nothing can enter the public treasury for the benefit of one citizen or one class unless other citizens and other classes have been forced to send it in."[11] (*The Law*, p. 30; *P.P.N.S.*, p. 350)

As Bastiat pointed out over a hundred years ago, once government steps over the clear line between the protective or negative role into the aggressive role of redistributing the wealth and providing so-called "benefits" for some of its citizens, it then becomes a means for what he accurately described

---

[11]"If we can prevent the government from wasting the labors of the people, under the pretence of taking care of them, they must become happy." (Thomas Jefferson, To Thomas Cooper, November 29, 1802; *Works* 4:453)

as legalized plunder. It becomes a lever of unlimited power which is the sought-after prize of unscrupulous individuals and pressure groups, each seeking to control the machine to fatten his own pockets or to benefit its favorite charities — all with the other fellow's money, of course.[12]

Listen to Bastiat's explanation of this "legal plunder."

> When a portion of wealth is transferred from the person who owns it — without his consent and without compensation, and whether by force or by fraud — to anyone who does not own it, then I say that property is violated; that an act of plunder is committed. . . .
>
> How is this legal plunder to be identified? Quite simply. See if the law takes from some persons what belongs to them, and gives it to other persons to whom it does not belong. See if the law benefits one citizen at the expense of another by doing what the citizen himself cannot do without committing a crime. . . . (*The Law,* pp. 21, 26; *P.P.N.S.,* p. 377)

As Bastiat observed, and as history has proven, each class or special interest group competes with the others to throw the lever of governmental power in their favor, or at least to immunize itself against the effects of a previous thrust. Labor gets a minimum wage, so agriculture seeks a price support. Consumers demand price controls, and industry gets protective tariffs. In the end, no one is much further ahead, and everyone suffers the burdens of a gigantic bureaucracy and a loss of personal freedom. With each group out to get its share of the spoils, such governments historically have mushroomed into total welfare states. Once the process begins, once the principle of the protective function of government gives way to the aggressive or redistributive function, then forces are set in motion that drive the nation toward totalitarianism. "It is impossible," Bastiat correctly observed, "to introduce into society . . . a greater evil than this: the conversion of the law

---

[12]"The state [government] is the great fictitious entity by which everyone seeks to live at the expense of everyone else." (Frederic Bastiat, 1848; *Selected Essays on Political Economy,* p. 144)

into an instrument of plunder."[13] (*The Law,* p. 12)

Students of history know that *no government in the history of mankind has ever created any wealth. People who work create wealth.* James R. Evans, in his inspiring book, *The Glorious Quest,* gives this simple illustration of legalized plunder:

> Assume, for example, that we were farmers, and that we received a letter from the government telling us that we were going to get a thousand dollars this year for ploughed up acreage. But rather than the normal method of collection, we were to take this letter and collect $69.71 from Bill Brown, at such and such an address, and $82.47 from Harry Jones, $59.80 from a Bill Smith, and so on down the line; that these men would make up our farm subsidy.
>
> Neither you nor I, nor would 99 per cent of the farmers, walk up and ring a man's doorbell, hold out a hand and say, "Give me what you've earned even though I have not." We simply wouldn't do it because we would be facing directly the violation of a moral law, "Thou shalt not steal." In short, we would be held accountable for our actions.

The free creative energy of this choice nation "created more than 50 percent of all the world's products and possessions in the short span of 160 years. The only imperfection in the system is the imperfection of man himself."

The last paragraph in this remarkable Evans book — which I commend to all — reads:

> No historian of the future will ever be able to prove that the ideas of individual liberty practiced in the United States of America were a failure. He may be able to prove that we were not yet worthy of them. The choice is ours.

According to Marxist doctrine, a human being is primarily an economic creature. In other words, his material well-being is all important; his privacy and his freedom are strictly

---

[13]"Many men, especially if they are ambitious of honour and glory, lavish on one the spoils of another, expecting to obtain credit as benefactors, if only they enrich their friends by fair means or by foul. Such conduct is absolutely opposed to duty. Let us therefore remember to practice that kind of liberality which will be beneficial to our friends and injurious to no one. Neither Sulla nor C. Caesar [government officials] deserves to be called *liberal* for transferring property from its rightful owners into the hands of strangers. For without justice there is no liberality. (Cicero, *On Moral Duties,* I, 14)

secondary. The Soviet constitution reflects this philosophy in its emphasis on security: food, clothing, housing, medical care — the same things that might be considered in a jail. The basic concept is that the government has full responsibility for the welfare of the people and, in order to discharge that responsibility, must assume control of all their activities. It is significant that in actuality the Russian people have few of the rights supposedly "guaranteed" to them in their constitution, while the American people have them in abundance even though they are not guaranteed. The reason, of course, is that material gain and economic security simply cannot be guaranteed by any government. They are the result and reward of hard work and industrious production. Unless the people bake one loaf of bread for each citizen, the government cannot guarantee that each will have one loaf to eat. Constitutions can be written, laws can be passed and imperial decrees can be issued, but unless the bread is produced, it can never be distributed.

Why, then, do Americans bake more bread, manufacture more shoes and assemble more TV sets than Russians do? They do so precisely because our government does not guarantee these things. If it did, there would be so many accompanying taxes, controls, regulations and political manipulations that the productive genius that is America's would soon be reduced to the floundering level of waste and inefficiency now found behind the iron curtain. As Henry D. Thoreau explained:

> This government never of itself furthered any enterprise, but by the alacrity with which it got out of its way. *It* does not keep the country free. *It* does not settle the West. *It* does not educate. *The character inherent in the American people has done all that has been accomplished: and it would have done somewhat more, if the government had not sometimes got in its way.* For government is an expedient by which men would fain succeed in letting one another alone; and, as has been said, when it is most expedient, the governed are most let alone by it. (Quoted by Clarence B. Carson, *The American Tradition,* p. 100; *P.P.N.S.,* p. 171)

In 1801 Thomas Jefferson, in his First Inaugural Address, said:

> With all these blessings, what more is necessary to make us a happy and prosperous people? Still one thing, fellow citizens — a wise and frugal government, which shall restrain men from injuring one another, which shall leave them otherwise free to regulate their own pursuits of industry and improvement, and shall not take from the mouth of labor the bread it has earned. (*Works* 8:3)

The principle behind this American philosophy can be reduced to a rather simple formula:

1. Economic security for all is impossible without widespread abundance.
2. Abundance is impossible without industrious and efficient production.
3. Such production is impossible without energetic, willing and eager labor.
4. This is not possible without incentive.
5. Of all forms of incentive — the freedom to attain a reward for one's labors is the most sustaining for most people. Sometimes called the profit motive, it is simply the right to plan and to earn and to enjoy the fruits of your labor.
6. This profit motive diminishes as government controls, regulations and taxes increase to deny the fruits of success to those who produce.
7. Therefore, any attempt *through governmental intervention* to redistribute the material rewards of labor can only result in the eventual destruction of the productive base of society, without which real abundance and security for more than the ruling elite is quite impossible. (See G. Edward Griffin, *The Fearful Master,* p. 128)

We have before us currently a sad example of what happens to a nation which ignores these principles. Former FBI agent, Dan Smoot, succinctly pointed out on his broadcast number 649, dated January 29, 1968, as follows:

> England was killed by an idea; the idea that the weak, indolent, and profligate must be supported by the strong, industrious, and frugal — to the degree that tax consumers will have a living standard comparable to that of taxpayers; the idea that govern-

ment exists for the purpose of plundering those who work to give the product of their labor to those who do not work.

The economic and social cannibalism produced by this communist-socialist idea will destroy any society which adopts it and clings to it as a basic principle — any society.

Nearly two hundred years ago, Adam Smith, the Englishman, who understood these principles very well, published his great book, *The Wealth of Nations,* which contains this statement:

> The natural effort of every individual to better his own condition, when suffered to exert itself with freedom and security, is so powerful a principle, that it is alone, and without any assistance, not only capable of carrying on the society to wealth and prosperity, but of surmounting a hundred impertinent obstructions with which the folly of human laws too often incumbers its operations; though the effect of these obstructions is always more or less either to encroach upon its freedom, or to diminish its security. (Book 4, chap. 5, IV)

On the surface this may sound heartless and insensitive to the needs of those less fortunate individuals who are found in any society, no matter how affluent. "What about the lame, the sick and the destitute?" is an often-voiced question. Most other countries in the world have attempted to use the power of government to meet this need. Yet, in every case, the improvement has been marginal at best and has resulted in the long run creating more misery, more poverty, and certainly less freedom than when government first stepped in. As Henry Grady Weaver wrote in his excellent book, *The Mainspring of Human Progress:*

> Most of the major ills of the world have been caused by well-meaning people who ignored the principle of individual freedom, except as applied to themselves, and who were obsessed with fanatical zeal to improve the lot of mankind-in-the-mass through some pet formula of their own. . . . *The harm done by ordinary criminals, murderers, gangsters, and thieves is negligible in comparison with the agony inflicted upon human beings by the professional "do-gooders,"* who attempt to set themselves up as gods on earth and who would ruthlessly force their views on all others — with the abiding assurance that the end justifies the means. (pp. 40-41; *P.P.N.S.,* p. 313)

By comparison, America traditionally has followed Jefferson's advice of relying on individual action and charity. The result is that the United States has fewer cases of genuine hardship per capita than any other country in the entire world of throughout all history. Even during the depression of the 1930's, Americans ate and lived better than most people in other countries do today.

In reply to the argument that just a little bit of socialism is good so long as it doesn't go too far, it is tempting to say that, in like fashion, just a little bit of theft or a little bit of cancer is all right, too! History proves that the growth of the welfare state is difficult to check before it comes to its full flower of dictatorship. But let us hope that this time around, the trend can be reversed. If not, then we will see the inevitability of complete socialism, probably within our lifetime.

Three factors may make a difference. First, there is sufficient historical knowledge of the failures of socialism and of the past mistakes of previous civilizations. Secondly, there are modern means of rapid communications to transmit these lessons of history to a large literate population. And thirdly, there is a growing number of dedicated men and women who, at great personal sacrifice, are actively working to promote a wider appreciation of these concepts. The timely joining together of these three factors may make it entirely possible for us to reverse the trend.

This brings up the next question: How is it possible to cut out the various welfare-state features of our government which have already fastened themselves like cancer cells onto the body politic? Isn't drastic surgery already necessary, and can it be performed without endangering the patient? In answer, it is obvious that drastic measures *are* called for. No halfway or compromise actions will suffice. Like all surgery, it will not be without discomforts and perhaps even some scar tissue for a long time to come. But it must be done if the patient is to be saved, and it can be done without undue risk.

Obviously, not all welfare-state programs currently in force can be dropped simultaneously without causing tremendous economic and social upheaval. To try to do so would be like finding oneself at the controls of a hijacked airplane and attempting to return it by simply cutting off the engines in flight. It must be flown back, lowered in altitude, gradually reduced in speed and brought in for a smooth landing. Translated into practical terms, this means that the first step toward restoring the limited concept of government should be to freeze all welfare-state programs at their present level, making sure that no new ones are added. The next step would be to allow all present programs to run out their term with absolutely no renewal. The third step would involve the gradual phasing-out of those programs which are indefinite in their term. In my opinion, the bulk of the transition could be accomplished within a ten-year period and virtually completed within twenty years. Congress would serve as the initiator of this phase-out program, and the President would act as the executive in accordance with traditional constitutional procedures.

As I summarize what I have attempted to cover, try to visualize the structural relationship between the six vital concepts that have made America the envy of the world. I have reference to the foundation of the Divine Origin of Rights; Limited Government; the pillars of Economic Freedom and Personal Freedom, which result in Abundance; followed by Security and the Pursuit of Happiness.

America was built upon a firm foundation and created over many years from the bottom up. Other nations, impatient to acquire equal abundance, security and pursuit of happiness, rush headlong into that final phase of construction without building adequate foundations or supporting pillars. Their efforts are futile. And, even in our country, there are those who think that, because we now have the good things in life, we can afford to dispense with the foundations which have made them possible. They want to remove any recognition of God from governmental institutions. They want to expand the scope and reach of government which will undermine and erode our economic and personal freedoms. The abundance which is ours, the carefree existence which we have come to accept as a matter of course, *can be toppled by these foolish experimenters and power seekers.* By the grace of God, and with his help, we shall fence them off from the foundations of our liberty, and then begin our task of repair and construction.

As a fitting summary to this discussion, I present a declaration of principles which have recently been prepared by a few American patriots, and to which I wholeheartedly subscribe.

As an independent American for constitutional government I declare that:

(1) I believe that *no people can maintain freedom unless their political institutions are founded upon faith in God and belief in the existence of moral law.*[14]

(2) I believe that God has endowed men with certain unalienable rights as set forth in the Declaration of Independence and that no legislature and no majority, however great, may morally limit or destroy these; that *the sole function of government is to protect life, liberty, and property, and anything more than this is usurpation and oppression.*

(3) I believe that the Constitution of the United States was prepared and adopted by men acting under inspiration from Almighty God; that it is a solemn compact between the peoples of the states of this nation which all officers of government are under duty to obey; that the eternal moral laws expressed therein must be adhered to or individual liberty will perish.[15]

---

[14]"The most learned men have determined to begin with Law. . . . Law is the highest reason, implanted in Nature, which commands what ought to be done and forbids the opposite. This reason, when firmly fixed and fully developed in the human mind, is Law. . . . Law is intelligence, whose natural function it is to command right conduct and forbid wrong-doing. . . . the origin of Justice is to be found in Law, for Law is a natural force; it is the mind and reason for the intelligent man, the standard by which Justice and Injustice are measured. . . . But in determining what Justice is, let us begin with that supreme Law which had its origin ages before any written law existed or any State had been established." (Cicero, *Laws,* I, 19)

[15]"This law of nature, being coeval with mankind, and dictated by God himself, is of course superior in obligation to any other. It is binding over all the globe, in all countries, and at all times: no human laws are of any validity, if contrary to this; and such of them as are valid derive all their force, and all their authority, mediately or immediately, from this original." (William Blackstone, 1765; *Commentaries on the Laws of England,* Book I, Sec. 2, No. 41)

(4) I believe it a violation of the Constitution for government to deprive the individual of either life, liberty, or property except for these purposes:

   (a) Punish crime and provide for the administration of justice;

   (b) Protect the right and control of private property;[16]

   (c) Wage defensive war and provide for the nation's defense;

   (d) Compel each one who enjoys the protection of government to bear his fair share of the burden of performing these functions.

(5) I hold that the Constitution denies government the power to take from the individual either his life, liberty or property except in accordance with moral law; that *the same moral law which governs the actions of men when acting alone is also applicable when they act in concert with others;* that no citizen or group of citizens has any right to direct their agent, the government, to perform any act which would be evil or offensive to the conscience if that citizen were performing the act himself outside the framework of government.[17]

(6) I am hereby resolved that under no circumstances shall the freedoms guaranteed by the Bill of Rights be infringed. In particular I am opposed to any attempt on the part of the federal government to deny the people their right to bear arms, to worship and pray when and where they choose, or to own and control private property.

(7) I consider ourselves at war with international communism which is committed to the destruction of our govern-

---

[16]"In the nature of things, those who have no property and see their neighbors possess much more than they think them to need, cannot be favorable to laws made for the protection of property. When this class becomes numerous, it grows clamorous. It looks on property as its prey and plunder, and is naturally ready, at time, for violence and revolution." (Daniel Webster, 1820; *Great Quotations,* p. 181)

[17]"My lords, let us consider just law. Does it bring tranquillity, good order, piety, justice and liberty and prosperity to a people? Does it nourish patriotism and the way of a manly and upright life? Then it is a good law, and deserves our utter obedience.

"But if it brings pain, intolerable burdens, injustice, sleepless anxiety and fear and slavery to a people, then it is an evil law passed and upheld by evil men, who hate humanity and wish to subjugate and control it." (Cicero, Quoted in *A Pillar of Iron,* p. 163)

ment, our right of property, and our freedom; that it is treason as defined by the Constitution to give aid and comfort to this implacable enemy.

(8) I am unalterably opposed to socialism, either in whole or in part, and regard it as an unconstitutional usurpation of power and a denial of the right of private property for government to own or operate the means of producing and distributing goods and services in competition with private enterprise, or to regiment owners in the legitimate use of private property.

(9) I maintain that every person who enjoys the protection of his life, liberty, and property should bear his fair share of the cost of government in providing that protection; that the elementary principles of justice set forth in the Constitution demand that all taxes imposed be uniform and that each person's property or income be taxed at the same rate.

(10) I believe in honest money, the gold and silver coinage of the Constitution, and a circulating medium convertible into such money without loss. I regard it as a flagrant violation of the explicit provisions of the Constitution for the federal government to make it a criminal offense to use gold or silver as legal tender or to issue irredeemable paper money.

(11) I believe that each state is sovereign in performing those functions reserved to it by the Constitution and it is destructive of our federal system and the right of self-government guaranteed under the Constitution for the federal government to regulate or control the states in performing their functions or to engage in performing such functions itself.[18]

(12) I consider it a violation of the Constitution for the federal government to levy taxes for the support of state

---

[18]"I declare that the maintenance inviolate of the rights of the States, and especially the right of each state to order and control its own domestic institutions according to its own judgment exclusively, is essential to that balance of powers on which the perfection, and endurance of our political fabric depends — and *I denounce the lawless invasion, by armed force, of the soil of any State or Territory, no matter under what pretext, as the gravest of crimes.*" (Abraham Lincoln, December 28, 1860; *Collected Works* 4:162)

or local government;[19] that no state or local government can accept funds from the federal and remain independent in performing its functions, nor can the citizens exercise their rights of self-government under such conditions.

(13) I deem it a violation of the right of private property guaranteed under the Constitution for the federal government to forcibly deprive the citizens of this nation of their property through taxation or otherwise, and make a gift thereof to foreign governments or their citizens.[20]

(14) I believe that no treaty or agreement with other countries should deprive our citizens of rights guaranteed them by the Constitution.[21]

(15) I consider it a direct violation of the obligation imposed upon it by the Constitution for the federal government to dismantle or weaken our military establishment below that point required for the protection of the states against invasion, or to surrender or commit our men, arms, or money to the control of foreign or world organizations or governments.

These things I believe to be the proper role of government. We have strayed far afield. We must return to basic con-

---

[19]"When more of the people's substance is exacted through the form of taxation than is necessary to meet the just obligations of the Government and the expense of its economical administration, such exaction becomes ruthless extortion and a violation of the fundamental principles of a free government." (President Grover Cleveland, Second Annual Message, December 6, 1886; *Messages and Papers* 8:509)

[20]"We are taxed in our bread and our wine, in our income and our investments, on our land and on our property, not only for base creatures who do not deserve the name of men, but for foreign nations, for complaisant nations who will bow to us and accept our largesse and promise to assist us in the keeping of the peace — these mendicant nations who will destroy us when we show a moment of weakness or our treasury is bare, and it surely is becoming bare! . . .

"Is the heart of our nation worth these? . . . Were they bound to us with ties of love, they would not ask our gold. They would ask only our laws. They take our very flesh, and they hate and despise us. And who shall say we are worthy of more?" (Cicero, quoted in *Success,* September 4, 1967)

[21]"By the general power to make treaties, the Constitution must have intended to comprehend only those objects which are usually regulated by treaty, and cannot be otherwise regulated. It must have meant to except out of these the rights reserved to the States; for surely the President and Senate cannot do by treaty what the whole government is interdicted from doing in any way. And also to except those subjects of legislation in which it gave a participation to the House of Representatives." (Thomas Jefferson, 1800, *A Manual of Parliamentary Practice,* Sec. LII; *Works* 9:80-1)

cepts and principles — to eternal verities. There is no other way. The storm signals are up. They are clear and ominous.

As Americans — citizens of the greatest nation under heaven — we face difficult days. Never since the days of the Civil War — a hundred years ago — has this choice nation faced such a crisis. . . .

Can we cope with these realities? Yes!

In closing I wish to refer you to the words of the patriot Thomas Paine, whose writings helped so much to stir into a flaming spirit the smoldering embers of patriotism during the days of the American Revolution:

> These are the times that try men's souls. The summer soldier and the sunshine patriot will in this crisis, shrink from the service of his country; but he that stands it NOW, deserves the love and thanks of man and woman. Tyranny, like hell, is not easily conquered; yet we have this consolation with us, that the harder the conflict, the more glorious the triumph. What we obtain too cheap, we esteem too lightly; 'tis dearness only that gives everything its value. Heaven knows how to put a proper price upon its goods; and it would be strange indeed, if so celestial an article as FREEDOM should not be highly rated. (*The Political Works of Thomas Paine*, p. 55)

President Theodore Roosevelt warned that:

> The things that will destroy America are prosperity-at-any-price, peace-at-any-price, safety-first instead of duty-first, and love of soft living and the get-rich-quick theory of life. (*The Red Carpet*, p. 315)

I intend to keep fighting. My personal attitude is one of resolution — not resignation.

I have faith in the American people. I pray that we will never do anything that will jeopardize in any manner our priceless heritage.[22] If we live and work so as to enjoy the ap-

---

[22]"To preserve it must be the responsibility of every citizen. Each step in the public administration of government concerns us dearly. The steady management of a good government is the most anxious, arduous and hazardous vocation on this side of the grave. It becomes necessary to every subject to be in some degree a statesman, and to examine and judge for himself of the tendency of political principles and measures." (John Adams, 1763; quoted by Catherine Drinker Bowen, *John Adams and the American Revolution*, p. 265)

probation of a Divine Providence, we cannot fail. Without that help we cannot long endure.

So I urge all Americans to put their courage to the test. Be firm in our conviction that our cause is just. Reaffirm our faith in all things for which true Americans have always stood.

I urge all Americans to arouse themselves and stay aroused. We must not make any further concessions to communism at home or abroad. We do not need to. We should oppose communism from our position of strength for we are not weak.

"We are not cowards," said Ted Dealey of the *Dallas Morning News,* "and will not wallow in the sloughs of degradation. We do not want to be lulled to sleep any more. We are awake and angry and intend to remain so."

There is much work to be done. The time is short. Let us begin — in earnest — now and may God bless our efforts, I humbly pray. . . .

CHAPTER 9

UNITED STATES FOREIGN POLICY[1]

"Observe good faith and justice towards all Nations. Cultivate peace and harmony with all. — Religion and Morality enjoin this conduct; and can it be that good policy does not equally enjoin it? — It will be worthy of a free, enlightened, and, at no distant period, a great nation, to give to mankind the magnanimous and too novel example of a People always guided by an exalted justice and benevolence. . . . Can it be that Providence has not connected the permanent felicity of a Nation with its virtue?" (President George Washington, Farewell Address, September 17, 1796)

In the "Virginia Bill of Rights," drafted by George Mason and adopted by the Virginia Convention on June 12, 1776, there appears this statement in Article 15:

No free government, or the blessings of liberty, can be preserved to any people, but by a firm adherence to justice, moderation, temperance, frugality and virtue, and by frequent recurrence to fundamental principles. (*Documents of American History,* [Henry S. Commager, Editor], 1:104)

"The paramount need today," recently wrote David Lawrence, "is for the United States to clear the air by emphasizing fundamental principles. Until there are acts that implement those principles — not just words — diplomacy will accomplish nothing and the world will remain continually on the brink of war." (*U.S. News and World Report,* January 27, 1964)

It has been truly said that

We cannot clean up the mess in Washington, balance the budget, reduce taxes, check creeping Socialism, tell what is muscle

---

[1]Address delivered on June 21, 1968, at the Farm Bureau Banquet in Preston, Idaho.

or fat in our sprawling rearmament programs, purge subversives from our State Department, unless we come to grips with our foreign policy, upon which all other policies depend. (Senator Robert A. Taft, quoted by Phyllis Schlafly, *A Choice Not An Echo,* p. 26)

Ever since World War I, when we sent American boys to Europe supposedly "to make the world safe for democracy," our leaders in Washington have been acting as though the American people elected them to office for the primary purpose of leading the entire planet toward international peace, prosperity and one-world government. At times, these men appear to be more concerned with something called world opinion or with their image as world leaders than they are with securing the best possible advantage for us, that they are not "nationalistic" in their views, that they are willing to sacrifice narrow American interests for the greater good of the world community. Patriotism and America-first have become vulgar concepts within the chambers of our State Department. It is no wonder that the strength and prestige of the United States has slipped so low everywhere in the world.

In this connection, it is well to remember that on June 25, 1787, during the formulation of the Constitution at the Philadelphia Convention, Charles Pinckney, of South Carolina, made the famous speech in which he asserted:

> We mistake the object of our government, if we hope or wish that it is to make us respectable abroad. Conquest or superiority among other powers is not or ought not ever to be the object of republican systems. If they are sufficiently active and energetic to rescue us from contempt and preserve our domestic happiness and security, it is all we can expect from them, — it is more than almost any other Government ensures to its citizens. (*The Records of the Federal Convention* [Max Farrand, Editor], 1:402)

In his book, *A Foreign Policy for Americans,* the late Senator Robert A. Taft correctly reasoned that

> No one can think intelligently on the many complicated problems of American foreign policy unless he decides first what he considers the real purpose and object of that policy. . . . There has been no consistent purpose in our foreign policy for a

good many years past. . . . Fundamentally, I believe the ultimate purpose of our foreign policy must be to protect the liberty of the people of the United States. (p. 11)

There is one and only one legitimate goal of United States foreign policy. It is a narrow goal, a nationalistic goal: the preservation of our national independence. Nothing in the Constitution grants that the President shall have the privilege of offering himself as a world leader. He's our executive; he's on our payroll, if necessary; he's supposed to put our best interests in front of those of other nations. Nothing in the Constitution nor in logic grants to the President of the United States or to Congress the power to influence the political life of other countries, to "uplift" their cultures, to bolster their economies, to feed their peoples or even to defend them against their enemies. This point was made clear by the wise father of our country, George Washington:

> I have always given it as my decided opinion that no nation has a right to intermeddle in the internal concerns of another; that every one had a right to form and adopt whatever government they liked best to live under themselves; and that, if this country could, consistently with its engagements, maintain a strict neutrality and thereby preserve peace, it was bound to do so by motives of policy, interest, and every other consideration. (August 25, 1796; *Writings* 13:263)

The preservation of America's political, economic and military independence — the three cornerstones of sovereignty — is the sum and total prerogative of our government in dealing with the affairs of the world. Beyond that point, any humanitarian or charitable activities are the responsibility of individual citizens voluntarily without coercion of others to participate.

The proper function of government must be limited to a defensive role — the defense of individual citizens against bodily harm, theft and involuntary servitude at the hands of either domestic or foreign criminals. But, to protect our people from bodily harm at the hands of foreign aggressors, we must maintain a military force which is not only capable of crushing an invasion, but of striking a sufficiently powerful counterblow as to make it unattractive for would-be conquerors to try their luck with us.

As President Washington explained in his Fifth Annual Address to both Houses of Congress,

> There is a rank due to the United States among nations, which will be withheld, if not absolutely lost, by the reputation of weakness. If we desire to avoid insult, we must be able to repel it; if we desire to secure peace, one of the most powerful instruments of rising prosperity, it must be known, that we are at all times ready for war. (December 3, 1793; *Writings* 12:352; *P.P.N.S.,* p. 442)

He had earlier, in his First Annual Address, strongly warned that

> To be prepared for war is one of the most effectual means of preserving peace. A free people ought not only to be armed, but disciplined. (January 8, 1790; *Writings* 11:456)

To protect our people from international theft, we must enter into agreements with other nations to abide by certain rules regarding trade, exchange of currency, enforcement of contracts, patent rights, etc. To protect our people against involuntary servitude or the loss of personal freedom on the international level, we must be willing to use our military might to help even one of our citizens no matter where he might be kidnapped or enslaved.

For those of you who have never heard or do not remember it, the story of Ion Perdicaris instructs us what an American President can and should do to protect the lives of its citizens. It seems that in the early years of the century, a North African bandit named Raisuli kidnapped Perdicaris, a naturalized American of Greek extraction.

Teddy Roosevelt was our President at that time, and he knew just what to do. He did not "negotiate." And he did not send any "urgent requests." He simply ordered one of our gunboats to stand offshore, and sent the local sultan the following telegram: "Perdicaris alive, or Raisuli dead." They say Raisuli didn't waste any time getting a healthy Perdicaris down to the dock. (*Review of the News,* February 7, 1968, pp. 20-21)

Certainly we must avoid becoming entangled in a web of international treaties whose terms and clauses might reach inside our own borders and restrict our freedoms here at home.[2]

This is the defensive role of government expressed in international terms. Interestingly enough, these three aspects of national defense also translate directly into the three aspects of national sovereignty: military, economic and political.

Applying this philosophy to the sphere of foreign policy, one is able almost instantly to determine the correct answer to so many international questions that, otherwise, seem hopelessly complex. If the preservation and strengthening of our military, economic and political independence is the only legitimate objective of foreign policy decisions, then, at last, those decisions can be directed by a brilliant beacon of light that unerringly guides our ship of state past the treacherous reefs of international intrigue and into a calm open sea.

Should we disarm? And does it really make any difference whether we disarm unilaterally or collaterally? Either course of action would surrender our military independence. Should we pool our economic resources or our monetary system with those of other nations to create some kind of regional common market? It would constitute the surrender of our economic independence. Should we enter into treaties such as the U.N. Covenants which would obligate our citizens to conform their social behavior, their educational systems, their treatment of the news, and even their religious practices to rules and regulations set down by international agencies? Such treaty obligations amount to the voluntary and piece-meal surrender of our political independence. The answer to all such questions is a resounding "no," for the simple reason that *the only way America can survive in this basically hostile and topsy-*

---

[2]"Against the insidious wiles of foreign influence, I conjure you to believe me, fellow-citizens, the jealousy of a free people ought to be *constantly* awake, since history and experience prove that foreign influence is one of the most baneful foes of republican Government.—But that jealousy, to be useful, must be impartial; else it becomes the instrument of the very influence to be avoided, instead of a defense against it." (President George Washington, Farewell Address, September 17, 1796; *Writings* 13:315)

turvy world is to remain militarily, economically and politically strong and independent.

We must put off our rose-colored glasses, *quit repeating those soothing but entirely false statements about world unity and brotherhood,* and look at the world as it is, not as we would like it to become. Such an objective, and perhaps painful, survey leads to but one conclusion. We would be committing national suicide to surrender any of our independence, and chain ourselves to other nations in such a sick and turbulent world. President George Washington, in his immortal Farewell Address, explained our true policy in this regard:

> The great rule of conduct for us, in regard to foreign Nations, is, in extending our commercial relations, to have with them as little *Political* connection as possible. . . .
>
> It is our true policy to steer clear of permanent alliances, with any portion of the foreign world. . . . Taking care always to keep ourselves, by suitable establishments on a respectably defensive posture, we may safely trust to temporary alliances for extraordinary emergencies. (September 17, 1796; *Writings* 13:316-318; *P.P.N.S.,* p. 547)

President Thomas Jefferson, in his First Inaugural Address, while discussing what he deemed to be "the essential principles of our government,"[3] explained that as far as our relations with foreign nations are concerned this means:

> Equal and exact justice to all men, of whatever state or persuasion, religious or political; peace, commerce, and honest friendship, with all nations — entangling alliances with none. . . . (March 4, 1801; *Works* 8:4)

The world is smaller, you say? True, it is, but if one finds himself locked in a house with maniacs, thieves and murderers — even a small house — he does not increase his chances of survival by entering into alliances with his potential attackers and becoming dependent upon them for protection to the point where he is unable to defend himself. Perhaps the analogy between nations and maniacs is a little strong for some to accept. But if we put aside our squeamishness over strong

[3]See Appendix I for Thomas Jefferson's full statement concerning "the essential principles of our government."

language, and look hard at the real world in which we live, the analogy is quite sound in all but the rarest exceptions.

Already, I can hear the chorus chanting "Isolationism, isolationism, he's turning back the clock to isolationism." How many use that word without having the slightest idea of what it really means! *The so-called isolationism of the United States in past decades is a pure myth.* What is isolationism? Long before the current trend of revoking our Declaration of Independence under the guise of international cooperation, American influence and trade was felt in every region of the globe. Individuals and private groups spread knowledge, business, prosperity, religion, good will and, above all, respect throughout every foreign continent. It was not necessary then for America to give up her independence to have contact and influence with other countries. It is not necessary now. Yet, many Americans have been led to believe that our country is so strong that it can defend, feed and subsidize half the world, while at the same time believing that we are so weak and "inter-dependent" that we cannot survive without pooling our resources and sovereignty with those we subsidize. If wanting no part of this kind of "logic" is isolationism, then it is time we brought it back into vogue.

Senator Robert A. Taft clearly explained our traditional foreign policy:

> Our traditional policy of neutrality and non-interference with other nations was based on the principle that this policy was the best way to avoid disputes with other nations and to maintain the liberty of this country without war. From the days of George Washington that has been the policy of the United States. It has never been isolationism; but it has always avoided alliances and interference in foreign quarrels as a preventive against possible war, and it has always opposed any commitment by the United States, in advance, to take any military action outside of our territory. It would leave us free to interfere or not interfere according to whether we consider the case of sufficiently vital interest to the liberty of this country. It was the policy of the free hand. (*A Foreign Policy for Americans,* p. 12)

"But that is nationalism," chants the chorus. "And nationalism fosters jealousy, suspicion and hatred of other countries which in turn leads to war."[4] How many times has this utter nonsense been repeated without challenge as though it were some kind of empirical and self-evident truth! What kind of logic assumes that loving one's country means jealousy, suspicion and hatred of all others? Why can't we be proud of America as an independent nation and also have a feeling of brotherhood and respect for other peoples around the world? As a matter of fact, haven't Americans done just that for the past 200 years? What people have poured out more treasure to other lands, opened their doors to more immigrants, and sent more missionaries, teachers and doctors than we? Are we now to believe that love of our own country will suddenly cause us to hate the peoples of other lands?

It was the late Herbert Hoover who pointed out the social poison in the current derision of American nationalism:

> We must realize the vitality of the great spiritual force which we call nationalism. The fuzzy-minded intellectuals have sought to brand nationalism as a sin against mankind. They seem to think that infamy is attached to the word "nationalist." But that force cannot be obscured by denunciation of it as greed or selfishness — as it sometimes is. The spirit of nationalism springs from the deepest of human emotions. It rises from the yearning of men to be free of foreign domination, to govern themselves. It springs from a thousand rills of race, of history, of sacrifice and pride in national achievement. (Quoted by Eugene W. Castle, *Billions, Blunders and Baloney,* p. 259)

In order for a man to be a good neighbor within his community, he had better first love his own family before he tries to save the neighborhood. If he doesn't love his own, why should we believe he would love others? Theodore Roosevelt firmly believed that "it is only the man who ardently loves his country first who in actual practice can help any other country at all." (*P.P.N.S.,* p. 196)

Many well-intentioned people are now convinced that we are living in a period of history which makes it both possible and necessary to abandon our national sovereignty, to merge our nation militarily, economically, and politically with other

---

[4]Credit is given to G. Edward Griffin, *The Fearful Master,* for some of the thoughts expressed in this chapter.

nations, and to form, at last, a world government which, sup-posedly, would put an end to war. We are told that this is merely doing between nations what we did so successfully with our thirteen colonies. This plea for world federalism is based on the idea that the mere act of joining separate political units together into a larger federal entity will somehow prevent those units from waging war with each other. The success of our own federal system is most often cited as proof that this theory is valid. But such an evaluation is a shallow one.

First of all, the American Civil War, one of the most bloody in all history, illustrates that the mere federation of governments, even those culturally similar, as in America, does not automatically prevent war between them. Secondly, we find that true peace quite easily exists between nations which are not federated. As a matter of fact, members of the British Commonwealth of Nations seemed to get along far more peacefully after the political bonds between them had been relaxed. In other words, true peace has absolutely nothing to do with whether separate political units are joined together — except, perhaps, that such a union may create a common military defense sufficiently impressive to deter an aggressive attack. But that is peace between the union and outside powers; it has little effect on peace between the units, themselves, which is the substance of the argument for world government.

Peace is the natural result of relationships between groups and cultures which are mutually satisfactory to both sides. These relationships are found with equal ease within or across federal lines. As a matter of fact, they are the same relation-ships that promote peaceful conditions within the commu-nity, the neighborhood, the family itself. What are they? Just stop and think for a moment; if you were marooned on an island with two other people, what relationships between you would be mutually satisfactory enough to prevent you from re-sorting to violence in your relationships? Or, to put it the other way around, what would cause you to break the peace and raise your hand against your partners?

Obviously, if one or both of the partners attempted to seize your food and shelter, you would fight. Their reaction to similar efforts on your part would be the same. If they attempted to take away your freedom, to dictate how you would conduct your affairs, or tell you what moral and ethical standards you must follow, likewise, you would fight. And if they constantly ridiculed your attire, your manners and your speech, in time you might be sparked into a brawl. The best way to keep the peace on that island is for each one to mind his own business, to respect each other's right to be different (even to act in a way that seems foolish or improper, if he wishes), and to have compassion for each other's troubles and hardships — but not to force each other to do something! And, to make sure that the others hold to their end of the bargain, each should keep physically strong enough to make any violation of this code unprofitable.[5]

Now, suppose these three got together and decided to form a political union, to "federate" as it were. Would this really change anything? Suppose they declared themselves to be the United Persons, and wrote a charter, and held daily meetings and passed resolutions. What then? These superficial ceremonies might be fun for awhile, but the minute two of them out-voted the other, and started "legally" to take his food and shelter, limit his freedom or force him to accept an unwanted standard of moral conduct, they would be right back where they all began. Federation or no federation, they would fight.

Is it really different between nations? Not at all. The same simple code of conduct applies in all human relationships, large or small. Regardless of the size, be it international or three men on an island, the basic unit is still the human personality. Ignore this fact, and any plan is doomed to failure.[6]

---

[5]"It takes a combination of three factors to protect our national interests under all conditions and to maintain peace on *our* terms. The three factors are: credible military superiority along the entire spectrum of modern warfare; courageous and decisive diplomacy; and the active support of the American people." (General Thomas S. Power, *Design for Survival,* p. 6)

[6]"Those who have written on civil government lay it down as a first principle, and all historians demonstrate the same, that whoever would found a state and make proper laws for the government of it must presume that all men are bad by nature: that they will not fail to show that natural depravity of heart whenever they have a fair opportunity. . . . constant experience shows us that every man vested with power is apt to abuse it. He pushes on till he comes to something that limits him." (Machiavelli, 1469-1527; quoted by John Adams, *Works* 4:408)

It might be worthwhile at this point to mention that Washington's policy of neutrality and non-interference was adhered to by those who followed him. For instance, President John Adams, in his Inaugural Address, resolved "to do justice as far as may depend upon me, at all times and to all nations, and maintain peace, friendship, and benevolence with all the world." He later said, in a special message to Congress,

> It is my sincere desire, and in this I presume I concur with you and with our constituents, to preserve peace and friendship with all nations. . . .

To which the Senate, presided over by Thomas Jefferson, replied,

> Peace and harmony with all nations is our sincere wish; but such being the lot of humanity that nations will not always reciprocate peaceable dispositions, it is our firm belief that effectual measures of defense will tend to inspire that national self-respect and confidence at home which is the unfailing source of respectability abroad, to check aggression and prevent war. (Quoted by Clarence B. Carson, *The American Tradition*, p. 210)

When the thirteen colonies formed our Federal Union, they had two very important factors in their favor, neither of which are present in the world at large today. First, the colonies themselves were all of a similar cultural background. They enjoyed similar legal systems, they spoke the same language, and they shared similar religious beliefs. They had much in common. The second advantage, and the most important of the two, was that they formed their union under a constitution which was designed to prevent any of them, or a majority of them, from forcefully intervening in the affairs of the others. The original federal government was authorized to provide mutual defense, run a post office, and that was about all. As previously mentioned, however, even though we had these powerful forces working in our favor, full scale war did break out at one tragic point in our history.

The peace that followed, of course, was no peace at all, but was only the smoldering resentment and hatred that follows in the wake of any armed conflict. Fortunately, the common ties between North and South, the cultural similarities and the common heritage, have proved through the intervening years to over-balance the differences. And with the gradual passing away of the generation that carried the battle scars, the Union has healed.

Among the nations of the world today, there are precious few common bonds that could help overcome the clash of cross-purposes that inevitably must arise between groups with such divergent ethnic, linguistic, legal, religious, cultural, and political environments. To add fuel to the fire, the concept woven into all of the present-day proposals for world government (the U.N. foremost among these) is one of unlimited governmental power to impose by force a monolithic set of values and conduct on all groups and individuals whether they like it or not. Far from insuring peace, such conditions can only enhance the chances of war.[7]

In this connection it is interesting to point out that the late J. Reuben Clark, who was recently described as "probably the greatest authority on [the Constitution] during the past fifty years" (*American Opinion,* April 1966, p. 113), in 1945 — the year the United Nations charter was adopted — made this prediction in his devastating and prophetic "cursory analysis" of the United Nations Charter:

> There seems no reason to doubt that such real approval as the Charter has among the people is based upon the belief that if the Charter is put into effect, wars will end. . . . The Charter will not certainly end war. Some will ask — why not? In the first place, there is no provision in the Charter itself that contemplates ending war. It is true the charter provides for force to bring peace, but such use of force is itself war. . . . It is true the Charter is built to prepare for war, not to promote peace. . . . The Charter is a war document not a peace document. . . .

---

[7]"Power and law are not synonymous. In truth they are frequently in opposition and irreconcilable. There is God's law from which all equitable laws of man emerge and by which men must live if they are not to die in oppression, chaos and despair. Divorced from God's eternal and immutable Law, established before the founding of the suns, man's power is evil no matter the noble words with which it is employed or the motives urged when enforcing it.

"Men of good will, mindful therefore of the Law laid down by God, will oppose governments whose rule is by men, and, if they wish to survive as a nation they will destroy that government which attempts to adjudicate by the whim or power of venal judges." (Cicero, quoted in *A Pillar of Iron,* p. ix)

Not only does the Charter Organization not prevent future wars, but it makes it practically certain that we will have future wars, and as to such wars it takes from us the power to declare them, to choose the side on which we shall fight, to determine what forces and military equipment we shall use in the war, and to control and command our sons who do the fighting. (Unpublished Manuscript; quoted in *P.P.N.S.*, p. 458)

Everyone is for peace and against war — particularly the horrors of nuclear war. And what are the horrors of war? Why, death, destruction and human suffering, of course! But, wait a minute. Since the big "peace" began at the end of World War II, isn't it a fact that, behind the iron and bamboo curtains, there has been more death, destruction and human suffering than in most of the big wars of history combined? Yes, it is a fact — a horrible fact — which Martin Dies, the former long-time Chairman of the House Committee on Un-American Activities, described in these words:

In Russia, a minimum of 25,000,000 people have been starved to death and murdered in 45 years. In Red China, the figure is probably at least 35,000,000 in a short 12 years. These ruthless, inhuman atrocities have been investigated, documented and reported in print, by numerous committees of the Congress. Yet only a relative handful of Americans know where to look for the facts, or even know that the reports exist; and still fewer have read them. (*The Martin Dies Story*, p. 20)

A consideration of these facts means that we have to re-define our terms when we talk about "peace." There are two kinds of peace. If we define peace as merely the absence of war, then we could be talking about the peace that reigns in a communist slave labor camp. The wretched souls in prison there are not at war, but do you think they would call it peace?

The only real peace — the one most of us think about when we use the term — is a peace with freedom. A nation that is not willing, if necessary, to face the rigors of war to defend its real peace-in-freedom is doomed to lose both its freedom and its peace! These are the hard facts of life. We may not like them, but until we live in a far better world than

exists today, we must face up to them squarely and courageously.[8]

In a discussion of war and its effects these wise words of
James Madison should always be remembered:

> *Of all the enemies to public liberty war is, perhaps, the most*
> *to be dreaded, because it comprises and develops the germ of*
> *every other.* War is the parent of armies; from these proceed debts
> and taxes; and armies, and debts, and taxes are the known instru-
> ments for bringing the many under the domination of the few. In
> war, too, the discretionary power of the Executive is extended; its
> influence in dealing out offices, honors, and emoluments is multi-
> plied; and all the means of seducing the minds, are added to those
> of subduing the force, of the people. The same malignant aspect
> in republicanism may be traced in the inequality of fortunes, and
> the opportunities of fraud, growing out of a state of war, and in
> the degeneracy of manners and morals, engendered by both. No
> nation could preserve its freedom in the midst of continual war-
> fare. (April 20, 1795; *Works* 4:491-2; *P.P.N.S.,* p. 468)

Shortly after this, in a letter to Thomas Jefferson, James
Madison issued another warning which should never be
forgotten:

> The management of foreign relations appears to be the most
> susceptible of abuse of all the trusts committed to a Government
> because they can be concealed or disclosed, or disclosed in such
> parts and at such times as will best suit particular views; and be-
> cause the body of the people are less capable of judging, and are
> more under the influence of prejudices, on that branch of their
> affairs, than of any other. Perhaps it is a universal truth that
> the loss of liberty at home is to be charged to provisions against
> danger, real or pretended, from abroad. (May 13, 1798; *Works*
> 2:140-1; *P.P.N.S.,* p. 431)

Until all nations follow the concept of limited government, it is unlikely that universal peace will ever be realized
on this planet. Unlimited, power-grasping governments will

---

[8]"It is our duty . . . to endeavor to avoid war; but if it shall actually take
place, no matter by whom brought on, we must defend ourselves. If our house be
on fire, without inquiring whether it was fired from within or without, we must
try to extinguish it." (Thomas Jefferson, to James Lewis, May 9, 1798; *Works*
4:241)

always resort to force if they think they can get away with it.[9] But there can be peace for America. As long as our leaders faithfully discharge their duty to preserve and strengthen the military, economic and political independence of our Republic, the world's petty despots will leave us alone. What more could we ask of U.S. foreign policy?

From these primary policy pronouncements some general principles emerge. They can be reduced to a few heads and stated as imperatives in the following manner:

The United States should:

1. Establish and maintain a position of independence with regard to other countries.

2. Avoid political connection, involvement, or intervention in the affairs of other countries.

3. Make no permanent or entangling alliances.

4. Treat all nations impartially, neither granting nor accepting special privileges from any.

5. Promote commerce with all peoples and countries.

6. Cooperate with other countries to develop civilized rules of intercourse.

7. Act always in accordance with the "laws of nations."

8. Remedy all just claims of injury to other nations, and require just treatment from other nations, standing ready, if necessary, to punish offenders.

9. Maintain a defensive force of sufficient magnitude to deter aggressors.[10] (See *The American Tradition*, p. 212)

---

[9]"There is one safeguard known generally to the wise, which is an advantge and security to all, but especially to democracies as against despots. What is it? Distrust." (Demosthenes, 384-322 B.C.; *Familiar Quotations*, p. 277)

[10]"Deterrence is more than bombs and missiles and tanks and armies. Deterrence is a sound economy and prosperous industry. Deterrence is scientific progress and good schools. Deterrence is effective civil defense and the maintenance of law and order. Deterrence is the practice of religion and respect for the rights and convictions of others. Deterrence is a high standard of morals and wholesome family life. Deterrence is honesty in public office and freedom of the press. Deterrence is all these things and many more, for *only a nation that is healthy and strong in every respect has the power and will to deter the forces from within and without that threatens its survival.*" (General Thomas S. Power, *Design For Survival*, p. 242)

For the first hundred years and more of the existence of the Republic, Americans developed and maintained a tradition that was in keeping with the above principles. We can say with confidence that the United States established a tradition of foreign relations in keeping with the principles laid down by the founding fathers. In the words of Senator Taft:

> I do not believe it is a selfish goal for us to insist that the over-riding purpose of all American foreign policy should be the maintenance of the liberty and the peace of the people of the United States, so that they may achieve that intellectual and material improvement which is their genius and in which they can set an example for all peoples. By that example we can do an even greater service to mankind than we can by billions of material assistance — and more than we can ever do by war. (*A Foreign Policy For Americans,* p. 14)

It seems fitting in conclusion to refer you again to the inspired words of the wise father of our country. He said,

> My ardent desire is, and my aim has been . . . to keep the United States free from political connections with every other country, to see them independent of all and under the influence of none. In a word, I want an American character, that the powers of Europe may be convinced we act for ourselves, and not for others. This, in my judgment, is the only way to be respected abroad and happy at home. (October 9, 1795; *Writings* 13:119)

CHAPTER 10

VICTORY OVER COMMUNISM

"This enemy must be neutralized and ultimately defeated if our national security is to be maintained. It must be defeated if the national goal of peace and freedom . . . is ever to be achieved.

"This will happen only when we accept the fact that the current struggle is a struggle for the survival of our way of life. It will happen only after we proclaim our determination to win this struggle and act accordingly." (National Strategy Committee, American Security Council, *Peace and Freedom Through Cold War Victory*, p. 35)[1]

Let's get one thing straight at the very beginning. International communism is the self-avowed enemy of every loyal American. It has declared war against us and fully intends to win. The war in which we are engaged is *total*. Although its main battlefields are psychological, political and economic, it also encompasses revolution, violence, terror and limited military skirmishes. If we should lose this war, the conquering enemy's wrath against our people and our institutions will result in one of the greatest blood-baths of all history. Call it a "cold war" if it makes you feel better, but our freedom and our very lives are the stakes of this contest.[2]

---

[1]The National Strategy Committee consists, among others, of such prominent Americans as General Mark W. Clark, General Robert E. Wood, General Albert C. Wedemeyer, Lt. General Edward M. Almond, Admiral Ben Moreell, Admiral Felix P. Stump, Rear Admiral Chester C. Ward, Lloyd Wight, Patrick J. Frawley, Jr., Dr. Robert Morris, Dr. Stefan Possony and Dr. Edward Teller.

[2]"The words just haven't been invented to adequately describe the magnitude of torture, brutality and terror about to be loosed upon the world by the greatest system of organized evil in the history of the world — the Communist international; nor do words exist to describe the evil already committed. . . . Today the future not only of our free nation, but indeed of what remains of the free world, is directly at stake; and general misinformation or misunderstanding can and will result in the total destruction of present day society. We are dealing with a life or death matter. . . ."(Julia Brown, Former F.B.I. Undercover Agent; *I Testify*, p. xiv)

We didn't start this war, and we don't want to be in it. But, we have no choice. True, we can *pretend* that it doesn't exist. We can hope that, somehow, if we just don't fight back, if we keep smiling at the enemy and show him that we intend no harm, then maybe he will call off his war, and we can all live in peace. But the communists merely laugh at our naivete, take advantage of concessions, consolidate their gains and press toward ultimate victory.

In view of the life-and-death nature of this struggle, it is incredible that our leaders in Washington for over thirty years consistently have followed a policy of hopeful coexistence, of fearful containment, and now even of building bridges of trade and friendship to our enemies. Are they deaf and unable to hear the communists daily reaffirm their declaration of war against us? Are they blind and unable to see how the communists are maneuvering into strategic positions, both at home and abroad, from which to strike a fatal blow? Are they ignorant and unable to learn the lessons of history?[3]

Unfortunately, they are none of these. The problem could be easily corrected if it were merely a question of competency. Our leaders and opinion-molders are well aware of everything I have just outlined, but they are steering us along a course of non-resistance to communism just the same, due primarily to a conviction on their part that such a course is our only alternative to nuclear war. The basic argument used to support this conviction runs something like this:

1. We live in a new age. Modern knowledge and technology have made it impossible to live by the rules and stan-

---

[3]At the Lenin School of Political Warfare in Moscow this significant statement was reportedly made by Dimitry Z. Manuilsky, who represented the U.S.S.R. in presiding over the Security Council of the United Nations in 1949: "War to the hilt between communism and capitalism is inevitable. Today, of course, we are not strong enough to attack. . . . To win we shall need the element of surprise. The bourgeois will have to be put to sleep. So we shall begin by launching the most spectacular peace movements on record. There will be electrifying overtures and unheard of concessions. The capitalist countries, stupid and decadent, will rejoice to cooperate in their own destruction. They will leap at another chance to be friends. As soon as their guard is down, we shall smash them with our clenched fist!" (Quoted by W. Cleon Skousen, *The Naked Communist,* p. 208)

dards of yesterday. We cannot turn back the clock, etc. Things are different now.

2. One thing that is different now is the concept of war. The existence of super-weapons means that, if a major war should break out today, neither side would win. Both would be virtually destroyed. There would be only losers. Victory is impossible.

3. Since victory is not possible, we should quit acting as though it were. We should not risk triggering an accidental war by reaching for the unattainable. We must determine what is realistically attainable and work for that.

4. Probably the best we can hope for is the eventual merger of the two opposing systems into some kind of an international body, such as the U.N. This would, perhaps, leave much to be desired, since we would be required to surrender our national sovereignty and to adopt many of the totalitarian features of those with whom we merge, but it's better than nuclear war, and that's our only alternative.[4]

There, in a nutshell, is the argument for our present policy of containment and coexistence rather than victory. It has been described as a no-win policy, but it is worse than that. It is an anti-win policy. Those who formulate and execute our national strategy have made it quite clear that not only do we have no intention of winning this contest with communism, but we will do everything possible to avoid even the *appearance* of a will to win, so as not to give the enemy any cause to miscalculate our intentions.

The only real worry to the planners in Washington and Moscow is that the American people will not appreciate the "wisdom" of their long-range strategy and will insist on real anti-communist action for a change. And so, occasionally, the planners go through the motions of opposing communism to placate the voters at home, but make it clear to the enemy

---

[4]"To negotiate true peace with people who are utterly dedicated to the concept of the historical inevitability of class war and their victory is impossible. To think that we can do it is to indicate a failure to understand Communism so completely that it approaches mental illness. To the Communist, every negotiation is an act of war. Every delegation is an act of war. Every peace petition is an act of war. Every disarmament conference is an act of war." (Dr. Fred Schwarz, quoted by Frank J. Johnson, *No Substitute For Victory*, p. 45)

that they really do not intend to do anything rash — like winning. In the meantime, it is a race against the clock. While they are still in power, they are attempting to build a world organization and to transfer our military might to that organization just as rapidly as possible so that, even if the anti-communist public should finally wake up to their plans, it will be too late to do anything about it.

Fantastic? I agree, but that is exactly what is now going on behind such soft phrases as "containment," "disarmament," and "world community." Of course, one doesn't have to take my word for this. The following references are fairly typical of what our leaders themselves are saying on the subject.

As far back as 1959, Joseph E. Johnson, former Chief of the Policy Planning Division of our State Department, declared:

> From now on, every decision facing the U.S. in this field must be taken in the light of the fact that a good part of this country could be destroyed. . . . We must be prepared to fight limited wars; limited as to weapons and as to goals, to stabilize the situation temporarily, tide things over. But *victory is no longer possible.* (As quoted in *The Dan Smoot Report,* December 11, 1961)

On May 5, 1962, the State Department issued a report explaining that it was necessary to censor speeches of high-ranking military men to avoid "provocative statements." The report said that an expression of public belligerence toward the Soviets or any talk of "victory" over communism would only serve to "discredit our good faith" toward communist regimes. (*L.A. Herald Examiner,* May 6, 1952, p. A-9).

The New York Times, in an editorial reflecting the official policy of our government, phrased it this way:

> We must seek to discourage anti-communist revolts in order to avert bloodshed and war. We must, under our principles, live with evil, even if by doing so we help to stabilize tottering Communist regimes, as in East Germany, and perhaps even expose citadels of freedom, like West Berlin, to slow death by strangulation. (*New York Times* editorial August 16, 1961)

In 1962, Walt Rostow, Chief of the State Department's
Policy Planning Division under President Kennedy, proposed
officially that, in the interest of avoiding war, the United States
should not only refrain from opposing the Soviets in any way,
but should go one step further and actually help them achieve
their objectives. He said:

> Rising tensions or pleas of our allies or of the American
> public must be ignored in any crisis with Russia. The temptation
> must be avoided to prolong or expand any crisis in an effort to
> degrade or embarrass the Soviets in the eyes of the world. (*New
> York Times,* June 22, 1962)

In November of 1965, a fifteen-member advisory group
on arms control appointed by President Johnson made public
its recommendations. The top-level advisory committee cau-
tioned the President to de-emphasize our military alliances in
Europe so as not to disturb or provoke the Soviets, and it was
suggested that part of the U.S. defense budget be turned over
to the U.N. to help finance a strong and permanent U.N.
Army. (*U.S. News and World Report,* December 6, 1965,
p. 6)

If there is still any doubt in anyone's mind as to where
all this is heading, note carefully these words spoken in 1966
by Secretary of Defense McNamara:

> Regional and international organizations for peacekeeping
> purposes are as yet rudimentary, but they must grow in experience
> and be strengthened by deliberate and practical co-operative
> action. . . .
>
> The Organization of American States in the Dominican Re-
> public, the more than 30 nations contributing troops or supplies
> to assist the Government of South Vietnam, indeed even the
> parallel efforts of the United States and the Soviet Union in the
> Pakistan-India conflict — these efforts together with those of the
> U.N., are the first attempts to substitute multinational for uni-
> lateral policing of violence. *They point to the peacekeeping pat-
> terns of the future.*
>
> We must not merely applaud the idea. We must dedicate
> talent, resources, and hard, hard practical thinking to its imple-
> mentation. (*U.S. News and World Report,* May 30, 1966)

Let us return for a moment to the basic premise. It must be remembered that all these policies of helping to stabilize tottering communist regimes and eventually merging our military forces into a multinational or international world body — all of these are predicated upon the premise that *victory is impossible*. If that premise is correct, then there is considerable force to the proposals. It would be futile to complain about our gradual but consistent retreat and loss of influence around the world since World War II. It would be useless to expect anything better in Berlin, Korea, Cuba, Vietnam or anywhere else we have "confronted" the Soviets with "limited objectives" and "limited wars." Under this concept we would have to agree with Secretary of State Dean Rusk when he said to Undersecretary George Ball, "We have won a considerable victory. You and I are still alive." (As quoted by Elie Abel, *The Missile Crisis* [Bantam Books, N.Y., 1966], p. 110.) But if that premise is in error, then, fellow Americans, we have some fast house-cleaning to do in Washington!

The first fallacy of our present anti-win policy is that an all-out war with the communists is likely to be a nuclear war. Nothing could be further from reality. As previously pointed out, *we are already engaged in an all-out war with the communists*. The thought that it might shift its present emphasis from the psychological, economic and political arenas to the military arena is totally inconsistent with an understanding of how the communists work. This is not their game. They have taken over one-third of the world without a single Soviet invasion. Their formula has been takeover from within by inspiring civil wars, revolution and through acts of treason. Countries fall into the Red slave empire, not at the hands of invading Russians, but at the hands of native communists who secretly work for the overthrow of their own government. This has been their successful pattern of operation for over fifty years, and they certainly are not going to abandon it now.

Nikita Khruschev explained it this way:

> It is not an army, but peace that is required to propagate communist ideas, disseminate them, and establish them in the minds of men. . . .

War will not help us reach our goal — it will spoil it. . . .

Marxism-Leninism is our main weapon. We will conquer the capitalist world by using this mighty ideological weapon and not a hydrogen bomb. . . .

We produce the hydrogen bomb with the sole object of cooling the ambitions of some excessively zealous politicians and generals in the Capitalist countries. (*Conquest Without War,* compiled and edited by N. H. Mager and Jacques Kotel [Simon and Schuster, N.Y., 1961], pp. 68, 69, 58, 51, 56)

This leads us to fallacy number two. Considering the non-military nature of the total war in which we are already engaged, we are forced to the conclusion that victory is not only *possible, it is inevitable — for one side or the other!* Let me repeat that, for it is one of the most vital and least understood facts of our present struggle against communism. *Victory is inevitable* — for one side or the other! The communists have said that it is inconceivable that this contest can go on indefinitely. I agree. Common sense dictates that, sooner or later, one of us must perish. The question is — and has been all along — not *can* we win, but *who* will win. Isn't it about time we turned our attention and energies to that issue instead of preparing for an accommodation or a merger that will only turn out to be surrender?[5]

Just as we have been losing through non-military means, so too, we can win through non-military means. A good place to begin is to stop foreign aid to communist countries; stop sending wheat to bail them out of their agricultural problems; stop building steel mills, synthetic rubber factories and truck plants for them, stop selling them vital machinery; stop building nuclear reactors and power generating stations for them; stop sending them jet fighters, and stop training their pilots and army officers. In other words, if we would just stop helping

---

[5]*"The ultimate weapon in our design for survival are the American people, individually and collectively.* They must be made to understand that, in the nuclear age, the primary mission of the military is no longer to win wars but to help deter them, and that the military can no longer do its job alone. It must be impressed on every citizen that he or she is a soldier in the battle for survival, because that battle must be waged on many fronts in addition to the military front and must be fought with many weapons in addition to military weapons." (General Thomas S. Power, *Design For Survival*, p. 243)

communist nations, there is every reason to believe that they would soon collapse under the sheer weight of their own failures and under the pressures of the restless captive peoples looking for a chance to revolt. Our strongest allies are not those in the free world whose leaders are seeking an accommodation with communism; they are the people of the captive nations — those who know what communism really is, and who are willing to give their lives to destroy their captors if they only thought that we might come to their aid.

There are some Americans who have been so effectively frightened by the extensive A-bomb propaganda that they have become convinced that it is "better Red than dead." Perhaps they wouldn't want to express it quite that bluntly, but that's what it boils down to. They have forgotten that there are other horrible ways to die. They have forgotten that, right now, as a matter of calculated policy, the communists are perpetrating horrible atrocities every bit as sickening as those carried out in the torture chambers and gas ovens of the Nazi regime. The details of these refined methods of human extermination are so gruesome, it is difficult to even describe them. Because so many Americans have forgotten this fact — or perhaps because they preferred not to believe it in the first place — they are willing to accept the possibility of living under communism rather than run the risk of death in an unlikely nuclear war. Apparently they do not comprehend the object lesson of tens of thousands of people risking their lives to escape from behind the iron and bamboo curtains.

Americans have always accepted Patrick Henry's choice of "Liberty or Death." As a result, we now have liberty. If we should ever come to place mere survival above all else, if we should now make our national slogan "Better Red than dead," we shall end up Red and only wish that we were dead.

As for the hard choices that confront us as a nation of free men, things really are no different now than in the past. The enemy may have more powerful weapons and more refined methods of conducting total war within our borders, but the hardest part of any battle is still the decision to fight or surrender. As George Washington expressed it in 1776:

> Our cruel and unrelenting enemy leaves us only *the choice of a brave resistance, or the most abject submission.* We have, therefore, to resolve to *conquer or to die.*[6] (As quoted by Stefan T. Possony, *A Century of Conflict* [Henry Regnery Co., Chicago, 1953] p. XIX.)

---

[6]"If you will not fight for the right when you can easily win without bloodshed; if you will not fight when your victory will be sure and not too costly; you may come to the moment when you will have to fight with all the odds against you and only a precarious chance of survival. There may be even a worse fate. You may have to fight when there is no hope of victory, because it is better to perish than live as slaves." (Winston Churchill, quoted in *P.P.N.S.*, p. 258)

CHAPTER 11

DISARMAMENT — BLUEPRINT FOR SURRENDER

"To be prepared for war is one of the most effectual means of preserving peace. A free people ought not only to be armed, but disciplined; to which end a uniform and well-digested plan is requisite; and their safety and interest require, that they should promote such manufactories as tend to render them independent on others for essential, particularly for military, supplies."[1] (President George Washington, Speech To Congress, January 8, 1790)

The first step toward formulating an intelligent attitude toward current disarmament proposals is to examine what the word "disarmament" really means. As it is used today by those who are its foremost advocates, the word "disarmament" can be defined simply as "the transfer of our national military apparatus to the control of the U.N."

In September of 1961, our State Department published the text of its proposal for disarmament as presented before the U.N. General Assembly. Entitled *Freedom From War — The United States Program for General and Complete Disarmament,* this proposal set down four objectives. Without mincing words, it advocated: (1) that all nations, including the United States, disband their national armed forces except for what would be earmarked for "a United Nations peace force"; (2) that all nations, including the United States, elim-

---

[1]"I can summarize my views on national security planning into two sentences. The leaders of an organized conspiracy have sworn to destroy America and the Free World by one means or another, and there is no real evidence available at this time to indicate that their objective has been changed. Therefore, we had better be prepared to fight to maintain our liberty." (General Nathan F. Twining, *Neither Liberty Nor Safety,* pp. 275-276)

inate their nuclear weapons and missiles "other than those required for a United Nations peace force"; (3) that all nations, including the United States, acknowledge the U.N. authority to supervise and direct this transfer of military power; and (4) that all nations, including the United States, carry out this transfer "to a point where no state would have the military power to challenge the progressively strengthened U.N. Peace Force."[2]

Most Americans find it hard to believe that our leaders in Washington would make such a fantastic proposal. This is merely part of the overall plan to resolve our conflict with communism, not by victory over it, but by merging with it into a world body, since it will have superior military force at its disposal, will become by definition a one-world government.

This plan is not new. It has been developed and gradually moved forward ever since the end of World War II and the creation of the U.N. President Kennedy described the "beneficial effects" in this way. Disarmament, he said, means

> . . . a revolutionary change in the political structure of the world; creation of a radically new international system; *abandonment of most of the old concepts of national states;* development of international institutions that would *encourage nations to give up much of their national sovereignty;* acceptance without question or reservation of the jurisdiction of the international court; willingness to *depend for national security on an international peace force* under an immensely changed and strengthened United Nations. (As quoted in Washington *News,* April 19, 1962)

Commenting further on these proposals, Walt Rostow — then chairman of our State Department Policy Planning Board — wrote:

> It is a legitimate American national objective to remove from all nations — including the U.S. — the right to use substantial

---

[2]"Some people seem to believe that the possession of arms and armament creates a circumstance which can lead to war. They seem to think that if our Government could eliminate military forces and armaments it would have eliminated war itself. This logic is totally at variance with the history of man. Under the terms of this logic the nation could eliminate its police force and thereby eliminate crime. This viewpoint also contradicts military history from well before the time of Caesar." (General Nathan F. Twining, *Neither Liberty Nor Safety,* p. 285)

military force to pursue their own interests. Since this residual right is the root of national sovereignty and the basis for the existence of an international arena of power, *it is, therefore, an American interest to see an end to nationhood as it has been historically defined.* (Entered into the Congressional Record, June 6, 1963, pp. A-362,3.)

In 1961, Adlai Stevenson spelled it out for even the most thick-headed to understand when, describing our proposals for disarmament, he said: "In short, the U.S. program calls for *total elimination of national capacity to make international war.*" And then, as though inscribing the epitaph on our national tombstone, he added: "It is presented in dead earnest." (*Documents on Disarmament,* 1961 [U.S. Arms Control and Disarmament Agency], Publication No. 5, p. 623)

There is yet another grim aspect to our disarmament proposals. While the major long-range thrust is the transfer of our military might to the U.N., the secondary short-range thrust is to weaken our military might so that, even if real anti-communists should somehow regain control of our government before the transfer is complete, they would not be able to pose any real threat to the communist empire. For just a glimpse into this phase of disarmament, consider this item taken word-for-word from the Department of State, *Foreign Policy Briefs,* May 10, 1965:

> *The United States is determined to work for general and complete disarmament* in order to achieve a better and safer world through the application of U.N. Charter principles and the steady development of international law and effective peace-keeping arrangements, the U.N. Disarmament Commission was told on April 26 by Ambassador Stevenson. . . .
>
> Reviewing the contributions of the U.S. toward the limitation and reversal of the arms race and urging other nations to take reciprocal action, Ambassador Stevenson said:
>
> ". . . by mid-1966 the U.S. will have inactivated or destroyed over 2,000 B-47 bomber-type aircraft. I might also add that none have been provided as potential strategic nuclear vehicles to other countries. In addition, the U.S. will make a reduction during 1965 in the number of B-52 heavy strategic bomber aircraft in the existing forces. These reductions also will be accomplished by destruction of aircraft.

"Moreover, the U.S. now plans to forego the construction of some advanced design Minuteman missiles which were included in our plans, as well as further increments of such missiles for the future."

That was 1965. The following year, *all* strategic bombers were phased out of our military program, and our total defense capabilities were placed upon missiles which were not yet fully operational. Since that time, missile research and weapons development have been severely curtailed to the point where, today, it is generally acknowledged that the Soviets very well may be better equipped than we in nuclear hardware that can be relied upon. Whether they really are, is beside the point. The mere fact that there can be speculation on the matter is serious enough. Don't let anyone say that there was a "miscalculation," though. *The record is quite clear that our sagging nuclear defense was calculated as part of our proposals for general and complete disarmament!*[3]

This is not the place to examine the pros and cons of maintaining economic or political sovereignty among divergent systems in a hostile world. But the question of military sovereignty or independence is very much to the point of this discussion. Putting aside all the arguments for sovereignty *per se,* let's look at just one narrow but highly practical question — the question of power.

Lord Acton often has been summoned to remind us that "Power tends to corrupt and absolute power corrupts absolutely." (*Essays on Freedom and Power,* p. 364) The wisdom of this statement is rather generally accepted today, but seldom applied. It needs to be applied to our thinking regarding the creation of an all-powerful international police force.[4]

---

[3] "If we keep trying to appease the Soviets with foolish offers and concessions, and keep reducing our military capabilities toward their level, and also keep tying our military technology into unrealistic cost-effectiveness straitjackets, I believe we can look forward to a major crisis. Such a crisis will be far more serious than any we have been through before. . . . There could be war. I believe that such a crisis is coming. I also believe that such a crisis need not come. But if we are to prevent it, we have no time to lose. The hour is late, and the enemy is watching the clock." (General Nathan F. Twining, *Reader's Digest,* March 1967, p. 55)

[4] "Those who voluntarily put power into the hands of a tyrant or an enemy, must not wonder if it be at last turned against themselves." (Aesop, *Great Quotations,* p. 746)

Even if we assume that all of the people at the U.N. representing the various nations were of the highest moral caliber and prompted only by the most pure and selfless motives, there still is every reason to believe that the concentration into their hands of the absolute power of a nuclear monoply, plus a military land, air, and naval force superior to any nation, would be a mighty tempting influence.[5] In time, the flesh could weaken, even the best of men would be caught up in the inevitable struggle for world power, and finally, the whole planet would be subject to an unchallengeable dictatorship of the few over the many. True, such a development conceivably might not materialize for years, but it *would* materialize. The only legitimate question open to speculation is how soon.[6]

That is, of course, assuming that all the people running the U.N. start out entirely pure and high-principled. Anyone who has watched the U.N. in action, however, hardly needs to be reminded that such an assumption is rather humorous. Out of the 120 or so nations which send delegates and staff employees, a shockingly large number of them are, themselves, military dictatorships. How could we expect them to resist the same thing at the international level? Others are still quite backward and primitive nations, not really nations at all, but more like a grouping of semi-savage tribes ruled by chieftains and witch doctors using a combination of terror and ancient superstitions to perpetuate their leadership. Oh, I know we aren't supposed to say such things for fear we might hurt their feelings and damage our good diplomatic relationships, but they are facts just the same. We had better not ignore those facts when we think about giving these people a voice equal to ours in the control of a world-monopoly of nuclear weapons.

These are all practical considerations which are reason enough to reject our current program called disarmament. But there is still one more aspect of this issue which is so

---

[5]"Constant experience shows us that every man invested with power is apt to abuse it, and to carry his authority as far as it will go. . . . To prevent this abuse, it is necessary from the very nature of things that power should be a check to power." (Montesquieu, 1748; *The Spirit of Laws* XI, 4)

[6]"The truth is that all men having power ought to be mistrusted." (James Madison, *Great Quotations*, p. 753)

alarming, that all other considerations are dwarfed by comparison. With all this talk about creating a super U.N. army, practically no attention has been given to *who* would be in charge of that army. Let's take a look.

On the surface, at least, the U.N. military structure is similar to that in our own country. The Military Staff Committee (comparable to our Joint Chiefs of Staff) is made up of military men, but it is subject to civilian control. There is a man at the U.N. who holds the position roughly comparable to our own Secretary of Defense. His post is known as the Undersecretary General for Political and Security Council Affairs. Appointed by the Secretary General, this man has, in addition to wide and unspecified duties in the political field, three primary responsibilities in the field of military activity: (1) He directs the Military Staff Committee in the performance of U.N. military action authorized by the Security Council; (2) He is in charge of all disarmament moves which I have just outlined; and (3) He is in charge of all atomic energy which already has been turned over to the U.N. and that which is to be turned over in the future.

It should be obvious that these three functions centered in the office of U.N. Undersecretary General for Political and Security Council Affairs may soon place into the hands of the man who holds that office absolute power of life and death over every one of us. I should think that Americans would want to know something about this man; that they ought to be passingly curious, at least.

Since 1945 there have been nine men appointed to this position. They are:

1. Arkady Sobolev — USSR (Resigned April 1949)
2. Konstantine Zinchenko — USSR (Resigned May 1953)
3. Ilya Tchernychev — USSR (Finished above term to 1954)
4. Dragoslav Protich — Yugoslavia (Resigned July 1958)

5. Anatole F. Dobrynin — USSR (Resigned Feb. 1960)
6. Georgi P. Arkadev — USSR (Resigned March 1963)
7. Eugeny D. Kiselev — USSR (Died April 17, 1963)
8. Vladimir P. Suslov — USSR (Appointed May 21, 1963)
9. Alesksie Nestorenko — USSR (Appointed August 17, 1965 — presently in office)[7]

What in heaven's name does it take to wake up the slumbering American spirit of resistance? Does not this list cause anyone to feel a chill of uneasiness? How much longer must we sit by and passively permit the international planners to get away with such gross perfidy. *It is no longer enough simply to declare an opinion against disarmament. It is too late for mere gestures and admonitions. The hour calls for men of action to step forward and turn our ship away from the treacherous reef dead ahead!*[8]

---

[7]Since this was written number ten has been appointed.

[8]"When the affairs of the nation are distracted, private people are, by the spirit of that law, justified in stepping a little out of their ordinary sphere. They enjoy a privilege, of somewhat more dignity and effect, than that of idle lamentation over the calamities of their country. They may look into them narrowly; they may reason upon them liberally; and if they should be so fortunate as to discover the true source of the mischief, and to suggest any probable method of removing it, though they may displease the rulers for the day, they are certainly of service to the cause of government." (Edmund Burke, 1770; *Works* 1:435)

CHAPTER 12

VIETNAM—WHY NOT VICTORY?

"Once war is forced upon us, there is no other alternative than to apply every available means to bring it to a swift end. *War's very object is victory* — not prolonged indecision. *In war, indeed, there can be no substitute for victory."* (General Douglas MacArthur, April 19, 1951; *A Soldier Speaks*, p. 251)

When are we going to win in Vietnam — and why not? For some time this provocative question has been making the rounds in the form of bumper stickers. It's more than just a slogan, for it dramatizes one of the most shocking aspects of our war in Vietnam. Hidden behind the barrage of confusing and self-contradictory policy statements, is the plain fact that we are *not* going to win in Vietnam, or anywhere else, for that matter on our present course. Elsewhere I have explored the rationalization behind our present no-win policy toward communism. Briefly stated: our leaders are supposedly convinced that any strong anti-communist action that would actually roll back the iron or bamboo curtain would certainly lead to nuclear war. Therefore, they have contented themselves with strictly the defensive policy of resistance, not counter-attack; of containment, not victory.

To better understand how this no-win policy is working in Vietnam, it is well to recall what happened in Korea. The Communists invaded South Korea, leaving behind a trail of murder, plunder and destruction. We responded to South Korea's plea for help, but we made it clear from the beginning that our objectives were "limited" to the point that the enemy invaders really had little to fear. If they wanted to retreat behind the 38th parallel to regroup and prepare another attack, we would not pursue them. If they wanted a breathing spell, we would agree to a cease-fire. They knew that our military commanders were forbidden to destroy their supply routes — the bridges over the Yalu River. In other words, the communists knew that their aggression would never be punished — that the very worst they would have to face was a stalemate and a settlement negotiated at a peace table where the aggressor and the victim are treated as respectable equals.

The whole situation should have been absurd, even to the casual observer. It was like having someone enter your home, attack your wife and shoot your children; but when you call for help, the police merely place the intruder back outside your house and ask him not to return. When he breaks in a second time, stabs you in the shoulder and sets your house on fire, the police react by setting up a committee to negotiate your differences. Such is the policy of containment; and as anyone can see, this approach to world problems encourages potential aggressor nations to try their luck at military conquest. After all, they have everything to gain and literally nothing to lose.

Our no-win policy, instead of promoting peace, actually increases the chances for war.[1] If we had forced North Korea to the peace table as a vanquished power instead of coaxing them to the negotiating table as an equal power, we would have demonstrated to communist leaders that aggression does not pay. By pursuing limited objectives in Korea, however, we made the prospect of future wars in Asia most promising to the communists. The seeds of our present war in Vietnam were sown in Korea. And, unless we change our present no-win policy in Vietnam, we will be setting the stage for future wars and commitment of American men to battle not only in Asia, but all around the globe — especially Latin America.

Make no mistake about it, our war in Vietnam, in principle, is no different than Korea. We have the military capacity,

---

[1]"I submit that it is politically immoral to use less force than is necessary to achieve a military objective when adequate force is available. It is immoral because more of our young men are killed or wounded or submitted to a cruel captivity than would have been necessary if *more* than enough force were used. Also, in a protracted struggle our total losses are greatly increased over the losses sustained in a quick, decisive war." (General Curtis E. LeMay, *America Is In Danger*, p. 309)

our leaders tell us, to wipe North Vietnam off the face of the map *without nuclear weapons*. Yet, almost a decade later and after thousands of American casualties, we are still fighting the war less than twenty-five miles from where it began.

Secretary of State Dean Rusk explains it this way: "What we face in Vietnam is what we have faced on many occasions before — the need to check the extension of communist power in order to maintain a reasonable stability in a precarious world." (*U.S. News and World Report,* February 28, 1966, p. 77)

General Maxwell D. Taylor, President Johnson's special consultant on Vietnam, tells a meeting of American business-men that he opposes unlimited bombing of communist North Vietnam because "it would destroy the Hanoi Government." (As quoted in *Review of the News,* April 6, 1966, p. 16)

Secretary of Defense McNamara says that the United States has "a very limited objective in Southeast Asia — very, very limited. We are not seeking to destroy the Government of North Vietnam." (*Review of the News,* March 8, 1967, p. 15)

President Johnson says: "We're not asking any uncondi-tional surrender on the part of the adversary. We're just saying to 'em, 'Come into the room and let's reason together. Let's talk out our difficulties." (*Review of the News,* November 16, 1966, p. 7)

U.N. Ambassador Arthur Goldberg says, "We're ready for unconditional negotiations," (*Review of the News,* March 8, 1967, pp. 1, 2) and then assures us three months later, "We are not engaged in a 'holy war' against communism." (*Review of the News,* February 22, 1967, p. 4)

Could the picture be more plain than that?

Asking men to offer their lives in a war which is deliber-ately prolonged to avoid victory is bad enough. Unfortunately, there is more to Vietnam than that. Although it receives little attention in the headlines, our long-range goal in Vietnam is to set up a communist coalition government. Everyone talks about the need to negotiate, but what is there to negotiate? Our leaders have already stated that we will fight forever, if necessary, to prevent the communists from taking over South Vietnam *by force.* But we have no objection if they do it through subversion, infiltration, or coalition government. Since we will not concede one inch of the physical boundaries of South Vietnam, the only thing left to negotiate is how many communists will be entitled to hold which positions in the new government.

Senator Robert Kennedy said: "One of the facts of life that you have to face up to is that the communists, or dissident elements, will play some role in the Government at some point as the result of a negotiated settlement. . . . What we have to be prepared for is the sharing of power with them in South Vietnam." (*U.S. News and World Report,* March 14, 1966, p. 68)

Vice President Hubert Humphrey explains: "North Vietnam undoubtedly will be, should be, at the negotiating table; and if North Vietnam wishes to bring in its stooge, its agent, which is the Viet Cong, we have said that would be no insurmountable obstacle." (*U.S. News and World Report,* March 14, 1966, p. 72)

Secretary McNamara explains it in these words: "I'm sure the Government of South Vietnam would welcome them [the Viet Cong] as voters. And surely we would do nothing to prevent that." (*Review of the News,* April 27, 1966, p. 2)

Sometimes we get the impression that there is a national debate going on between the "doves" and the "hawks." But where are the hawks? The doves say we should get out of Vietnam immediately and turn that country over to the communists *right now.* The so-called hawks come back and say, "Oh, no. Let's not do that. Let's stand firm *and negotiate—* Let's set up a coalition government, and turn the country over to the communists through a more gradual process." What kind of a debate is that? *The emblem of the United States is the American eagle.*

All right, let's get down to brass tacks. It's wrong to find fault and to criticize unless one has something better to offer. Let's take a look now at a few specific proposals.

The key to a solution of the problems in Vietnam is an understanding that we have no business being there in the first place — at least not under the present conditions or authority.[2] Nevertheless, we *are* there and we *are* involved, so what do we do now? Since we shouldn't be there in the first place, *we should now concentrate on doing whatever is necessary to bring our boys home. But* — and this is just as important — we must bring our boys home in such a manner as to make it unlikely that they will have to go back either to Vietnam or Thailand or the Dominican Republic or Mexico, or anywhere else to fight communist guerillas. That means that, before we bring our men home, we should let them finish the job most of them thought they were sent there to do. Let Ho Chi Minh and all the other communist underlings around the world see what good-natured old Uncle Sam still can do when a bully picks a fight with him. In other words, drop those suicidal "limited political objectives" and launch a massive military campaign. *Without having to resort to nuclear weapons,* topple the Hanoi regime, and dictate rather than negotiate the peace terms.[3] *Then* bring our boys home.

Will this bring Red China into the war? Red China already is in the war![4] The best way to get her out of the war is to let Chiang Kai-shek join us as he has requested. Chiang has stated many times that America's real enemy in Vietnam

---

[2]"We Americans have no commission from God to police the world." (Benjamin Harrison, 1888; *Great Quotations,* p. 21)

[3]"Regardless of how we have backed into this war we must now recognize, unequivocally, that we *are* in it and our only exit with honor and world respect is to win it. How can we do this?

"The first step is to reverse our objective. Instead of the negotiating table we must aspire to decisive victory. We must make the war so costly to North Vietnam that it will sue for peace. The Communists started this war. Let them wish they never had. Let the Communists end it.

"Second, we must fight the war from our position of strength, not theirs. We must fight it at the lowest cost to ourselves and at the greatest cost to the enemy. We must change the currency in this contest, from men to materials." (General Curtis E. LeMay, *America Is In Danger,* p. 257)

[4]"I don't believe the Red Chinese — who appear on the verge of civil war — are ready or willing to take on the United States in an all-out war. . . . I don't believe that the chance of Russia or China's going to war with us over this question is very high, and I'd be willing to accept the risk." (General Curtis E. LeMay, *Human Events,* January 28, 1967, pp. 8-9)

is mainland China. Chiang Ching-kuo, Free China's Defense Minister, has said:

> In order to solve the Vietnam problem and to safeguard U.S. security and prestige in Asia, it is imperative that the Chinese Communists be destroyed. And this is the best time for us to deal them a fatal blow. If the United States does not help us with logistical support in our effort to destroy the Chinese Communist regime now, it will later find a war against the Chinese Communists unavoidable. Then the loss of American lives will far surpass casualties in World War II, Korea or Vietnam. (*U.S. News and World Report,* October 10, 1966, p. 34)

Chiang Kai-shek, himself, has declared: "So long as the Peking regime continues, there can be no satisfactory solution in Vietnam. North Vietnam must be isolated from the Chinese Communists. There is no need for American combat troops. On the mainland it is between us and the Chinese Communists. We have enough strength once we reach the mainland." (*Review of the News,* April 13, 1966, p. 13)

So, in answer to the fear of bringing Red China into the war, I say we should grant Chiang permission to come into it for the purpose of getting Red China out![5]

We should not kid ourselves into thinking that the war isn't serious business. It is inconceivable to me that a man as high in government as is Walt Rostow, now President Johnson's assistant for national security affairs, could go to Leeds, England, and tell an audience: "I come from a government which, contrary to a widespread view, is not overwhelmed and obsessed by the problem of Vietnam." Our government had better *become* obsessed by Vietnam! When we ask American men to don the uniform of their country and lay down their lives for the cause, that cause had better be awfully important and we'd better put those men at the very top of our list in all that we do. To those at the front line, there is no such thing as limited war. When you're facing an enemy bent on killing you, war is total — death is final.

---

[5]"It is a reasonable assumption that the [Red] Chinese will not enter the war in a combat role. For them to do so would mean, I trust, immediate destruction by the U. S. of their atomic potential and limited air power, a setback they are not willing to face as they look into the future." (General John K. Waters, *U.S. News and World Report,* December 19, 1966, p. 56)

General Curtis E. LeMay, former Chief of Staff of the U.S. Air Force, has laid down four basic principles of warfare that we should all understand and be prepared to apply in Vietnam. (*U.S. News and World Report*, October 10, 1966, pp. 36-38) The first is, as I have just mentioned, that war is serious and dangerous business, and it does not lessen its seriousness — especially to those who are on the front line — by calling it a "police action" or a "limited" war. War, *any* war, should have objectives that are both clear and worthy of the sacrifice of human lives.[6]

Secondly, even small wars are cruel and must be fought in such a way as to win them as quickly as possible. Under no circumstances do so-called political considerations justify prolonging the slaughter when it is possible to have victory.

General LeMay's third precept, in his own words, is "Never to point a gun at someone unless you are prepared to shoot him dead. A bluff in warfare should never be attempted unless one fully intends to back it up, if need be."

The fourth doctrine of warfare is probably the most important of them all. We should never accept battle in a small war unless we are fully prepared for it to develop into a large war. As LeMay phrased it:

> The popular philosophy that we can, by cautious and timid military tactics, keep the war from escalating into a larger conflict is the ultimate in military blindness. The only way to win a war is to escalate it in one way or another above what the enemy can take. If we feel that we can't win without unacceptable risk, we have no business fighting in the first place. . . . Thus, whenever we commit our young men to mortal combat, we should be equally prepared to commit our leaders, our cities, our families and civilians — our own or the enemy's. Modern war is that serious, and we should not forget it.

Is your life and mine more valuable than that of the G.I. in Vietnam? If we are so fearful of a possible escalation of the Vietnam war to the point where our lives might be in dan-

---

[6]"The only proper rule is never to fight at all if you can honorably avoid it, but never under any circumstances to fight in a half-hearted way. When peace comes it must be the peace of complete victory." (Theodore Roosevelt, 1917; *Theodore Roosevelt Cyclopedia*, p. 633)

ger here at home, if the "limited objectives" which our leaders have declared are not important enough to risk our own hides, then how in heaven's name can we have the gall to dress our sons in uniform, give them a rifle, pat them on the back and send them into battle for the same cause!

The sharp point of our Vietnam dilemma is that the limited objectives of containment are *not* worth risking anyone's life for — ours nor those of our fighting men. What we need is a new goal — and, as that great American Douglas MacArthur once said, *"There can be no substitute for victory."*[7] As Francis Cardinal Spellman states: *"Total victory means peace."* (*The Tidings,* January 6, 1967, p. 3)

---

[7]"Now, oblivious to the lessons of military history and the American tradition, a new concept has arisen from outside our ranks which tends to disavow victory as the combat objective and to advocate in its stead a new kind of tactic on which to base the battle. The result can be nothing but failure, nothing to repay the terrible human sacrifice of war. We of the military shall always do what we are told to do. But *if this nation is to survive, we must trust the soldier once our statesmen fail to preserve the peace.* We must regain our faith in those lessons and traditions which have always sustained our victorious march through the military perils which have beset our past. *We must recapture the will and the determination to win come what may once American arms have been committed to battle.* We must reject the counsels of fear which strange and alien doctrines are attempting to force upon us. We must proclaim again and again and again an invincible adherence to the proposition that *in war there can be no substitute for victory."* (General Douglas MacArthur, March 14, 1953; *A Soldier Speaks,* pp. 302-303)

CHAPTER 13

CIVIL RIGHTS — TOOL OF COMMUNIST DECEPTION[1]

"There is no grievance that is a fit object of redress by mob law. In any case that arises . . . one of two positions is necessarily true; that is, the thing is right within itself, and therefore deserves the protection of all law and all good citizens; or, it is wrong, and therefore proper to be prohibited by legal enactments; and in neither case, is the interposition of mob law, either necessary, justifiable, or excusable." (Abraham Lincoln, January 27, 1838; *Collected Works* 1:113)

In the Book of Mormon the Prophet Nephi exclaims: "O Lord, I have trusted in thee, and I will trust in thee forever. I will not put my trust in the arm of flesh; for I know that cursed is he that putteth his trust in man or maketh flesh his arm." (2 Nephi 4:34)

Prophecying of our day, Nephi said, "They have all gone astray save it be a few, who are humble followers of Christ; nevertheless, they are led, that in many instances they do err because they are taught by the precepts of men." (2 Nephi 28:14)

Yes, *it is the precepts of men versus the revealed word of God.* The more we follow the word of God the less we are deceived, while those who follow the wisdom of men are deceived the most.

Increasingly, the Latter-day Saints must choose the reasoning of men and the revelations of God. This is a crucial

---

[1]An address delivered on September 29, 1967, at the General Conference of The Church of Jesus Christ of Latter-day Saints, in the Tabernacle, Salt Lake City, Utah, and printed in pamphlet form by Deseret Book Company.

choice, for we have those within the Church today who, with their worldly wisdom, are leading some of the members astray. President J. Reuben Clark warned that, "The ravening wolves are amongst us, from our own membership, and they, more than any others, are clothed in sheep's clothing, because they wear the habiliments of the Priesthood. . . . We should be careful of them." (*Conference Report,* April 1949, p. 163)

The Lord does not always give reasons for each commandment. Sometimes faithful members, like Adam of old, are called upon to obey an injunction of the Lord even though they do not know the reason why it was given. Those who trust in God will obey him, knowing full well that time will provide the reasons and vindicate their obedience.

The arm of flesh may not approve, not understand, why God has not bestowed the Priesthood on women or the seed of Cain, but God's ways are not man's ways. God does not have to justify all his ways for the puny mind of man. If a man gets in tune with the Lord he will know that God's course of action is right even though he may not know all the reasons why.

The Prophet Joseph Smith understood this principle when he said,

> The curse is not yet taken off from the sons of Canaan, neither will be until it is affected by as great a power as caused it to come; and the people who interfere the least with the purposes of God in this matter, will come under the least condemnation before Him; and those who are determined to pursue a course, which shows an opposition, and a feverish restlessness against the decrees of the Lord, will learn, when perhaps it is too late for their own good, that God can do His own work, without the aid of those who are not dictated by His counsel. (Prophet Joseph Smith, 1836, *History of the Church* 2:438)

The world largely ignores the first and great commandment — to love God — but talks a lot about loving their brother. They worship at the altar of man. Would Nephi have slain Laban if he put the love of neighbor above the love of God? Would Abraham have taken Isaac up for a sacrifice if he put the second commandment first?

The attitude of the world is reflected in a phrase of false-hood which reads, "Presume not God to scan; the proper study of mankind is man." (Alexander Pope, *Essays on Man*) But only those who know and love God can best love and serve his children. For only God fully understands his children and knows what is best for their welfare. Therefore, one needs to be in tune with God to best help his children. That's why the Church, under the inspiration of the Lord, encourages its members to first look to themselves, then their family, then the Church, and if need be to other voluntary agencies to help solve the problems of poverty, unemployment, hunger, sickness and distress. Those who are not moved by that same inspiration turn instead to government. Such man-made course of action does little good compared to the Lord's approach and often results in doing great harm to our Father's children even though the intentions may seem to have been noble.

Therefore, if you desire to help your fellowmen the most, then you must put the first commandment first.

When we fail to put the love of God first, we are easily deceived by crafty men, who profess a great love of humanity, while advocating programs that are not of the Lord.

In 1942, President Heber J. Grant, J. Reuben Clark, and David O. McKay warned us about the increasing threat to our Constitution, caused by the revolutionists who, the First Presidency said, were "using a technique that is as old as the human race — a fervid, but false solicitude for the unfortunate, over whom they thus gain mastery, and then enslave them. They suit their approaches to the particular group they seek to deceive." (First Presidency, *Conference Report,* April 1942, p. 90)

That timely counsel about a "fervid, but false solicitude for the unfortunate" could have saved China and Cuba if enough people knew what the communist "master of deceit" really had in mind when they promised agrarian reform. Such timely counsel could help save our country from communism, as the same "masters of deceit" are showing the same false solicitude for the unfortunate in the name of civil rights.

Now there is nothing wrong with civil rights — it is what's being done in the name of civil rights that is alarming. *There is no doubt that the so-called Civil Rights movement as it exists today is used as a communist program for revolution in America,* just as agrarian reform was used by the communists to take over China and Cuba.[2]

This shocking statement can be confirmed by an objective study of communist literature and activities and by knowledgeable Negroes and others who have worked within the communist movement.[3]

As far back as 1928, the communists declared that the cultural, ceonomic, and social differences between the races in America could be exploited by them to create the animosity, fear, and hatred between large segments of our people that would be necessary beginning ingredients for their revolution.[4]

Briefly, the three broad objectives were — *and are* — as follows:

Create Hatred

Trigger Violence

Overthrow Established Government

1. *Create Hatred.* Use any means to agitate blacks into hating whites and whites into hating blacks. Work *both* sides of the split. Play up and exaggerate real grievances. If neces-

---

[2]"From the beginning of the so-called Negro Revolution and the insane antics identified with it . . . I had opposed all of the marches on Washington and other mob demonstrations, recognizing them as part of the Red techniques of agitation, infiltration, and subversion. That was indicated by the fact that invariably they were proposed, incited, managed, and led by professional collectivist agitators, whose only interest in the workers was to exploit them; backed by the proliferation of 'liberals' of position and influence who always run interference for them by 'explaining' and defending their course." (George S. Schuyler, Negro Journalist; *Black and Conservative,* p. 341)

[3]Manning Johnson, now deceased, spelled out this blueprint in his book, *Color, Communism and Common Sense* (Western Islands, Belmont, Mass.). Leonard Patterson, Mrs. Julia Brown and Mrs. Lolabelle Holmes are currently active on lecture tours carrying this unhappy truth about the Civil Rights movement to as many of the American people as they can reach.

[4]The two classic communist manuals explaining this diabolic plot are *American Negro Problems,* by John Pepper (1928) and *Negroes in a Soviet America,* by James Ford and James Allen (1935). Both originally were published by the Communist party and now may be obtained as photographic reprints from American Opinion, Belmont, Mass. 02178.

sary, don't hesitate to manufacture *false* stories and rumors about injustices and brutality. Create martyrs for both sides. Play upon mass emotions until they smolder with resentment and hatred.

2. *Trigger Violence.* Put the emotional masses into the streets in the form of large mobs, the larger the better. It makes no difference if the mob is told to demonstrate "peacefully" so long as it is brought into direct confrontation with the antagonist. Merely bringing the two emotionally charged groups together is like mixing oxygen and hydrogen. All that is needed is one tiny spark. If the spark is not forthcoming from purely spontaneous causes, create it.[5]

3. *Overthrow Established Government.* Once mob violence becomes widespread and commonplace, condition those who are emotionally involved to accept violence as the only way to "settle the score" once and for all. Provide leadership and training for *guerrilla warfare.* Institute discipline and terrorism to insure at least passive support from the larger inactive segment of the population. Train and battle-harden leadership through sporadic riots and battles with police. Finally, at the appointed time, launch an all-out simultaneous offensive in every city.[6]

---

[5]"At this moment in history, the communists are ecstatic over their success in helping to retard our progress in improving racial relations in this country. . . . The present dangerous decline in black-white relations in the United States could well lead us into a disastrous racial civil war, which is exactly what the communists want and are willing to gamble on at the present moment. A racial civil war in the United States could only breed one thing — anarchy. And once anarchy sweeps this country, the battle will be over to all intents and purposes. . . . Certainly while the rest of the country was involved in trying to salvage itself from a civil war, the communists would remain intact as a functioning revolutionary cadre and would await the chance to seize power from a government incapable of governing or defending itself from internal tyranny." (Phillip Abbott Luce, ex-communist; *The Intelligent Student's Guide To Survival,* p. 60)

[6]"The Communists are counting on the premise that most Americans will discount the possibility of a guerrilla war in their country. The notion of a guerrilla war in the United States is so outrageous and improbable to Americans that they would receive it as the product of a deranged mind. The Communists are fully aware of this and are counting heavily on the fact that most of our citizens will be mentally, as well as physically, unprepared. The shock effect of the initial onslaught will work in favor of the guerrillas." (Phillip Abbott Luce, *Road to Revolution: Communist Guerrilla Warfare in the U.S.A.,* p. 13)

Police and national guard units will never be adequate to handle such widespread anarchy — especially if a large part of our men and equipment are drained away in fighting a foreign war. In self-defense, larger numbers are brought into fighting on both sides. The appearance of a nationwide civil war takes form. In the confusion, potential anti-communist leaders of both races are assassinated, apparently the accidental casualties of race war.

Time the attack to coincide with large-scale sabotage of water supplies, power grids, main railroad and highway arteries, communication centers, and government buildings. With fires raging in every conceivable part of town, with wanton looting going on in the darkness of a big city, without routine police protection, without water to drink, without electrical refrigeration, without transportation or radio or TV, the public will panic, lock its door in trembling fear, and make it much easier for the small but well-led and fully disciplined guerrilla bands to capture the power-centers of each community. Overthrow the government! After complete control is consolidated, (and that may take many months, as in Cuba), only then allow the people to discover that it was a communist revolution after all.

If communism comes to America, it will probably *not* happen quite like that. Even though this is the basic formula used in so many other countries now part of the communist empire, there is one very important difference. In China, in Cuba, and in Algeria the segment of the population which the communists used as the "battering ram" of their revolution of force and violence was the majority segment.[7] In America, though, the Negro represents only 10 percent of the population. In any all-out race war which might be triggered, there isn't a chance in the world that communist-led Negro guerilla units could permanently hold on to the power centers of government, even if they could capture them in the first place.

---

[7]"There is nothing more odious than the majority. It consists of a few powerful men who lead the way; of accommodating rascals and submissive weaklings; and of a mass of men who trot after them without in the least knowing their own minds." (Johann Wolfgang Von Goethe, 1749-1832; *Great Quotations,* p. 624)

It would be a terribly bloody affair, with all Americans suffering mightily, but with Negroes paying the highest toll in human life. And the communists know this better than anyone else. They do not really expect to take America with a "War of National Liberation," (which is their term for internal conquest through force and violence), unless the aggressive revolutionary force can be broadened to include, not only the minority of Negroes, but migratory farm laborers, the poor, the unemployed, those on welfare, other minority groups, students, the so-called "peace movements," and anyone who can be propagandized into mob action against established government. But unless and until they manipulate an overwhelming majority of the population into at least sympathizing with their revolutionary activities, they will use violence, anarchy, and sabotage, *not* as a means of seizing power, but merely as a support operation or a catalyst to an entirely different plan.

In such countries as Czechoslovakia, the communists have used an entirely different method of internal conquest. Instead of the force and violence of a bloody revolution (a "War of National Liberation") parliamentary and political means were used to bring about a more peaceful transition to communism. The communist sympathizers call this alternate plan a "Proletarian Revolution."[8]

The plan is as follows: Using unidentified communist agents and non-communist sympathizers in key positions in government, in communications media, and in mass organizations — such as labor unions and civil rights groups — demand more and more government power as the solution to all civil rights problems. Total government is the objective of communism. Without calling it by name, build communism

---

[8]For a detailed understanding of this phase of communist strategy, the student is urged to research the Party's official pronouncements on the subject of Proletarian Revolution. Perhaps the easiest and best place to begin, however, is with one of the actual textbooks used to teach communist cadres in Czechoslovakia. It is entitled, *About the Possible Transition to Socialism by Means of the Revolutionary Use of Parliament,* written by Jan Kozak, official Historian of the Czech Communist Party and member of the National Assembly. Reprints of the pertinent parts of this textbook may be obtained from the U. S. Printing Office in the form of a government pamphlet entitled, *The New Role of National Legislative Bodies in the Communist Conspiracy,* published by the House Committee on Un-American Activities, December 30, 1961.

piece by piece through mass pressures for presidential decrees, court orders, and legislation which appear to be aimed at improving civil rights and other social reforms. If there is social, economic, or educational discrimination, then advocate more government programs and control.

And what if riots come? Then more government housing, government welfare, government job training, and finally, federal control over police. Thus, the essential economic and political structure of communism can be built entirely "legally" and in apparent response to the wishes of the people who have clamored for some kind of solution to the problems played-up, aggravated or created outright by communists for just that purpose. After the machinery of communism is firmly established, then allow the hidden communists one-by-one to make their identities known. Liquidate first the anti-communists and then the non-communist sympathizers who are no longer needed in government. The total state mechanism can now openly and "peacefully" be transferred into the hands of communists. Such is the so-called Proletarian Revolution. Such has happened in other once free countries. It has already started here.

The communists are not entirely certain whether force and violence or the use of government or a combination of both would be best for the internal conquest of America. At first, there was talk of splitting away the "Black Belt," those Southern states in which the Negro held a majority, and calling that a Negro Soviet Republic. But, as conditions changed and more Negroes migrated to the Northern states, they applied this same strategy to the so-called "ghetto" areas in the North. It now seems probable that the communists are determined to use force and violence to its fullest, coupled with a weakening of the economy and military setbacks abroad, in an effort to create as much havoc as possible to weaken America internally, and to create the kind of psychological desperation in the minds of all citizens that will lead them to accept blindly government measures which actually help the communists in their take-over.

Some wonder if it can happen here. Just take a good look at what has been going on around us for the past few years.

IT IS HAPPENING HERE! If it is to be prevented from running the full course, we must stop pretending that it doesn't exist.

Let us consider some suggestions for our survival. The hour is late.

The communist program for revolution in America has been in progress for many years and is far advanced. While it can be thwarted in a fairly short period of time merely by exposure, the evil effects of what has already been accomplished cannot be removed overnight. The animosities, the hatred, the extension of government control into our daily lives — all this will take time to repair. The already-inflicted wounds will be slow in healing. But they can be healed; that is the important point.

1. First of all, we must *not* place the blame upon Negroes. They are merely the unfortunate group which has been selected by professional communist agitators to be used as the primary source of cannon fodder. Not one in a thousand Americans — black or white — really understands the full implications of today's civil rights agitation. The planning, direction and leadership come from the communists, and most of those are white men who fully intend to destroy America by spilling Negro blood, rather than their own.

2. Next, we must not participate in any so-called "backlash" activity which might tend to further intensify inter-racial friction. Anti-Negro vigilante action, or mob action, of any kind fits perfectly into the communist plan. This is one of the best ways to force the decent Negro into cooperating with militant Negro groups. The communists are just as anxious to spearhead such anti-Negro action as they are to organize demonstrations which are calculated to irritate white people.

3. We must insist that duly authorized legislative investigating committees launch an even more exhaustive study and expose the secret communists who are directing the Civil Rights movement. The same needs to be done with militant anti-Negro groups. This is an effective way for the American

people of both races to find out who are the false leaders among them.[9]

4. *We must support our local police in their difficult task of keeping law and order in these trying times.* Police should not be encumbered by civilian review boards,[10] or asked to be social workers. They have their hands full just trying to keep the peace. Recent soft-on-crime decisions of the Supreme Court which hamper the police on protecting the innocent and bringing the criminal to justice should be reversed. Persistent cries of "police brutality"[11] should be recognized for what they are — attempts to discredit our police and discourage them from doing their job to the best of their ability. Salaries should be adequate to hold on to and attract the very finest men available for police work. But, in questions of money, great care should be taken not to accept grants from the federal government. Along with federal money, inevitably there will come federal controls and "guidelines" which not only may get local police embroiled in national politics, but may even lead to the

-----

[9]"It is the proper duty of a representative body to look diligently into every affair of government and to talk much about what it sees. It is meant to be the eyes and the voice, and to embody the wisdom and will of its constituents. . . . The informing function of Congress should be preferred even to its legislative function." (Woodrow Wilson, quoted by Justice Frankfurter at the October 1952 Term of the Supreme Court)

[10]"A questionable move currently being championed in some localities is the establishment of *civilian review boards* to hear complaints against law enforcement officers. . . . When carefully considered, it is clear this drive for external boards is an ill-advised maneuver. It amounts to the usurpation of authority rightfully belonging to the police commander. It is a practice which could damage effective law enforcement and reduce the orderly processes of community life to petty bickering, suspicion, and hatred. The police executive cannot become a mere pawn of bureaucratic committees. He must have full responsibility for the performance, discipline, and control of his officers. . . . Such panels represent a backward step for law enforcement toward ineptness and mediocrity. Moreover, one of the major weaknesses of these boards is their inherent political overtones." (J. Edgar Hoover, *FBI Law Enforcement Bulletin,* January 1, 1965)

[11]"We know there is a calculated and deliberate attempt by some groups to inflame hostility against law enforcement by charging '*police brutality*' without cause. To a large degree they have succeeded. The term is bandied about in all media of communication without serious consideration as to its true meaning or its harmful effect on a profession which is charged with enforcing the basic rules of civilized living." (J. Edgar Hoover, *FBI Law Enforcement Bulletin,* June 1, 1966)

eventual creation of a national police force.[12] Every despotism requires a national police force to hold the people in line. Communism is no exception. Our local police should remain free from federal control.

5. Further encroachment of government should be stopped and the entire process reversed. The solution to most, if not all, of the current problems involving civil rights is *less government,* not more.

6. Lastly, we need a vast awakening of the American people as to the true nature of the communist blueprint for revolution. Considering the degree to which the controlling influences of the federal government and the communications media are now furthering this communist revolution, it is unrealistic to expect most of our present leaders or the networks to bring about this awakening. In fact, they may be expected to resist it. That means that individual citizens must stand up and assume more than their share of the responsibility. The speaker's platform, and distribution of literature, study clubs, home discussions — all must be pressed into service. All of us should read the new book, *Communist Revolution in the Streets,* written by Gary Allen, with an introduction by W. Cleon Skousen.

Each of us must be willing to discuss the problem openly with our friends — especially those of the Negro race. The success or failure of Americans of all races to meet this challenge may well determine the fate of our country. If we fail, we will *all* lose our civil rights, black man and white man together, for we will live under perfect communist equality — the equality of slaves.

---

[12]"America has no place for, nor does it need, *a national police force.* It should be abundantly clear by now that in a democracy such as ours effective law enforcement is basically a local responsibility. In the great area of self-government reserved for States, counties, and cities, the enforcement of the laws is not only their duty but also their right. Law-abiding citizens and local officials should vigorously oppose concerted attacks against law enforcement and the devious moves to negate local authority and replace it with Federal police power. . . . Since local law enforcement represents the first line of defense of our social order, it becomes a primary target of those who challenge established authority." (J. Edgar Hoover, *FBI Law Enforcement Bulletin,* February 1, 1968)

As President David O. McKay has stated, "The position of this Church on the subject of communism has never changed. We consider it the greatest Satanical threat to peace, prosperity and the spread of God's work among men that exists on the face of the earth." (*Conference Report,* April 1966, p. 109)[13] He has also counseled that, "next to being one in worshipping God, there is nothing in this world upon which this Church should be more united than in upholding and defending the Constitution of the United States!" (President David O. McKay, *The Instructor,* 1956, p. 94)

May we unite behind the Prophet in opposing the communist conspiracy and preserving our freedom and our divine Constitution, I pray.

---

[13]See Appendix III for full text of President David O. McKay's "Statement Concerning the Position of the Church on Communism."

CHAPTER 14

THE UNITED NATIONS — PLANNED TYRANNY

"When we resist . . . concentration of power, we are resisting the powers of death, because concentration of power is what always precedes the destruction of human liberties." (Woodrow Wilson, May 9, 1912; *Great Quotations,* p. 603)

The United Nations has been the recipient of so much lavish praise and favorable publicity, most of us have come to regard it as the embodiment of our own hopes for peace and a better future world. Who could have the audacity to speak out against this wonderful organization?

Occasionally, of course, we hear what at first appears to be opposition to the U.N., but upon closer examination, we find that most of the talk is about how weak the U.N. is, how is has failed to do this or do that, how it needs to be strengthened and given more authority — perhaps even a standing army so it could really accomplish something. In other words, this criticism is not opposition at all. It is merely a plea for us to support the U.N. even more.

No political opportunist would dare to speak out completely against the U.N. so long as public sentiment is so solidly for it. Yet the public, to a large extent, depends upon our leaders in Washington to speak forthrightly about the important issues of the day. So, we find ourselves on a kind of merry-go-round where practically everyone is in favor of the U.N. because they have never heard anyone speak out against it, and no one will speak out against the U.N. because almost everyone endorses it.

After many years of observing the U.N. in operation, after carefully researching the less publicized aspects of this organization, and after a great deal of soul-searching, *I reluctantly have been forced to the conclusion that the U.N.'s potential for evil far outweighs its potential for good.* Furthermore, the very nature of the organization is such that this evil cannot be corrected without disbanding and starting all over from the bottom up.

I wish with all my heart that this were not true, but it *is* true, and the issue is far too important for the future of mankind to allow sentimentality to cloud our vision. *It's about time someone placed principle above popularity and came right out and spoke the truth.*

During my early re-evaluation of the U.N., one of the hardest things for me to do was to separate the *dream* of nations united from the *reality* of the United Nations. Like most Americans, to me the idea of a world united in peace and brotherhood was so appealing that it was extremely difficult to be objective about the organization that claimed it was the fulfillment of that dream. I so fervently wanted the U.N. to be what it said it was, I was far from receptive to anti-U.N. sentiment. This is, perhaps, the U.N.'s greatest protection — the ease with which the dream can be confused with the reality.[1]

The first step, therefore, in accurately appraising the U.N. is to separate the two. We must distinguish in our thinking the vital difference between the *idea* of the United Nations, or *a* United Nations, or even some *future* United Nations — between these and the *existing* United Nations. Unfortunately, they are not at all the same.

With this as a starting frame of reference, then, what is there about the existing U.N. — an organization of disunited nations — that could lead me to such an unpopular conclusion? Let's look at the facts.

Supporters of the U.N. often tell us how wonderful it is that all nations can come together under a single room and air their problems in open debate. The implication, of course, is that this procedure is a way of "blowing off steam," a safety

---

[1]"The people never give up their liberties but under some delusion." (Edmund Burke, 1784; *Familiar Quotations*, p. 261)

valve that somehow reduces the international tensions that otherwise might lead to war. How utterly absurd! Consider what would happen if every time a small spat arose between a husband and wife they called the entire neighborhood together and took turns airing their complaints in front of the whole group. Would there be much real chance of reconciliation? Instead of working out their problems together, the necessity of saving face, proving points and winning popular sympathy would likely drive them further apart. Not only that, by the time the issue was put to a vote, the neighbors would be forced into taking sides. Suddenly their own ranks would be divided, and they would return to their own homes to continue a quarrel that, previously, wasn't even known to them. What starts out as an argument between two people now infects the entire neighborhood with bitterness and dissension.

Exactly the same kind of thing happens daily as the U.N. diplomats stand in front of the General Assembly, shake their fingers at each other, hurl insults at each other, and then ask all nations of the world to choose up sides. Far from being a procedure calculated to preserve peace, this kind of madness can only increase the likelihood of war.

What is wrong with the traditional methods of maintaining contact between nations through the use of ambassadors, envoys and a diplomatic corps? The United States has such contacts in all the major capitals of the world. Why not use them? Quiet diplomacy always has been and still is far more conducive to real international progress than diplomacy on the stage.

It has always been a source of amazement to me how so many Americans properly are concerned over the growth of big government and the welfare state here at home, but continue to give their unqualified support to the U.N. which incorporates every doctrine which they abhor. The reason, I suppose, is that too few of us have taken the time or felt the need to find out just what *is* the concept of government at the U.N.

On the surface, the U.N. Charter and the structure of its various departments bears a strong resemblance to those of

our own federal government. But the similarity goes no further than outward form. Whereas the United States is founded
on the concept of limited government, the U.N. concept is one
of *unlimited* government power with virtually no meaningful
restraints to protect individual liberty.[2]

For instance, Article 4, Section 4 of our Constitution
states: "The United States shall guarantee to every State in this
union a Republican form of government. . . . " This means a
government with *limited* powers. The framers knew that the
Union would not last if the individual states were allowed to
become despotic and unrestrained. To provide protection
against the creation of a super-federal government, the Ninth
Amendment further stipulates: "The enumeration in the Constitution of certain rights shall not be construed to deny or
disparage others retained by the people." And more of the
same in the Tenth Amendment: "The powers not delegated
to the United States by the Constitution, nor prohibited by it
to the States, are reserved to the States respectively, or to the
people."

Compare this with the ideological foundation upon which
the U.N. is built. Instead of insuring that all member states
have limited forms of government, the U.N. assumes that most
of them have unlimited power over their subjects. The U.N.
is not the least bit concerned over the fact that a majority of its
members are governments which rule with police-state methods. Instead of assuming that any power not specifically mentioned in the Constitution is reserved to the individual citizens
or their smaller governmental units, the U.N. operates under
the doctrine that its Charter is sufficiently vague and broad
so as to authorize doing absolutely anything. This concept of
unlimited power was made unmistakably clear when the U.N.
World Court declared:

> Under international law, the (U.N.) organization must be
> deemed to have those powers which, though not expressly pro-

---

[2]"I insist, that if there is ANYTHING which it is the duty of the WHOLE
PEOPLE to never entrust to any hands but their own, that thing is the preser-
vation and perpetuity, of their own liberties, and institutions. (Abraham Lincoln,
October 16, 1854; *Collected Works* 2:270)

vided in the Charter, are conferred upon it by necessary implication as being essential to the performance of its duties. (*Repara-
tions for Injuries Suffered in the Service of the United Nations,* International Court of Justice Opinion; as quoted by Abraham Feller,
general legal counsel for the U.N., in his book *United Nations
and World Community* [Little, Brown & Co., Boston, 1952],
p. 41)

As a result, the U.N. has become a professional politician's paradise. Glancing through the publications of the
various U.N. specialized agencies and commissions, one can
find daily reports on proposals for setting prices, production
quotas, inventories, stockpiles of raw materials, labor standards, wages and monetary policies. Every conceivable sphere
of human activity is being analyzed and then planned for so
that it will come under the ultimate control of the United Nations. It is becoming a world legislature, world court, world
department of education, world welfare agency, world planning center for industry, science and commerce, world finance
agency, world police force, and world anything else anyone
might want — or might *not* want.

It has more-or-less become accepted without particular
concern that communists are present at the U.N., not only as
delegates, but as full-time employees on the Secretariat staff.
We have even become conditioned to accept as routine those
newspaper accounts of how one or another of them is forever
being caught "red-handed" in acts of espionage against our
country. We have resigned ourselves to accept these as merely
the price we must be willing to pay in exchange for the privilege of having the U.N. on American soil.

Let's take another look. Each year for the last ten years.
J. Edgar Hoover has testified before the appropriations sub-
committees of both Houses of Congress and warned the American people that the U.N. is not merely an occasional haven for
a Soviet agent, but is, in fact, the *center* of communist espionage in America! The diplomatic immunity afforded to these
people due to their U.N. status automatically protects them
against arrest for violating the laws of this country. In other
words, these communist espionage agents at the U.N. *are above*

the law! Police files are full of proven cases of kidnapping and suspected cases of outright murder committed by U.N. communists where nothing could be done even to question the guilty parties. (See *The Episode of the Russian Seaman,* SISS Report, May 12, 1956; also *Soviet Political Agreements and Results,* SISS publication, 1959, p. VII)

Diplomatic immunity also prevents customs officials from inspecting the personal baggage of these espionage agents. How convenient for them! How idiotic for us!

I am convinced that nuclear war is not the major threat to this country. The communists are following a far more subtle and potentially successful plan of internal takeover, using a combination of riots, revolution and parallel political manipulations to convert our government into a totalitarian regime, which then can be merged comfortably into a one-world government of the same characteristics. *Nuclear blackmail, however, cannot be disregarded.* If the communists can maneuver us into weakening our own military posture and, at the same time, convince us that they hold an absolute nuclear superiority and ability to destroy our cities without our ability to retaliate, then they could well simply issue an ultimatum to surrender — or else![3]

With this in mind, let's go back and look at those suitcases U.N. espionage agents bring into this country under the protection of diplomatic immunity. *If* the Soviets should decide to launch an all-out nuclear attack on the United States, or *if* they should decide to detonate only one or two as an ultimatum for surrender — and that is at least possible if we con-

---

[3]"I am . . . firmly convinced that *the threat of nuclear war, sparked by Communist aggression is very real and that it is, in fact, growing* rather than diminishing as some people like to believe. . . . If the Soviets should become convinced that they cannot subdue the United States through their present strategy, they will have no choice but to resort to all-out military action and they have long prepared for such a contingency. . . . Because of their nuclear weapons and modern delivery systems, especially missiles, *the Soviets now have the capability to launch a surprise attack on the United States.* . . . The greatest mistake we can make in this respect is to underestimate the Soviet's intentions and their determination as well as their capability to pursue these intentions. . . . *This direct threat will continue to mount in the days ahead.*" (General Thomas S. Power, *Design For Survival,* pp. 25-36)

tinue to disarm — then they wouldn't have to send the bombs over in missiles, they could bring them *in suitcases,* and there would be literally no defense against them!

We tend to overlook the obvious fact that there are many communists at the U.N. from the "non-communist" nations of the world, too. Not openly pro-communist countries like Algeria, Egypt, Ethiopia, Guinea, Kenya, Mali, Somalia, Tanzania, Tibet, Yemen, and Zambia — to mention just a few — but even many of the countries supposedly anti-communist like Cyprus, Finland, France, Iceland, Italy, Morocco, Panama, the Philippines, Singapore, Sudan, Syria, Tunisia, and Venezuela all have strong communist influences within their governments. In both France and Italy, for example, the communists are accepted as a legitimate political party and have open members elected to Parliament and city government posts. They constitute the third largest political party in France and hold the balance of power in Italy. In addition, we can be certain that they have hidden members lodged within the other political parties as well. Do they come to the U.N. to represent these "non-communist" countries? Certainly! They are there openly. It's all a matter of record.

When one stops to consider the degree of communist influence at the U.N., not only from countries that are totally behind the iron curtain, but from many of the non-communist countries as well, it is no wonder that the U. N. has *never* performed a real anti-communist act. How could it? On the other hand, it has helped the forces of communism on many occasions — helped either by direct action, as in the Congo, or by total paralysis, as in Hungary, Tibet and Israel.

The U.N. record should start us to thinking. Is it an accident? Is it planned — or is it merely the product of historical forces? It is both! *It is the product of historical forces which were planned many years ago.* Those forces were made inevitable by the very nature and structure of the U.N. Allowing members of the world's greatest peace-destroying force to help a "peacekeeping" organization makes about as much sense as appointing members of the Mafia to a police commissioner's board to control crime in Chicago!

As long as communists are permitted to hold membership in and allowed to help direct the activities of the U.N., it can never keep the peace, and it can never promote the high ideals so glibly written into the Charter and the Declaration of Human Rights.

We should get out of the U.N. and get the U.N. out of the United States.[4]

---

[4]Some of the thoughts contained in this chapter were adapted from material in the excellent book by G. Edward Griffin, *The Fearful Master: A Second Look At The United Nations.*

CHAPTER 15

DEFICIT SPENDING AND INFLATION

"As a very important source of strength and security, cherish public credit. — One method of preserving it is, to use it as sparingly as possible: — avoiding occasions of expense by cultivating peace, but remembering also that timely disbursements to prepare for danger frequently prevent much greater disbursements to repel it — avoiding likewise the accumulation of debt, not only by shunning occasions of expense, but by vigorous exertions in time of Peace to discharge the debts which unavoidable wars may have occasioned, not ungenerously throwing upon posterity the burden which we ourselves ought to bear." (President George Washington, Farewell Address, September 17, 1796)

The value of the American dollar has declined in its purchasing power from 100 cents in 1939 to approximately 40 cents in 1967. Projected into the future, it will be worth only a nickel by 1985. (*National Program Letter* [Harding College. Searcy, Arkansas], March, 1966)

It is important to understand that the wage-price spiral is *not* the cause of inflation. The rise of wages and prices are the result, not the cause. There is one and *only* one cause of inflation — expansion of the money supply faster than the growth of the nation's material assets. Whether those assets are gold and silver, or food, machines and structures, the creation of money more rapidly than the creation of tangible items of value which people may want to purchase, floods the market place with more dollars than goods and dilutes the accepted value of money already in existence.

In America, only the federal government can increase the money supply. *Only government can create inflation.*

The most common method of increasing the money supply today is by spending more than is in the treasury, and then merely printing extra money to make up the difference. Technically this is called "deficit spending." *Ethically, it is counterfeiting. Morally, it is wrong.*

Often we are admonished not to worry about deficit spending and the national debt since, after all, we only owe it to ourselves. What utter nonsense! If that were the case, why don't we just cancel the debt to ourselves and stop paying all that interest?

By 1962, the United States, the most productive and richest nation in the world, owed $303.4 billion dollars, more than the total indebtedness of all other nations on earth! (Letter from Representative Otto E. Passman, dated April 5, 1963, as quoted in *The Dan Smoot Report,* October 21, 1963, p. 332) By 1964, the true national debt, including the funded debt plus all future fiscal commitments for which no funds yet exist, had climbed to one trillion 140 billion dollars. (California Free Enterprise Association [P.O. Box 1831, Santa Ana, California], Leaflet No. 14) To pay off the national debt will require a stack of one-thousand dollar bills that would rise more than 144 miles into space. Each and every family in America already owes the federal government over $20,000.

Interest alone on the national debt is climbing at the rate of $27,000 per minute, *compounded!* (*U.S. News and World Report,* January 16, 1967, p. 53) Yet every year or so, politicians in Washington who claim they are opposed to inflation, ritualistically vote in favor of raising the so-called "permanent" national debt ceiling another twenty or thirty billion dollars.[1]

Deficit spending, and the inflation it produces, constitutes a hidden tax against all Americans — especially those who own insurance policies, have savings accounts, or who are retired on fixed incomes. Every time the dollar drops another penny in value, it is the same as if the government had counted up all the money that you and I had in our pockets, in sav-

---

[1]"There does not exist an engine so corruptive of the government and so demoralizing of the nation as a public debt. It will bring on us more ruin at home than all the enemies from abroad against whom this army and navy are to protect us." (Thomas Jefferson, To Nathaniel Macon, August 19, 1821)

ings, or investments, and then taxed us one cent on each dollar. The tax in this case, however, does not show up on our W-2 forms. It is hidden from view in the nature of higher and still higher prices for all that we buy.

Most tables show an increase of the average family income from $2,500 in 1932 to over $7,000 today. Don't be fooled! In terms of 1932 dollars, the average income is now only $2,800. (*National Program Letter*, March 1967.)

The rise in our standard of living during that time has been due in large part to an increase in productivity, the ability to produce goods for less money (*real* money, not inflated dollars.) Automation, new techniques, and more efficient methods of production are the causes of our prosperity, not the rising wages and prices which are the symptoms of deficit government spending and hidden taxation.

It is true that a little inflation is not as harmful as a great deal of inflation. But, in *principle*, there is no difference. I am opposed to *all* inflation — and that means *all* deficit spending — because (1) it is a hidden tax which is a deceitful and immoral method of collecting revenue; (2) it is an unfair tax which shifts the heaviest burden of payment onto the shoulders of the thrifty who are attempting to save for the future, and upon the retired who are living on fixed incomes; and (3) it is an irresponsible act which saddles future generations with the payments of our own fantastic debts.

Few policies are more capable of destroying the moral, political, social and economic basis of a free society than the debauching of its currency. And *few tasks, if any, are more important for the preservation of freedom than the preservation of a sound monetary system.*

Why should any government resort to such immoral and destructive policies? The answer to this crucial question must be sought in the tremendous popularity of easy money and government spending.

Every one of the Great Society features require government spending. The large number of federal programs places a heavy financial burden on the public treasury, which may suffer deficits.

In short, the federal government resorts to inflation to cover its deficits. This unsound policy is fraught with great danger for us as individuals and the nation as a whole.[2]

---

[2]"I place economy among the first and most important of republican virtues, and public debt as the greatest of the dangers to be feared. . . . To preserve our independence, we must not let our rulers load us with perpetual debt. We must make our election between economy and liberty, or profusion and servitude. . . . The same prudence, which, in private life, would forbid our paying our money for unexplained projects, forbids it in the disposition of the public moneys. . . . We [must endeavor] to reduce the government to the practice of a rigorous economy, to avoid burthening the people, and arming the magistrate with a patronage of money, which might be used to corrupt and undermine the principles of our government. . . . The multiplication of public offices, increase of expense beyond income, growth and entailment of a public debt, are indications soliciting the employment of a pruning knife. . . . It is incumbent on every generation to pay its own debts as it goes." (Thomas Jefferson, *The Jeffersonian Cyclopedia*, pp. 227, 234, 235, 271, 272, 649)

CHAPTER 16

GOLD AND THE BALANCE OF PAYMENTS

"Manifestly nothing is more vital to our supremacy as a nation and to the beneficent purpose of our Government than a sound and stable currency. Its exposure to degradation should at once arouse to activity the most enlightened statesmanship, and the danger of depreciation in the purchasing power of the wages paid to toil should furnish the strongest incentive to prompt and conservative precaution." (President Grover Cleveland, Inaugural Address, March 4, 1893)

An entire volume could be written on the present dilemma we now find surrounding the nation's unfavorable international balance of payments and the dwindling gold supply.[1] The highlights of these problems, however, and the sequence of events that led up to them are here summarized:[2]

1. The root of all evil is money, some say. But *the root of our money evil is government.* The very beginning of our troubles can be traced to the day when the federal government overstepped its proper defensive function and began to manipulate the monetary system to accomplish political objectives.[3]

---

[1] "All the perplexities, confusions, and distresses in America arise, not from defects in the Constitution or confederation, not from want of honor or virtue, as much as from downright ignorance of the nature of coin, credit, and circulation." (John Adams, *Works* 8:447)

[2] "If we could first know *where* we are, and *whither* we are tending, we could then better judge *what* to do, and *how* to do it." (Abraham Lincoln, June 16, 1858; *Collected Works* 2:461)

[3] "Gentlemen, it is the *currency,* the currency of the country, — it is this great subject, so interesting, so vital, to all classes of the community, which has been destined to feel the most violent assaults of executive power. The consequences are around us and upon us. Not unforeseen, not unforetold, here they come, bringing distress for the present, and fear and alarm for the future . . . its object was merely to increase executive power." (Daniel Webster, March 15, 1837; *Works* 1:362)

The creation of the Federal Reserve Board made it possible for the first time in America for men arbitrarily to change the value of our money. Previously, that value had been determined solely by the natural interplay of (1) the amount of precious metals held in reserve, (2) the value men freely placed on those precious metals, and (3) the amount of material goods which were available for sale or exchange.

2. One of the first arbitrary and politically motivated interferences with the natural value of money was to peg the price of gold at $35.00 per ounce. At first, this made little difference because it was quite possible for men to mine gold profitably at this price. But as the government moved into a program of deficit spending, the motivation for fixing the price of gold became obvious. The artificial increase of the money supply caused the value of each dollar to decrease in relationship to the total supply of material goods which that dollar could purchase. This relative decrease in purchasing power, of course, is known as inflation. But, if gold were not held by law at a fixed price, then its value would have risen in direct proportion to the artificial increase in paper money, and as long as gold was guaranteed backing behind each dollar, the government wouldn't have been able to benefit one iota from deficit spending. The whole process would have been a bookkeeping operation similar to that of a corporation with assets of $100,000 suddenly doubling its number of stock-shares. Since the assets wouldn't increase, the *value* of each share simply would be cut in half. But, if the corporation somehow could force by law all persons to purchase each new share at the same price as the old, then it could realize a tremendous profit through sale of the new issue. This is exactly the kind of fraudulent practice that was and is perpetrated on the American people by forcing the price of gold to remain at $35.00 per ounce.

3. The natural result of this con game was that the mining of gold gradually came to a halt. Actually, the *real* cost of mining, due to technological advances, has decreased, but the cost *in terms of inflation-ridden dollars* has increased to approximately twice the artificially set level.

4. With practically no new gold moving into the Treasury to keep pace with the expanding paper money supply, it was essential for the government manipulators to have the nation go off the gold standard; that is, to remove gold as a guaranteed backing. The dollar was "cut loose" from gold by 75 percent. In other words, for every $1.00 of paper money, only 25 cents worth of gold is now legally required to back it. It is important to note, however, that Americans are not permitted to cash in their dollars for even that token amount. And if gold cannot be obtained in exchange for paper bills, then it is not really "backed" by gold at all. To say that it is, is merely to deceive oneself. The 25 percent so-called backing of gold is merely a bookkeeping ledger account designed to sustain the people's psychological confidence in and acceptance of our money system.[4]

Since there was no way for the federal government to *force* foreign investors to accept American dollars, or international credits based upon American dollars, and since they surely would not do so if there was no gold to back it, the new law applied only to American citizens. That's right, Americans were forced by their government to abandon any claim to gold behind their paper dollars, but foreign holders of these dollars are still entitled to "cash in" for gold if they wish — and at the full price, too.

5. Sensing that American paper money was now literally "worthless," many people began to put their savings into gold itself. If allowed to continue, this might have led to a parallel monetary system dealing in the private exchange of gold or credits against gold instead of government paper money. So the next step for the government manipulators was to make it illegal for Americans even to own gold. People of other nations may demand and receive gold bullion from Fort Knox for whatever American money they hold, but our own citizens are not permitted even to own an ounce of gold, except in the form of jewelry, art objects, or a few rare collector's coins.

---

[4]"They that can give up essential liberty to obtain a little temporary safety deserve neither liberty nor safety." (Benjamin Franklin, *Familiar Quotations,* p. 226)

6. During and since World War II, our leaders in Washington have seen fit to give away to other nations over $130 billion dollars. (*U.S. News and World Report,* August 15, 1966, p. 46) According to *Information Please World Almanac,* this is approximately $25 billion more than the total assessed valuation of all land and personal property in the 50 largest cities of the United States. Much of this money has found its way back to our country, not in the form of purchases for American goods, but in the form of international credits which can at any time be converted into demands for gold.

7. Through a continued policy of giving away money to other countries, through gigantic military expenditures in other lands to supposedly protect them against aggression, through building up foreign industries to where they can compete effectively with our own industries (which not only pay higher labor costs, but also pay the taxes used to build up their foreign competitors), our leaders have finally brought us to the position where we no longer have enough gold left to pay off our solemn promise to foreign holders of U.S. dollars. Out of approximately $13 billion total gold stock, about $9 billion is required by law to back up our domestic money supply, and about $4 billion is left to meet claims of foreigners. But — and mark this well — the claims held by foreigners against this supply are already in excess of $29 billion and rising rapidly! Even counting *all* the gold — including that which supposedly is held as reserve against our domestic money supply — there is more than twice as much claim by foreigners than ability to pay. Internationally, we are bankrupt! (*U.S. News and World Report,* July 12, 1965, p. 39, and October 17, 1966, p. 63)

8. The pending economic crisis that now faces America is painfully obvious. If even a fraction of potential foreign claims against our gold supply were presented to the Treasury, we would have to renege on our promise. We would be forced to repudiate our own currency on the world market. Foreign investors who would be left holding the bag with American dollars would dump them at tremendous discounts in return for more stable currencies or for gold, itself. The American dol-

lar both abroad and at home, would suffer the loss of public confidence. If the government can renege on its international monetary promises, what is to prevent it from doing the same on its domestic promises? How really secure would be government guarantees behind FHA loans, Savings and Loan Insurance, government bonds, or even Social Security?

Even though American citizens would still be forced by law to honor the same pieces of paper as though they were real money, instinctively they would rush and convert their paper currency into tangible material goods which could be used as barter. As in Germany and other nations that have previously traveled this road, the rush to get rid of dollars and acquire tangibles would rapidly accelerate the visible effects of inflation to where it might cost $100 or more for a single loaf of bread. Hoarded silver coins would begin to reappear as a separate monetary system which, since they have *intrinsic value* would remain firm, while printed paper money finally would become worth exactly its proper value — the paper it's printed on! Everyone's savings would be wiped out totally. No one could escape.[5]

One can only imagine what such conditions would do to the stock market and to industry. Uncertainty over the future would cause the consumer to halt all spending except for the barest necessities. Market for such items as TV sets, automobiles, furniture, new homes and entertainment would dry up almost over night. With no one buying, firms would have to close down and lay off their employees. Unemployment would further aggravate the buying freeze, and the nation would plunge into a depression that would make the 1930's look like prosperity. At least the dollar was sound in those days. In fact, since it was a firm currency, its value actually

---

[5]"I have already endeavored to warn the country against irredeemable paper; against the paper of banks which do not pay specie for their own notes; against that miserable, abominable, and fraudulent policy, which attempts to give value to any paper, of any bank, one single moment longer than such paper is redeemable on demand in gold and silver. . . . We are in danger of being overwhelmed with irredeemable paper, mere paper, representing not gold nor silver; no, Sir, representing nothing but broken promises, bad faith, bankrupt corporations, cheated creditors, and a ruined people." (Daniel Webster, February 22, 1834; *Works,* 3:541-2)

went *up* as related to the amount of goods which declined through reduced production. Next time around however, the problems of unemployment and low production will be compounded by a monetary system that will be utterly worthless. All the government controls and so-called guarantees in the world will not be able to prevent it, because every one of them is based on the assumption that the people will continue to honor printing press money. But once the government, itself, openly refuses to honor it — as it must if foreign demands for gold continue — then it is likely that the American people will soon follow suit.

This, in a nutshell, is the so-called "Gold Problem." It's no wonder that our leaders who have gotten us into this mess don't talk about it very much, except to show the proper amount of public concern, and to assure us from time to time that they are "watching the situation closely."

The question that is uppermost in the minds of everyone familiar with the foregoing facts is "How can we prevent this from happening?" The honest answer is, "We can't!" Like the drunkard at the end of a weekend spree, there is no way in the world to avoid the inevitable "morning after." We have been feeling the exhilarating effects of inflation and have become numbed to the gradual dissipation of our gold reserves. In our economic stupor, when we manage to think ahead about the coming hangover, we have merely taken another swig from the bottle to reinforce the artificial sensation of prosperity. But each new drink at the cup of inflation, and each new drain on the gold supply of our body strength does not prevent the dreaded hangover, it merely postpones it a little longer and will make it that much worse when it finally comes.

What should we do? *We should get a hold on ourselves, come to our senses, stop adding to our intoxication and FACE THE MUSIC!*

I realize this is an extremely unpopular answer. There are those — particularly among the government manipulators who endorse the policies that have brought us to our present unhappy state — who would have us believe that, somehow, if we just do a little *more* manipulating of our money, possibly even set up a world monetary system through the U.N., then we can avoid having to pay the fiddler; or, to be more precise, to pay the bartender. But such proposals are merely more of the same con game against the American people, and would not only fail to solve our economic problems, but could lead us into surrendering our economic independence as a nation to the dictates of a majority block in the U.N. which, conceivably, would be less interested in our recovery than in exploiting our misery.

No, there is no "happy" solution to our problems, but, if left to our own resources, the productive genius that is the product of the free enterprise system, coupled with the initiative and drive of the American people, can successfully lead us through the trying readjustment period that lies ahead, and then on to higher levels of *real* prosperity and security than we have ever known.

While politicians will continue to insist that our economy is not in the slightest danger, lest they be accused of being "negative," or "spreaders of doom," there is a sound and realistic course of action that we can follow to prepare for the coming readjustment period and to lessen the shock. As a nation, we must stop giving away money to foreign nations as though we had it. We should demand repayment of our loans to other countries — especially those, like France, which are making the heaviest demands upon our gold supply. We should cease giving them our gold until they pay their debts to us. We must stop the federal government from deficit spending, and begin immediately to pay off the national debt in a systematic fashion. This, of course, means increasing taxes *or* decreasing the size of government. It is doubtful that the American people can absorb more taxes without further injuring the productive base of our economy, but there is no doubt that government can be reduced without any such risk.

The price of gold must be allowed to seek its own level without artificial government restraint. Americans should be given back their freedom to own gold if they wish. Just as soon as the mining industry is able to respond to the higher price of gold and begins to extract it from the earth once again, it should be exchanged for 100 percent gold-redeemable paper dollars from the Treasury, payable upon demand to *anyone* who holds these dollars. Make it known that the federal government eventually will offer the same conversion privilege to holders of the present Federal Reserve Notes just as soon as the acquisition of gold bullion and the repayment of the national debt makes it possible.

So much for the nation. As individuals there is also much that can be done to lessen the shock. *The first and most obvious step is to get out of debt if it is at all humanly possible.* We have lived in an atmosphere of inflation for so long that many people now accept the benefits of permanent debt as a firm law of economics. But if inflation runs its full course and drops over into depression with little if any *real* income for millions of workers, the country may well have to start over with a brand new currency which will be in extremely short supply to pay off those existing debts. Even in times of economic stability it is sound practice to live within one's income and avoid unnecessary debt. Such practice is doubly sound in times like these.

Each of us should make every effort to become economically independent, at least within the family unit. Avoid looking to government for handouts or future security. Again, this is not only good practice in normal times, but especially important today. A government which is unable to pay its own bills can hardly be depended upon to pay yours.

Finally, when the going gets rough, we mustn't rush to Washington and ask Big Brother to take care of us through price controls, rent controls, guaranteed jobs and wages.[6] *Any government powerful enough to give the people all that they*

---

[6]"When the people are encouraged to turn to government to settle all of their problems for them, the basis for all revolutions is thereby established. For then the people expect the government to provide them with all of the material things they want. And when these things are not forthcoming, they resort to violence to get them. And why not — since the government itself has told them that these responsibilities belong to government rather than to them? I am convinced that a revolution would not be possible if the only relationship between government and the people was to guarantee them their loyalty and security." (Frederic Bastiat, quoted in *American Opinion*, February 1968, p. 22)

want is also powerful enough to take from the people all that they have. And it is even possible that some of the government manipulators who have brought us into this economic crisis are hoping that, in panic, we, the American people, literally will plead with them to take our liberties in exchange for the false promise of "security."[7] As Alexander Hamilton warned almost 200 years ago: "Nothing is more common than for a free people, in times of heat and violence, to gratify momentary passions by letting into the government principles and precedents which afterward prove fatal to themselves." (*Alexander Hamilton and the Founding of the Nation* [The Dial Press], p. 21) Let us heed this warning. Let us prepare ourselves for the trying time ahead, and resolve that, with the grace of God and through our own self-reliance, we shall rebuild a monetary system and a healthy economy which, once again, will become the model for all the world.[8]

---

[7]"Though liberty is established by law, we must be vigilant, for liberty to enslave us is always present under that very liberty! Our Constitution speaks of the 'general welfare of the people.' Under the phrase all sorts of excesses can be employed by lusting tyrants to make us bondsmen." (Cicero, quoted in *A Pillar of Iron,* p. 512)

[8]"No duty is more imperative on . . . Government, than the duty it owes the people, of furnishing them a sound and uniform currency." (Abraham Lincoln, December 26, 1839; *Collected Works* 1:164)

CHAPTER 17

TAXATION — A POWER TO DESTROY

"This is the history of governments — one man does something which is to bind another. A man who cannot be acquainted with me, taxes me; looking from afar at me ordains that a part of my labor shall go to this or that whimsical end — not as I, but as he happens to fancy. Behold the consequence. Of all debts men are least willing to pay the taxes. What a satire is this on government! Everywhere they think they get their money's worth, except in these." (Ralph Waldo Emerson, *Essay On Politics*)

Almost everyone agrees that taxes are too high. They are wrong. Taxes are merely the cost of government. Taxes are *not* too high; government is too big![1]

From 1900 through 1964, the gross national product increased about 33 times. During this same period, federal expenditures increased 234 times. During recent years, the rate of growth in the number of government employees has been approximately five times more rapid than our civilian labor force. (Henry J. Taylor, *Human Events,* February 20, 1965, p. 3) In the year ending January of 1966, the level of spending by all government agencies — federal, state and local — rose by an estimated 9.3 percent. This compares with a 5.5 percent rise for business and 5.7 percent for consumers. In other words, government spending is increasing approximately twice as fast as private spending. (*U. S. News and World Report,* January 10, 1966, pp. 24, 25) The total tax "bite," including federal, state and local taxes, has risen from 16 per-

---

[1]"Our history teaches us that when a government is honest and just and virtuous taxes are light. But when a government becomes powerful it is destructive, extravagant, and violent; *it is an usurer which takes bread from innocent mouths and deprives honorable men of their substance, for votes with which to perpetuate self.*" (Cicero, quoted in *A Pillar of Iron,* p. 102)

cent of the gross national product in 1939 to 30 percent projected for 1968. (*U.S. News and World Report,* February 27, 1967, p. 61) Many of the biggest federal spending programs are not included in the official budget. To get the real totals, one must include the net outgo of the Social Security fund, the highway fund, the deficit of the Post Office and similar government enterprises. *Total* federal spending is climbing at a staggering rate. If government continues to expand at the 1965-67 rate, by 1969 it will be taxing and spending $200 billion a year! And that doesn't include the additional "hidden tax" of inflation caused by deficit spending. (*U. S. News and World Report,* April 18, 1966, p. 107)

In 1932, the federal government had a budget of $4.6 billion. There were 30 million families. The average cost to each family, therefore, was $153. As the size and reach of government grew, so did the cost. The following figures graphically show what has happened since and need little comment. (Figures taken from *The National Program Letter* [Harding College, Searcy, Arkansas], March, 1967)

Year	Govt. Spent Billions	Millions of Families	Cost Per Family
1932	$4.6	30	$ 153
1936	8.4	32	262
1940	9	34.9	257
1944	94.1	37	2,540
1948	36	39	923
1952	68	44	1,545
1956	72.5	48	1,510
1960	95	53	1,792
1964	120.3	55	2,187
1967	170	57	2,980

All this plus the gigantic "non-budgeted" expenses of the federal government, plus the expenses of state and local governments, plus the hidden costs of inflation! And yet, this is merely the cost of government. Taxes are *not* too high! Government is too big.

Ever since the progressive income tax was instituted, the American people have been misled into believing that such a system would "soak the rich" and reduce the tax burden of the poor and the middle class.[2] It has never worked out that way. If our nation's millionnaires were forced to pay in taxes every last cent of their entire income, it would run the federal government for less than 39 hours. If all the income from those earning over $25,000 were taken in taxes, it would run the government only three days. In fact, if all personal income over $10,000 were confiscated, it would run the government for less than 18½ days. (Statistics provided by Congressman Ed Foreman, *Human Events,* May 9, 1964, p. 15) It is the little man that pays the largest part of the bill. Eighty-five percent of all the billions of dollars paid in income taxes come from the lowest rate — the 20 percent paid by all persons with taxable income. Only 15 percent is added by all the higher rates including up to 91 percent. (Press Release, Remington Rand Corp., July 30, 1957)

The progressive income tax does not reduce the tax burden of those in the lower income tax brackets. What it does accomplish, however, is to weaken the incentives of the wealthy to risk in new business ventures what money they already have. Why should they? If the venture should fail, they absorb the loss. But if it should succeed, they have to pay most of the profits in taxes. In a sense, they are penalized for success. It is much easier to sit back, avoid the extra work, live comfortably, and not take the risk.[3]

The progressive income tax is also an obstacle to private capital formation, the building of personal fortunes that could be used to finance new business enterprises. This coupled with the weakening of incentives, leads to a sharp reduction in the expansion of industry. The result is the creation of fewer and fewer *new* jobs for the working man. No matter how you look at it, the progressive income tax, in the end, always hurts the

---

[2]"Pretexts for taking away the property are never wanting; for he who has once begun to live by robbery will always find pretexts for seizing what belongs to others." (Machiavelli, 1513; *The Prince* XVII)

[3]"In the general course of human nature, a power over a man's subsistence amounts to a power over his will." (Alexander Hamilton, *The Federalist,* No. 79)

little man far more than the tycoon.[4] It should be abolished and replaced by a tax system that is proportionately fair for all citizens with no special favors, exemptions, gimmicks or loopholes for one group at the expense of another.

The only way to reduce taxes is to reduce the size and scope of government. That is why I support the Liberty Amendment which proposes, under Section 1: "The Government of the United States shall not engage in any business, professional, commercial, financial or industrial enterprise except as specified in the Constitution." Under Section 3, it stipulates: "The activities of the United States Government which violate the intent and purposes of this amendment shall, within a period of three years from the date of the ratification of the amendment, be liquidated and properties and facilities affected shall be sold." As incredible as this may seem, enactment of the Liberty Amendment[5] would cut the cost of government *more than half* and provide funds with which to pay off the national debt by more than 65 billion dollars! Cutting the size of the government is the only way to cut taxes, and don't let any politician tell you otherwise.

---

[4]"An unlimited power to tax involves, necessarily, the power to destroy." (Daniel Webster, 1819; *Great Quotations,* p. 905)

[5]For details on the Liberty Amendment, write to the National Committee for Economic Freedom, 6413 Franklin Ave., Los Angeles 28, California.

CHAPTER 18

SOCIAL SECURITY — FACT AND FICTION

"You will never get me to support a measure which I believe to be wrong, although by doing so I may accomplish that which I believe to be right." (Abraham Lincoln)

Social Security is unconstitutional. Why not end it by re-funding to all participants their equitable share?[1] The Social Security system in the U.S. is compulsory, unfair and immoral, yet no one can deny the great popularity of the program.

The Social Security system, as it is conceived and operated today, is not social, does not provide security, and does not qualify as a real system. It should be made voluntary in order to become social; it should be backed by reserves in order to become secure; and benefits should be computed on an actuarial basis to make it a system that is fair and impartial, to all participants, whether young or old.

The practice of setting aside a small portion of income during one's productive years in order to be self-sustaining in old age is not only commendable, but, in my opinion, it is an obligation to ourselves and to the younger generation that follows in our footsteps. Most people agree, but there are some who feel that the natural order of things calls for total investment in their children during productive years and a reliance upon the family unit in old age. Others prefer to prepare for retirement through investments in property and securities which they feel will expand in value and keep pace with inflation-shrinking dollars. Still others prefer to build up a retire-

---

[1]See Chapter 8 for an explanation of how it is possible to cut out the various welfare-state features of our government which "have already fastened themselves like cancer cells onto the body politic." (P. 141)

ment fund with private insurance policies which provide such flexible features as a sizeable cash payment to surviving dependents in the event of premature death. Why not let men and women in this land of the free *be* free to choose? (Participation in the Social Security system should be made entirely voluntary.)

It is truly ironic that the federal government requires insurance companies and private pension funds to maintain assets and reserves sufficient to pay off every last cent of their retirement contracts; yet it ignores this requirement when it comes to its own Social Security system. At the end of 1966, private pension plans covered 26 million workers and held reserve funds in excess of 90 billion dollars. (*U.S. News and World Report,* March 6, 1967, p. 67) At the beginning of 1967, just as greatly expanded benefits were being put into operation, the "unfunded liability" of the system — promises to pay benefits for which there are no reserves to draw upon — had already reached approximately $400 billion and were growing rapidly. The reserves on hand were inadequate to pay even one year's benefits, which simply means that the program is on a pay-as-you-go basis with virtually nothing to back it up except the future taxing power of the government. (*U.S. News and World Report,* January 30, 1967, pp. 42, 43) To put "Security" into the Social Security system, it would be required to maintain the same kind of assets and reserves as are now required of private pension funds.

Benefits to be paid under the Social Security system should be completed on an actuarial basis which takes into account the amount each person has paid in and the number of years he is expected to draw out. This is the only fair system that does not penalize some by forcing them to pay, not only for their own retirement, but for the retirement of others as well.[2] As the system operates today, new benefits are voted

---

[2]"To promote the welfare of one section of the citizens and neglect another is to bring upon the state the curse of revolution and civil strife. . . . This factious spirit it was that caused such bitter feuds at Athens and in our own republic fanned the flames of sedition and destructive civil wars. From such disasters a brave and earnest citizen worthy of supreme political power will turn with detestation." (*Cicero, On Moral Duties,* I, 25)

into existence by Congress and the older citizens begin to receive them immediately, even though their past contributions into the fund are nowhere adequate to cover the cost. This means that those in the next generation have to pay their full share plus the deficit created by their elders. This is politics at its worst.[3] Those who stand to benefit by an immediate increase clamor to the polls and pressure Congress into a yearly expansion of the program. But those of the next generation who will have to pay the bill are too young to vote. By the time they advance to the receiving end of the line, then they, too, press for even more benefits which, in turn, adds to the cost and passes the ever-growing deficit still one more generation into the future. Such madness cannot go on forever. Sooner or later — and probably much sooner than we would like to think — this irresponsible game of politics will cause the entire system to collapse.

Already, a young man with a family can get far more for his money from a private pension program than he can from the Social Security system. The break-even point, according to estimates by Professors James M. Buchanan and Colin B. Campbell, is 39 years of age. And it advances further with each new increase of benefits. At the present time anyone born after 1927 will pay more into Social Security than he stands to get out of it.

The time may be close at hand when young men will wake up to the fact that they are being played for suckers by the older generation. And who could blame them if they should decide to apply the political pressure of their greater numbers to call a halt to the con game and cancel the whole program? After all, since there are no real reserves and no binding contracts, there is no reason why this could not happen. The present arrangement is *not* insurance, it is *politics*.

---

[3]"Some eighty years ago, the Supreme Court of the United States in Savings and Loan Association vs. Topeka (22 Law. Ed. 461) declared, 'to lay, with one hand, the power of government on the property of the citizen, and with the other to bestow it upon favored individuals . . . is nonetheless a robbery because it is done under the forms of law and is called taxation.' " (W. C. Mullendore, *The Freeman,* January 1957, p. 8)

CHAPTER 19

EDUCATION FOR FREEDOM

"If a nation expects to be ignorant and free, in a state
of civilization, it expects what never was and never will be."
(Thomas Jefferson, To Colonel Yancey, January 6, 1816)

From the very beginning of recorded political thought, man has realized the importance of education as a tremendous potential for both good and evil. In a free and open society such as ours, a well-rounded education is an essential for the preservation of freedom against the chicanery and demogoguery of aspiring tyrants who would have us ignorantly vote ourselves into bondage.[1] On the other hand, should the educational system ever fall into the hands of the in-power political faction or into the hands of an obscure but tightly-knit group of professional social reformers, it could be used, not to educate, but to indoctrinate.

"All who have meditated on the art of governing mankind," said Aristotle, "have been convinced that the fate of empires depends on the education of youth." (As quoted in *The Public Speaker's Treasure Chest* [Harper & Bros., New York, 1942], p. 318) Lenin, the prophet of world communism wrote: "Give me a child for eight years and it will be a Bolshevist forever." (As quoted by J. Edgar Hoover, Testimony before House Sub-committee on Appropriations, March 4, 1965, p. 55) Adolph Hitler declared: "In my great educative work, I am beginning with the young." (As quoted by

---

[1]"On the diffusion of education among the people rest the preservation and perpetuation of our free institutions. . . . Education, to accomplish the ends of good government, should be universally diffused. Open the doors of the schoolhouse to all the children of the land. Let no man have the excuse of poverty for not educating his own offspring. Place the means of education within his reach, and if they remain in ignorance, be it his own reproach. (Daniel Webster, June 1, 1837; *Works* 1:403)

Herman Rauschning, Hitler's confidant, as printed in *The Voice of Destruction,* p. 251; reference taken from Newquist, *P.P.N.S.,* p. 217) And Khruschev wrote: "Like every other form of state-directed activity in the Soviet Union, education is conceived as a weapon serving the interests of the Communist Party and dedicated to a single objective — the victory of the Soviet system." (Khruschev, *Problems of Communism,* 1958, Vol. VII, No. 2, p. 42)

Could the educational system in America be used for similar purposes? Once that system is consolidated into one central source of authority, finance and direction, it is entirely possible.[2] The present trend of increasing federal control and the establishment of a federal Office of Education which is already beginning to dictate to previously independent local school systems should give all Americans cause for concern over the future.

Obviously, the best way to prevent a political faction or any small group of people from capturing control of the nation's educational system is to keep it decentralized into small local units, each with its own board of education and superintendent. This may not be as efficient as one giant super educational system (although bigness is not necessarily efficient, either) but it is far more safe. There are other factors, too, in favor of local and independent school systems. First, they are more responsive to the needs and wishes of the parents and the community. The door to the school superintendent's office is usually open to any parent who wishes to make his views known. But the average citizen would be hard pressed to obtain more than a form letter reply from the national Commissioner of Education in Washington, D.C.

Secondly, and by no means of little importance, there is absolutely nothing in the Constitution which authorized the federal government to enter into the field of education. Fur-

---

[2]"The most effectual means of preventing the perversion of power into tyranny are to illuminate, as far as practicable, the minds of the people." (Thomas Jefferson, 1799, Diffusion of Knowledge Bill; *Jefferson Cyclopedia,* p. 278)

thermore, the Tenth Amendment says: *"The powers not dele-gated to the United States by the Constitution, nor prohibited by it to the States, are reserved to the States respectively, or to the people."* Nothing could be more clear. It is unconstitutional for the federal government to exercise any powers over education.

The phrase "federal aid to education" is deceptive and dishonest. What is really meant is "federal *taxes* for education." The federal government cannot "aid" education. All it can do is tax the people, shuffle the money from one state to another and skim off its administrative costs from the top. Only the people can aid education. They can do it safer, faster and cheaper within their local communities than by going through the middleman in Washington. Federal taxes for education means federal control *over* education. No matter how piously the national planners tell us that they will not dictate policies to local school systems, it is inevitable that they will in the long run. In fact, they already are doing it. Whenever the federal government spends tax money for *any* purpose, it has an obligation to determine how and under what conditions that money is used. Any other course would be irresponsible.

In summary, this is what should be done:

1. Force the federal government to comply with the Constitution and get out of the business of education.

2. Through the elimination of federal taxes for education, reduce the federal tax load so that citizens can better their own local school systems.

3. Encourage private schools to compete with government schools. Not even state or city governments should have a monopoly on such a vital activity as education.

4. Reassert the primary right and responsibility of parents for the *total* education of their children, including social values, religious convictions and political

concepts.[3] Schools should be reminded that their primary field of competence is academic, not social adjustment, or world citizenship, or sex education. Parents should stand firm on this and not be intimidated by "professional educators." After all, it's their children and their money.

5. Restore to the teacher the authority to insist upon and administer discipline in the classroom.[4]

6. Frills and non-academic pursuits should be secondary to the basic tasks of real learning. Let no school system come complaining to the taxpayer about lack of funds as long as school curricula are cluttered with such as "driver-training," "fly-bait casting" and "square-dancing." A few less psychiatric counselors and personality analysts might also help raise the real academic level of our schools, at the same time lowering the cost.

7. Don't *force* children to attend school. Leave that up to the parents. If students realized that they could be expelled if they failed to live up to the rules, or that no one would beg them to return to class, more would realize that a tax-supported education is a privilege worth working for.

8. Raise academic standards by refusing to promote students for mere attendance. Students should get used to the facts of life where it is achievement that counts.

---

[3]"There is but one method of preventing crimes, and of rendering a republican form of government durable, and that is, by disseminating the seeds of virtue and knowledge through every part of the state by means of proper places and modes of education. . . ." (Benjamin Rush, 1745-1813; *Great Quotations*, p. 308)

[4]"Education does not mean teaching people what they do not know. It means teaching them to behave as they do not behave. It is not teaching the youth the shapes of letters and the tricks of numbers and then leaving them to turn their arithmetic to roguery, and their literature to lust. It means, on the contrary, training them into the perfect exercise and kindly continence of their bodies and souls. It is a painful, continual and difficult work, to be done by kindness, by watching, by warning, by precept, and by praise, but above all — by example." (John Ruskin, *Great Quotations*, p. 308)

9. Place more emphasis upon the glorious achievements and traditions of our American heritage.[5] World consciousness and international understanding are fine, but they should not blind us to the fact that in our own country we really *do* have something better than anywhere else, and we shouldn't be ashamed to say so — least of all to our youth.

---

[5]"Our liberties are safe until the memories and experiences of the past are blotted out and the Mayflower with its band of pilgrims forgotten; until our public-school system has fallen into decay and the Nation into ignorance." (Woodrow Wilson, *Great Quotations*, p. 604)

CHAPTER 20

MANAGEMENT AND LABOR

"What is the true condition of the laborer? I take it that it is best for all to leave each man free to acquire property as fast as he can. Some will get wealthy. *I don't believe in a law to prevent a man from getting rich;* it would do more harm than good. . . . I want every man to have the chance — and I believe a black man is entitled to it — in which he *can* better his condition — when he may look forward and hope to be a hired laborer this year and the next, work for himself afterward, and finally to hire men to work for him! That is the true system." (Abraham Lincoln, March 6, 1860; *Collected Works* 4:24)

One of the basic flaws in the communist doctrine espoused by Karl Marx was his theory of "class warfare" between "capitalists" and working men, between management and labor. Communist agitators preach class hatred between these two groups and attempt to mobilize the workers into a class war against their employers. In countries where they have succeeded, the workers soon discover that they have merely changed employers. Instead of working under the management of private owners of industry, they are now working under the management of members of the Communist party. The glowing promises of higher wages, better working conditions and a higher standard of living turn out to be empty political promises. Their new employers, since they are primarily politicians instead of industrialists, are more concerned with reports, forms and statistics to create on paper the appearance of progress than they are with real economy, efficiency, research for future development, and high productivity. As a result, production begins to slump, the economy begins to suffer and the workers find not only fewer goods to purchase but higher price tags on everything.[1]

In America, most informed persons realize that management and labor are not class enemies, but are equal partners in the mutual business enterprise of producing the goods and services that make our high standard of living possible. Neither can exist without the other. Likewise, neither can be hurt without the other eventually being hurt.[2] If management's wages (called profits) are squeezed to where management either raises the price of its product or goes out of business, then labor either pays a higher price for the product in the store or is out of a job. On the other hand, if labor's profits (called wages) are squeezed to where it is necessary either to reduce the standard of living or seek other employment, then management finds that either it is selling less of its product in the stores as the result of the reduced purchasing power of working men, or it loses its employees to higher paying firms, or both.

The relationship between employer and employee is based upon the natural laws of supply and demand. Each is interested in receiving from the other the very best possible terms, but that is determined by what is offered in return and by competition. Under such a system, the best employees receive the highest wages, the best paying employers attract the best workers, the best workers turn out the best product, the best product outsells the inferior products and produces the highest income to the best employer . . . and around it goes, a never-ending cycle of increasing productivity, abundance and security.

---

[1]No better case history can be found than "A Communist In A 'Worker's Paradise,' " the testimony of John Santo, a former high-ranking communist in Hungary, Hearings before the House Committee on the Un-American Activities, March 1, 4, & 5, 1963.

[2]"The strongest bond of human sympathy, outside of the family relation, should be one uniting all working people, of all nations, and tongues, and kindreds. Nor should this lead to a war upon property, or the owners of property. *Property is the fruit of labor — property is desirable — is a positive good in the world.* That some should be rich, shows that others may become rich, and hence is just encouragement to industry and enterprise. *Let not him who is houseless pull down the house of another; but let him labor diligently and build one for himself,* thus by example assuring that his own shall be safe from violence when built." (Abraham Lincoln, March 21, 1864; *Collected Works* 7:259)

The foregoing analysis, some will say, is overly idealistic. Indeed, there are times when it appears to be. Human nature is such that there always will be those who will attempt to cheat at this game called life so as to get something for nothing if they can, by artificially manipulating the natural economic laws in their favor. "Power tends to corrupt," wrote Lord Acton, "and absolute power corrupts absolutely." (*Essays On Freedom and Power,* p. 364) He was referring, of course, to political power, but the same can be said about economic power. Everyone is familiar with the dire consequences of past concentration of such economic power into the hands of certain giant industries.

The governments — both state and federal — by making grants and giving exclusive licenses to railroads, banks, public utilities, etc., created artificial, government monopolies. Free competition in these fields was prohibited by law. One had to possess a certificate of convenience and necessity to enter business and these were given to only a select few.

The results were only to be expected. With no competition to keep these monopolies in line, prices and rates were raised until the public clamor to halt these abuses brought about the anti-trust laws. The correct remedy, of course, would have been to withdraw all exclusive privileges and allow anyone who had the desire to enter into these fields of economic activity.

If every member of society and every group is allowed to compete, and if the consuming public is left completely free to select those with whom they do business, then the public will always be served by those who offer the best product at the cheapest price. When the exclusive power to make or break business concerns rests in the hands of the consumers, we may rest assured there will be no monopolies. Public opinion can break a business overnight unless the government steps in and forcibly prohibits competition.

Today the situation is almost completely reversed. Through a vast maze of regulations and a sizeable bureaucracy, the government now regiments and controls those monopolies which it had created in the first instance. But in place thereof the government has created a new power structure in our economy. It now issues exclusive licenses to certain labor unions to represent employees, and in the great majority of states the government empowers these unions to forcibly collect dues from anyone who works in these unionized industries. The police power is available to punish anyone who refuses to co-operate with the union leaders in compelling union members to pay for the privilege of working.

And so the inevitable has happened again. Labor bosses are abusing this government-granted monopoly power on a wide scale. In an annual ritual they are compelling industry to pay higher and higher wages and more and more benefits, thus forcing prices up and feeding the fires of inflation.

My conscience forbids me to consent to granting exclusive privileges to either business or labor unions. Since I would not forcibly prevent anyone from entering any legitimate business or joining any union they desired, and since I could never bring myself to dictate to the buying public who they could and who they could not purchase goods and services from, I consider it wrong to ask government to do these things on my behalf.

Economic wealth flows from thrift and productive investment. Many labor laws even hamper economic output and therefore cause poverty rather than wealth. Take, for instance, the minimum wage legislation. I am convinced that it does irreparable harm to young and unskilled people, especially Negroes and other minority groups.

In 1966, the Great Society Congress passed a new minimum wage law that raised the current minimum rate to $1.40 by February 1967 and to $1.60 by February 1968. In addition, the costs of fringe benefits, such as social security and unemployment compensation, paid holidays and vacations, insurance coverage, etc. usually amount to some 25 percent of wage rates, so that the minimum costs of employment of unskilled workers will reach $2 an hour. That is to say, the least skilled teenage worker costs $2 an hour. It should be obvious that this law seriously jeopardizes the employment of millions of untrained workers who produce less than this minimum.

This labor law not only causes mass unemployment and poverty, but also breeds racial conflict and strife. It is an unfortunate fact that many Negro youngsters lack the minimum level of education and training needed for the $2 minimum wage rate. Economists have estimated that their unemployment rate, which hovered around 25 percent under the old minimum wage law, will rise to at least 35 percent under the new law.

Considering that the proper function of government is limited purely to such defensive measures as the protection of life, liberty and property, the extent of government-interference into labor-management relationships also should be confined to this function. Playing the role of policeman and judge, it should see to it that both parties refrain from violence and that they live up to their contracts. Government should not go beyond that point. It should not act as an "umpire" giving either special favors or handicaps. Above all, it should not *force* either or both parties to negotiate, to settle, or to follow *any* prescribed course of action. *Government has no business making up rules for the game and then forcing the players to follow those rules.* If left completely alone, labor and management will work out their own agreements in the shortest possible time and with the least disruption to the economy. In time, a natural balance between the forces of supply and demand will result in the greatest benefit for business, for labor and for the country.

What can we expect as the result of this natural balance? Among other improvements in labor-management relations, we can predict the following concrete changes: (1) Freedom of association, (2) Equal bargaining, and (3) Political integrity.

Freedom of association means that a man will be free to join or not to join a union, as he sees fit. This will not only give each man his freedom of choice, but will force labor bosses to be more considerate of the wishes and needs of the working man. Poorly run unions or those that accomplish little except to spend the members' dues will have to improve or make way for better unions. Well run, uncorrupted unions need never worry about membership. Only those that have little to offer the workers need the government to force people to join them. If a company wishes to negotiate a closed shop agreement with a union, it should be free to do so. But the power of government should never be brought to bear to force it one way or the other.

Equal bargaining means that, as a result of the natural forces and counter-forces in the labor marketplace, without government interventions to aid or hinder either side, it is likely that the size of the labor union involved in a contract negotiation will equal the size of the management unit. In other words, instead of a giant nation-wide industry intimidating a tiny union of employees at just one of its plants, or instead of a giant nation-wide union intimidating a tiny company in just one community, there will tend to be a grouping and regrouping of unions *and* employers so that the forces on both sides will be approximately equal. While this could conceivably result in industry-wide negotiations between giant unions and giant employer associations, most of the natural economic pressures point in the opposite direction. Cost of living and cost of production factors vary so widely from one part of the country to the other that if a uniform compromise wage rate were set on a national basis, workers in the high cost areas would form a local union for more realistic negotiations, and employers in the low cost areas would form a local association for the same purpose. But whatever the final outcome, it would be the most flexible and the most responsible to the varying needs of both labor and management in all parts of the country.

Political integrity means that voluntary unionism would put an end to the present practice in some of the larger unions of spending huge amounts of the members' dues for political action which is pleasing to the labor bosses but may or may not be for the membership. No man should be forced to pay through union dues for political campaigns or philosophies which he opposes. Political contributions should be strictly voluntary. Just as corporation funds should not be spent for political action by the president of that corporation, so too, union funds should not be spent for political action by the president of that union.

In summary, *labor and management are equal partners in business.* They should be treated as equals with no special favors either way. Government, as a non-productive entity that lives off the income of both labor and management, has no business meddling in their affairs, except to make sure that public order is maintained and that contracts are honored.[3] Only in this way can both parties obtain the maximum mutual benefits from the natural laws of supply and demand which are at the heart of our successful free enterprise system.

---

[3]"With all these blessings, what more is necessary to make us a happy and prosperous people? Still one thing more, fellow citizens — a wise and frugal government, which shall restrain men from injuring one another, which shall leave them otherwise free to regulate their own pursuits of industry and improvement, and shall not take from the mouth of labor the bread it has earned. This is the sum of good government. . . ."(Thomas Jefferson, First Inaugural Address; *Works* 8:3)

CHAPTER 21

THE MONROE DOCTRINE AND BEYOND

"Our first and fundamental maxim should be, never to entangle ourselves in the broils of Europe. Our second, never to suffer Europe to intermeddle with cis-Atlantic Affairs. America, North and South, has a set of interests distinct from those of Europe, and peculiarly her own. She should therefore have a system of her own, separate and apart from that of Europe. While the last is laboring to become the domicil of despotism, our endeavor should surely be, to make our hemisphere that of freedom." (Thomas Jefferson, To President James Monroe, October 24, 1823)

For more than a hundred years the Monroe Doctrine provided a fundamental guidepost for American foreign policy. Designed to protect American security through opposition to outside intervention in the Western Hemisphere, the Doctrine was first enunciated by President Monroe in 1823. Presidents George Washington and Thomas Jefferson had made similar policy statements.[1]

The declaration was directed against the real danger of intervention by European powers in Central and South American affairs, and in particular, against any attempt at restoring to Spain its Latin American colonies, most of which had won their independence a few years earlier. President Monroe's message was a bold act, a striking example of open diplomacy

---

[1]"It would appear that neither Adams nor Monroe had any closer connection with this Doctrine than Jefferson had with the Declaration of Independence, except as to the colonization principle, which Mr. Adams seems to have developed. In each case, the drawing of the instrument was the work of the draughtsman; the principles cast into definite formulae had long been the common property of the American statesmen of the time, and even of European statesmen." (J. Reuben Clark, 1930, *Memorandum On The Monroe Doctrine*, p. xv)

in the face of danger that loomed large throughout the century of European supremacy. It became securely established in the minds of several generations of Americans.

Most people generally are quite familiar with the Monroe Doctrine. The basic facts are these. On December 2, 1823, President Monroe delivered his annual message to Congress and enunciated a policy which he and his cabinet had formulated regarding the official attitude of the United States toward future extension of European influence anywhere in the American hemisphere — both North and South America. In essence, that policy proclaimed that the United States look with disfavor upon any new European colonization in the future, and any attempt by European powers to extend their influence over existing independent countries. In return, the United States proclaimed that it would not interfere with existing European colonies or in the internal affairs of any country in the Western Hemisphere.[2] The purpose was to maintain the current balance of power so that we would not become the targets of future aggressive designs of European nations with massive strongholds on or near our borders. It was felt that the maintenance of an ocean between ourselves and European powers would safeguard us from becoming reluctantly entwined in the perennial intrigues and wars of the Continent.

Whenever the physical security of the United States is directly threatened, as it was in the Cuban crisis, we must not hesitate to uphold the traditional meaning of the Monroe

[2]"We owe it to candor and to the amicable relations existing between the United States and those powers [European] to declare that we should consider any attempt on their part to extend their system to any portion of this hemisphere as dangerous to our peace and safety. With the existing colonies or dependencies of any European power we have not interfered and shall not interfere. But with the Governments who have declared their independence and maintained it, and whose independence we have, on great consideration and on just principles, acknowledged, we could not view any interposition for the purpose of oppressing them, or controlling in any other manner their destiny, by any Eureopean power in any other light than as the manifestation of an unfriendly disposition toward the United States. . . .

". . . It is impossible that the allied powers should extend their political system to any portion of either continent [North or South America] without endangering our peace and happiness. . . . It is equally impossible, therefore, that we should behold such interposition in any form with indifference. . . . It is still the true policy of the United States to leave the parties to themselves, in the hope that other powers will pursue the same course." (President James Monroe, Seventh Annual Message, December 2, 1823)

Doctrine: our unilateral opposition to outside intervention in the Western Hemisphere. This Doctrine laid down as a broad principle of action and applied to world communism enjoys strong public support for foreign policy decisions. While the Monroe Doctrine may be subject to modification and divergent interpretation, it can and should continue to play a useful and significant role in the diplomacy of the United States.

The Monroe Doctrine was entirely within the constitutional prerogative of the President. He could not commit our armed forces to battle, for that is a legislative function. But, as spokesman to the world in matters of foreign policy, he not only had a right but had an obligation to advise other nations of this country's general position on such matters. Advance declarations of this kind serve a valuable function in the international relations of a non-aggressive nation. Hopeful of maintaining peace for ourselves, and with nothing to hide, there is much in favor of spelling out for other nations what conditions generally will be unacceptable to the point where non-peaceful acts will be contemplated. Other nations then can consider the probable consequences of their acts *prior* to making them, and thus avoid stumbling into a confrontation.

The Monroe Doctrine is based upon the principle, long recognized in international law journals, that a nation has a right to interfere in the affairs of another nation if such interference is within the framework of self-defense. In other words, if the establishment by a foreign power of unusually heavy military installations is observed on a nation's frontier, and if that nation has good reason to believe that those installations eventually are going to be used as part of an offensive attack against it, then it is justified in taking the initiative in destroying those installations, without waiting for the actual attack. Such action, although aggressive by itself, is viewed as part of a generally defensive maneuver.[3]

---

[3]"What we take to be pointed out by justice as the true international right of self-preservation is merely that of self-defense. A state may defend itself, by preventive means if in its conscientious judgment necessary, against attack by another state, threat of attack, or preparations or other conduct from which an intention to attack may reasonably be apprehended. In so doing it will be acting in a manner intrinsically defensive even though externally aggressive." (Westlake, *International Law;* quoted by J. Reuben Clark, *op. cit.,* p. xvi)

Naturally, whether a nation can successfully execute this policy of "preventive self-defense" depends ultimately upon its strength and the advantage of its position. But international law is concerned, not so much with what a nation *can* do as it is with what a nation *may* do and still abide by a code of conduct to which honorable men can subscribe. In this respect, the Monroe Doctrine neither added nor detracted one iota from what the United States had a right to do. All it accomplished was to inform other nations what conditions the United States would consider a sufficient threat to its long-range security to justify involving, if need be, the sovereign right of preventative self-protection. If other nations wished to test our resolve or our strength in these matters, that was up to them, but at least we went on record and laid our cards on the table so that no one could say they didn't know.

The important point, however, is that, even if the Monroe Doctrine had never been enunciated, the United States — or any nation for that matter — would still be justified in attempting to prevent an upset on the stable balance of power among its friendly bordering neighbors if it were convinced that such a shift in power eventually would result in a threat to its own security. That principle, which is at the heart of a nation's right to self-preservation, is just as valid today as ever before — and especially so for the United States.

It should be painfully obvious that the principle of preventative self-defense embodied in the Monroe Doctrine now has been deserted by our leaders in Washington. With a hostile communist regime in Cuba, firmly established only ninety miles from our borders, and with the United States Navy and Coast Guard actively protecting this enemy stronghold against anti-communist Cuban refugees who attempt to raid the island, it is futile any more to expect other nations to seriously believe that the Monroe Doctrine reflects the present attitude of the United States Government. *The Monroe Doctrine is right, it just needs to be applied.*[4]

---

[4]"The Monroe Doctrine is not a policy of aggression; it is a policy of self-defense. . . . It still remains an assertion of the principle of national security. . . . The decision of the question as to what action the United States should take in any exigency arising in this hemisphere is not controlled by the content of

There is no doubt in my mind that the American people would be angry if they fully realized the extent to which our leaders have abandoned the vital principle of preventative self-defense on behalf of our nation. If a man says he is going to shoot you, and then points a gun in your direction, you don't have to wait until he pulls the trigger before you take action to overpower him. When the communists say they are going to bury us and then move in a bearded gravedigger right next door, we should grab him by the hair on his chin and *throw him out!* And we don't have to apologize to anyone for our action.

What we need is a new application of the Monroe Doctrine — a declaration to the nations of the world to inform them that no longer are we going to tolerate communist or other hostile regimes on or near our borders. Give them fair warning. We don't need to tell them exactly *what* we intend to do. That should be determined by each situation and the need.[5] But there is no doubt that very quickly in the beginning we should have taken strong and swift action against communist Cuba, not only to eliminate that menace from our borders, but to demonstrate that we mean business with what we declare.

----

the Monroe Doctrine, but may always be determined on the grounds of international right and national security as freely as if the Monroe Doctrine did not exist. . . . The Monroe Doctrine rests 'upon the right of every sovereign state to protect itself by preventing a condition of affairs in which it will be too late to protect itself.' " (Secretary Hughes, 1923; quoted by J. Reuben Clark, *ibid.,* p. xv)

[5]"The United States itself determines by its sovereign will when, where, and concerning what aggressions it will invoke the Doctrine, and by what measures, if any, it will apply a sanction. In none of these things has any other state any voice whatever. . . . In other words, there is a broad domain occupied by self-preservation which is incapable of definite boundary as to its extent, or of definition as to the kind of act which lies within it. . . . As the law stands, whatever falls within the necessities of self-preservation, under existing or future conditions, lies within the boundaries of the domain of the principle." (J. Reuben Clark, *ibid.,* p. xx)

CHAPTER 22

NEW HORIZONS IN FARMING[1]

"Were we directed from Washington when to sow, and
when to reap, we should soon want bread." (Thomas Jefferson, *Autobiography; Works* 1:82)

I deeply appreciate this opportunity to talk with you
about this vitally urgent subject of farm policy. I do not claim
to have all the answers. No mortal has. But I am deeply concerned because some of the answers currently proposed are
clearly unsound.

It has been truly stated that "The issue is this: Are we going to have a government-planned, -licensed and -regimented
agriculture run from Washington; or, are we going to solve
farm problems in a way that will preserve freedom, expand
markets and increase opportunity for farmers to make needed
adjustments and to earn and get high per-family net incomes?"

I emphasize the importance of freedom in agriculture because we see today in this country a new threat against the
freedom to farm — a threat posed by unsound efforts to cope
with the problems of the agricultural technological revolution.

There is no question about the greater efficiency and increased abundance brought about by this technological
revolution.

Along with its benefits, however, this revolution, like all
changes, has also brought serious dislocations and problems.

*The modern mechanized farm requires heavy investment
of capital.* In general, the big producing farms are the larger

[1]An address delivered on January 28, 1963, at the 48th Annual Meeting of
the National Dairy Council, Salt Lake City, Utah.

farms and those with the most machinery and equipment. Over 90 percent of our marketed farm products come from less than half our farms. It is extremely common for these commercial family farms to have capital investments of $50,000 to $100.-000 and more. This does not mean that the family farm is disappearing. Today 96 percent of our farms are family type operations, the same percentage as 30 years ago. The family farm is here to stay. It is stronger today than ever before.

Today management has become a key factor in farming success. Machines save labor and speed up operations. But many machines are economical only if used at relatively full capacity. To use his time and machinery efficiently, a farmer may have to make important production shifts. He may have to get more land, or improve the land he has. He may have to increase his dairy herd. He may have to shift out of grains and over to production of beef cattle, hogs or poultry. To be successful, such adjustments often require capital. They *always* require skilled management. A sound economic unit is the objective. To achieve it, freedom in farming is essential.

Specialization is the new look in some phases of agriculture, especially in poultry, fruits, and vegetables. We are seeing something very strange to oldtime farmers. There have been tremendous developments in so-called "contract farming" in some phases of our agriculture.

In an effort to cope with the cost-price squeeze — occasioned by rising costs and falling prices brought on by the abundance produced by technology — government, through price and acreage control programs, is tempted to take over too many of the decisions farmers used to make for themselves. This impedes needed adjustments. The destination of some farm products thus becomes a government warehouse — which is not a market. Too many and too small allotments for some commodities result in a large number of relatively inefficient production units and a lessening of farmers' freedom to make their own decisions.

These trends — big investment, the growing need for skilled management, specialization, rising costs, and especially the impact of government on farmers' freedom — all have deep meaning for those of us devoted to the objective of an expanding, prosperous, and free agriculture.

The latest overall proposal by government is what is called a "supply management" program. As I view the new proposed program, part of which has now been passed by the Congress, I am convinced that our farmers are not going to be happy about a choice between rigid controls on the one hand and a price depressed by government dumping on the other. Many of them don't really understand it yet. But they will.

The mandatory feed grain proposal brought into the farm policy debate many livestockmen who grow their own feed and who previously thought they had little at stake in the controversy. They are generally anti-control. This has stirred them up.

For almost thirty years now, government has been attempting to solve what it calls the ills of agriculture by a socialistic and planned system of controls. But it is my conviction that a revolution has been brewing at the grassroots for ten years to free farmers from government shackles. It may well be — and I hope it is — that we are today seeing a strong and growing step by one segment of our population "to overthrow the all-consuming embracement of Federal Control over its very life. In recent years many polls of farmers have been taken and a growing number of them are demanding that government get out of agriculture altogether." (Elmer Price)

I have just received this letter from a couple living on the Long Lost Ranch, RFD 3, Lake Providence, Louisiana:

> Dear Friend, Mr. Benson: We have treasured the enclosed small clipping for a long time and you were right.
>
> Just last year we farmers had to fight for a free enterprise (farming) and nearly lost the battle to a compulsory Farm Program.
>
> With best regards,
> Lloyd Elliott

This is the clipping enclosed:

SECRETARY BENSON told a press conference in Dallas recently that he believes it is "indefensible to have a law on the books that says a farmer can't grow feed to be fed to livestock on his own farm."

Dr. Don Paarlberg has recently issued a summary statement on the so-called "supply management" proposals with which I agree and from which I will draw somewhat freely.

Presently production quotas and price supports are in effect for only a few farm products: wheat, cotton, rice, peanuts, and tobacco. Acreage restrictions have been put into effect — with pay — by producers of feed grain. Altogether these controlled and supported commodities bring in about 25 percent of our farm income. In several states less than five percent of farm income is from the so-called basic crops.

By contract, about three-fourths of our farm production decisions and more than half of our price decisions are made privately, competitively. In this category is found the bulk of our livestock, most of our eggs, vegetables for market, fruits, and many specialty products. Decisions as to how much of these products should be produced are made by the farm operators themselves, without attempted government regulations. Prices at which these products are sold are determined in the competitive markets, at freely fluctuating prices, without price support in any form.

The prevailing idea is that agriculture is almost universally supported and controlled. This just is not true. The misinterpretation comes from the fact that the controlled and supported crops, being constantly in trouble, are constantly in the news. The unsupported and uncontrolled part of agriculture, being less often in difficulty, receives much less attention in the press.

Based on the critical issues of how price and production decisions are made, there are five categories of farm products:

Apprx. percent of farm income

Price and production decisions made by farmers. (Livestock, poultry, fruits, vegetables, etc.) 40

Price and production decisions negotiated by contracts between farmers and processors. (Sugar crops, canning crops, certain fruits and vegetables, broilers, turkeys, etc.) 10

Price decisions referred by government through marketing orders; production decisions in farmers' hands. (Milk, specialty crops.) 15

Price decisions made by government through price supports; production decisions in farmers' hands. (Milk for manufacturing, soybeans, wool, dry beans, etc.) 10

Price decisions made by government in the form of price supports; production decisions made by government in the form of quotas. (Wheat, rice, cotton, peanuts, etc.) 25

_____

100

While the supported and controlled commodities bring in only 25 percent of the farm income, they are responsible for about 75 percent of the farm program costs and cause perhaps 90 percent of the controversy.[2]

There has been before the Congress the "Food and Agriculture Act of 1962," a proposal which would extend production quotas to include feed grains and dairy products, huge sectors of agriculture hereto free of controls. The feed-grain-livestock complex brings in nearly one-third of the nation's farm income; the dairy industry brings in about 13 percent. Thus the proposed extension is of truly major proportions. It is of even greater proportions when potatoes, turkeys and other

_____

[2]*"The lessons of paternalism ought to be unlearned and the better lesson taught that while the people should patriotically and cheerfully support their government its functions do not include the support of the people.* The acceptance of this principle leads to a refusal of bounties and subsidies, which burden the labor and thrift of a portion of our citizens to aid ill-advised or languishing enterprises in which they have no concern." (President Grover Cleveland, Inaugural Address, March 4, 1893)

commodities are added to the proposed list. What has been the experience with production controls? Experience is that, except for a few commodities and in a limited way, controls will not work.

For a quarter of a century we have been trying to control the production of wheat. Yet wheat is our major problem commodity. Despite controls and despite disposal overseas of all we can sell, barter, and give away, our wheat stocks are at fantastically high levels. If we had not harvested a bushel of wheat in 1962 we would still have all we could possibly eat and export, plus a substantial carryover.

Why have controls failed for wheat? Why were acreage allotments voted out by corn farmers? Why did the cotton people move in the direction of less restriction on production and a more modest price objective? Because in a country with a representative government and a tradition of freedom, strict controls are not wanted.

The plain truth is that when controls pinch too hard on volume, on income, on jobs, on efficiency, on the farm supply industry, on the rural community, or on the independent nature of our people, then public opinion rises in opposition. Then come critical editorials, angry resolutions from farm groups, ominous letters to the congressmen, stern delegations calling on the Secretary of Agriculture and telegrams of protest to the President. The machinery of representative government goes into action in behalf of individual freedom. And it is effective! This is fortunate for America — it is a safeguard to our God-given freedom.

The experience of the past quarter of a century is clear: The Congress will not vote, the administration cannot enforce, and the farmers will not accept the strict controls which would be needed to balance supply with demand at the levels of incentive price support promised by the politicians.

What happens is this: A national economic argument is made to the effect that a high price objective should be sought with strict controls to hold down production. The high price is real, but the controls are not. The high price stimulates production more than the weak controls restrain it. The result is surplus and the loss of markets.

This is not a quick judgment. It is the experience built up under two political parties over a period of more than a quarter of a century, by fifteen Congresses, six Secretaries of Agriculture, and four Presidents. The new "supply management" enthusiasts would do well to heed this record.

I have not said that it is unfair or immoral or illegal or unwise for farm people to be allowed to develop programs with the intended purpose of improving their economic position. This is a battle that has been fought and won. I applaud the victory.

Programs of education, research, some adjustments in land use, rural development with local and state direction and orderly marketing, all coupled with modest price objectives are less dramatic, but they are more effective.

But this hard-won victory should not be wasted in repeating or extending the errors of programs that have obviously failed. Rather, we should broaden outlets, improve the functioning of the market system and keep open the doors of opportunity for our farm people.

The forces of the market place should be permitted to allocate resources. Price should be permitted to play its normal role of directing production and consumption. We should keep our economy free.

The farms of the United States cannot be run from a desk in Washington. In fact the answer to farm and ranch problems caused or aggravated by the technological revolution and made worse by unwise government policy is to be found in the pursuit of three basic objectives:

1. Freedom.
2. Profit through efficiency.
3. Expansion of free markets and wise use of abundance.

Freedom is as fundamental to agriculture as soil and water. Agriculture does not flourish where the spirit of freedom is lacking. As we have seen in Soviet Russia, regimented agriculture is the weak spot of the economy. In Poland, the government had to move toward greater liberalization in agriculture before it could obtain greater production.

The farmer and Mother Nature have an alliance that frustrates efforts to weaken it. Nowhere has this been better illustrated than in the United States. For a quarter of a century, beginning in the 1930's, a continuing series of programs stimulated production and impeded adjustment, while the advance of technology made controls largely ineffective. The technological revolution in agriculture cannot be repealed by legislation.

A feeling of independence is the predominant characteristic of the 16 million farm and ranch people of the United States.

It is perfectly natural that farmers resist regimentation. I count their independence of spirit and action as one of our great strengths. Far from doing anything to weaken that independence, we should always look for opportunities to strengthen it.

The second objective is profit through efficiency. Increasing efficiency can lower production costs, expand markets and leave a greater margin of profit for farm operators.

Last year (1962) we observed the 100th anniversary of the United States Department of Agriculture. When President Abraham Lincoln in 1862 signed the paper that established that department, he released a spirit of agricultural advancement that has motivated our agriculture ever since.

Out of this spirit has developed our Land-Grant College System of research, education, and extension for the benefit of rural people and all of us. Our federal government, our state governments, and private industry work closely together in making available better plant material, livestock, and farming techniques. Our farmers live and move in an atmosphere of striving to do things better.

In the past two decades, the expanded use of science and technology on the part of the farmers has been phenomenal.

Our farmers are using more than three times as many tractors and motor trucks and over five times as many combines as they were in 1940. The horse and mule have all but disappeared from our farms.

Today's rancher and farmer produces more in one hour than he did in two hours in 1950, and three hours in 1940.

Technology is not something to be feared. History tells how the first power looms were broken by the cottage weavers of Lancashire, England, in a futile effort to restrain progress. Men have come far since then. We have learned that technology is a friend. It offers promise of better things to come for all who will put it to good purpose.

The third objective is market expansion and the wise use of abundance. This abundance is the product of the free spirit with which our farmers approach their tasks, the technology that they apply to their efforts, and the blessings of vast land and water resources provided by the Almighty.

I have heard some of my countrymen halfway apologize that we are what is termed a surplus-producing nation. All major exporting nations are surplus-producing nations. Were we not surplus producers, millions of the world's people would go hungry for lack of supplies that come from the United States. We are, in a sense, the breadbasket of the free world.

And we should give thanks that our problems are not those of scarcity but rather the positive challenge of how to make effective use of abundance.

Now I want to return again to the question of freedom — not just freedom for agriculture — but our basic freedom as a people, as a nation.

Whether we in this nation keep our freedom — the freedom to choose where we will go and how we will earn a living, what we will do with our savings and how we will spend our leisure — may depend to a significant degree on how our government in the years ahead approaches the farm problem.

The fundamental economics of the farm dilemma is simple — it is the politics of the problem that is baffling. What farmers and ranchers want and need is not more, but less government in the farming and ranching business — not more, but less politics in agriculture.[3]

Our real struggle, the paramount struggle of all, is between freedom and socialistic communism.

Our major danger is that we are currently — and have been for thirty years — transferring responsibility from the individual, local and state governments to the federal government.

There is no freedom under full socialism. *Our fight is freedom vs. creeping socialism.*

Socialism is simply: Government ownership and control of the means of production and distribution.

For thirty years we have aided the cause of atheistic, socialistic communists in high places in government; by giving away vital military secrets; by squandering much of our material resources; by recklessly spending ourselves to near bankruptcy; by weakening our free enterprise system through adoption of socialistic policies; by wasteful bungling of our foreign affairs; by ever increasing confiscatory taxation and by permitting the insidious infiltration of socialistic-communist agents and sympathizers into almost every segment of American life.

The amount of freedom depends upon the amount of socialism. A good measurement is to determine the amount, or percentage, of income of the people which is taken over and spent by the state.[4]

We have accepted a degree of socialism in the U.S. The question is how much. Russia, it is reported, takes well over

---

[3]"Agriculture, manufactures, commerce, and navigation, the four pillars of our prosperity, are the most thriving when left most free to individual enterprise." (President Thomas Jefferson, First Annual Message, December 8, 1801; *Works* 8:13)

[4]"We do not commonly see in a tax a diminution of freedom, and yet it clearly is one. The money taken represents so much labor gone through, and the product of that labor being taken away, either leaves the individual to go without such benefit as was achieved by it or else to go through more labor." (Herbert Spencer, 1850; *Great Quotations*, p. 905)

80 percent of the income of the people. Scandinavia takes about 60-65 percent, England some 50 percent. The U.S. is now approximately 35 percent. What will be our direction?

At present socialism seems to be decreasing a little in Russia to stimulate production, while increasing in the United States. The direction we are moving should be our real concern.

Some unsuspecting Americans say that the most important thing is peace. These misled dupes applaud the fact that we and Russia are moving closer together. This is an appalling statement. Someone has said that the ninth wonder of the world is the apparent willingness of the American people to give up our free enterprise, capitalistic system because of a lack of appreciation and understanding of how the system works. Are we guilty? I've even heard of American businessmen who apologize for our capitalistic free system which has built their own enterprises and given all of us the highest standard of living on this good earth. . . .

Agriculture is undergoing serious change. This is our most important farm problem.

Some are inclined simply to observe the changes and do nothing about them. Others meet them wisely and adjust to them. Resistance to change in the past 30 years has brought imbalance, controls, subsidies, and unrealistic price supports in agriculture and has been reflected in a series of congressional actions at the request of members of Congress and some farmers.

Where is the problem in agriculture? It is the 25 percent of our production where government tinkering and panaceas, based on unsound economics, have been applied. Our surplus is the result, in large measure, of these unsound government panaceas.

Does the program help farmers to adjust to new conditions? Some government programs do, but many do not. Particularly is this true with attempted production controls and price fixing. Fixing prices means rationing the right to produce. As a result markets shrink, surpluses accumulate and imbalance occurs. Production controls and price fixing do not work anywhere. Any segment of our economy can produce a surplus if prices are fixed above competitive levels, but under a free market system there may be temporary market gluts but not prolonged surplus — supplies clear the markets.

It is difficult to believe that an administration could push a socialistic supply management farm program which would destroy the free market when the President has said this:

> The free market is a decentralized regulator of our economic system. The free market is not only a more efficient decision maker than even the wisest central planning body, but even more important, the free market keeps economic power dispersed. (John F. Kennedy)

There seems to be a distrust of the market system by high government officials in agriculture.

> Those who would politically fix prices without regard to supply and demand, and ration the right to produce would destroy the market system — whether or not they know that such is the inevitable endpoint of what they propose. (Roger Fleming, AFBF.)

The major issue is this: Is the market system based on freedom of choice — to be preserved or destroyed "in the face of attacks by federal bureaucrats dedicated to government price fixing" and regimentation of farm production?

I say, let's go back to a system that works. Soybeans is a good example. When price supports were realistic, the surplus disappeared; production and marketing increased. Realistic supports may serve a need on certain storable commodities — in helping to facilitate orderly marketing — if they are below competitive markets.

Dairying is another example where supports were high, markets were declining, and we have a billion pounds of stocks in government storage. Supports were lowered, the surplus disappeared, consumption increased and production leveled out and declined slightly. Equilibrium was established in the markets, and the dairy industry moved forward.

But when unwise action raised dairy supports in 1961 above competitive levels, purchases by government soared and government stocks again accumulated. Trouble again faced the dairy industry. When will we ever learn? Every farm commodity must be competitive in price, in quality, and in promotion.

When will we learn that economic laws are just as immutable as moral laws or the laws of nature or the Ten Commandments?

Interventionists and socialists vary by degrees. Some don't know what it's all about. Others do. We can't have agriculture partly free and partly controlled. Berlin is an example. Most interventionists don't have any confidence that people know best how to spend their own money. They would take their money away from them and then gratuitously return a portion of it.

We have one government worker today in agriculture for every eight farm families, and with the billion dollar feed grain fiasco and further controls on our farmers, the number of federal employees is increasing. This is not good — for agriculture or for America. An extended supply management program would increase government employees and multiply and complicate our problems. When a congressman from our top farm state makes the following statement we have cause for alarm: "This," said Congressman Hosmer of California, "is a national disgrace and a national scandal paid for by U.S. taxpayers twice — once with subsidy checks and once again by higher food prices. No amount of patchwork can cure the situation."

We all want an agriculture that is dynamic, forward-looking, prosperous, and free; where there is continuing opportunity to live on the land — and live well.

But that kind of agriculture can be achieved only when the farms are run, decisions are made, and responsibilities are borne by the families on the farms — when price is permitted to play its normal role in directing production and consumption.

There are many ways in which government can help to promote agriculture. When I left Washington, three-fourths of agriculture was free and doing fairly well. All of agriculture should be free in the best interests of farmers and all of us. But when government steps in and takes over — dictates, controls — that is not promoting agriculture, it is strangling it.

Farmers want government at their *side* not on *their back.* Surveys show that eight out of ten farmers are opposed to governmental regimentation and control.

This nation will never reach its full strength until our farmers have more freedom to plant, to market, to compete and to make their own decisions. The farms of the United States cannot be run from a desk in Washington, D.C.

I am convinced that the old road for agriculture — the road of the economic strait jacket and the political blind alley, the old road disguised in the trapping of the so-called New Frontier, supply management — can only bring results that are distasteful to real farm people.

Economic and technological progress cannot be stopped with legislative blockades. The day will no doubt come when the rapid growth of our economy and population will call for all available farm production. When that day comes, our farmers must be free and strong and ready — but, above all, free.

Neither the vigor of farm families nor the march of modern science should be impeded. That is why we must build markets, not curtail them. That is why we must help producers promote and sell farm commodities. That is why we must push agricultural research — with special emphasis on market expansion and new uses for farm commodities. That is why we must move toward more freedom for farmers.

Our freedom was not achieved, and it cannot be maintained, by simple short-cuts that attempt to bypass basic eternal truths. We cannot — we must not — ignore sound, basic economic principles. These economic laws are immutable.

If our country, so blessed with opportunity and purpose, is to progress and prosper for the benefit of all, it cannot, it must not, replace integrity with cynicism, principles with catch-words, ideals with doles, and liberty with controls.

Charles B. Shuman, president of the AFBF has wisely said:

> The basic fallacy of government price fixing and production controls in agriculture is the denial of the market price system as the most efficient and equitable means yet known to bring about the shifts in agricultural production that are necessary to meet the ever changing pattern of human needs.
>
> The market price system is the most important means of letting producers know of the changes in consumer needs. When a product or service is no longer needed, the price declines. Those who insist on continuing as usual will suffer the most.
>
> Economic laws are closely related to moral and natural laws. They are as surely God-given as are the great truths that have been recorded and demonstrated in the Bible.
>
> The greatest good for all will result from a system where changes are dictated by human needs rather than by the political decisions of a dictator or a bureaucracy.
>
> Production for the competitive market is production for consumption — not production in response to bureaucratic decisions of a dictator or a bureaucracy.
>
> God has given men the power to choose — this is the essential ingredient of freedom.
>
> If we use this power of choice to continually transfer responsibility to the federal government, we will most surely relinquish our freedom.

We should not expect an overly paternalistic government to be the divider over us.

This is what we *must* do:

1. Get government out of price fixing and futile attempts at production controls.

2. Increase efficiency.

3. Expand markets.

4. Work for increased bargaining power in agriculture.

5. Control monopolies in major industries, labor, and elsewhere.

6. Check inflation — deficit spending is the principal cause.

7. Support the competitive price, free market, capitalistic system as the best system in this world.

Our people must remain free. Our economy must remain free. Free of excessive government paternalism, regimentation, and control. We must not encourage "agricultural dictatorship administered by socialists in Washington. . . . "

This is America — the land of opportunity! A land choice above all other lands. Let us keep it so!

That we may do so, is my humble prayer.

CHAPTER 23

THE SUPREME COURT — A JUDICIAL OLIGARCHY

> "The candid citizen must confess that if the policy of
> the government, upon vital questions, affecting the whole
> people, is to be irrevocably fixed by decisions of the Supreme
> Court, the instant they are made, in ordinary litigation be-
> tween parties, in personal actions, the people will have
> ceased to be their own rulers, having, to that extent, prac-
> tically resigned their government into the hands of the emi-
> nent tribunal." (Abraham Lincoln, First Inaugural Address,
> March 4, 1861)

Almost everyone recognizes that *something is wrong with
the Supreme Court. One does not have to be a constitutional
lawyer to sense it.* After a decade or more of Court decisions
following a consistent and recognizable pattern, crime now
runs rampant in the street, subversives who are openly dedicated to the destruction of our way of life operate in our midst
with complete impunity, and government has grown to gigantic proportions never envisaged by the framers of our Constitution. People are beginning to wonder who is master and
who is servant. If one looks closely, the hand of the *modern*
Supreme Court can be found in all of these major developments.[1]

---

[1]"At the establishment of our constitutions, the judiciary bodies were supposed to be the most helpless and harmless members of the government. Experience, however, soon showed in what way they were to become the most
dangerous; that the insufficiency of the means provided for their removal gave
them a freehold and irresponsibility in office; that their decisions, seeming to
concern individual suitors only, pass silent and unheeded by the public at large;
that these decisions, nevertheless, become law by precedent, sapping, by little
and little the foundations of the constitution, and working its change by construction, before any one has perceived that that invisible and helpless worm has
been busily employed in consuming its substance. *In truth, man is not made to
be trusted for life, if secured against all liability to account.*" (Thomas Jefferson,
To M. Coray, October 31, 1823; *Works* 7:322)

Decisions of the modern Supreme Court have undermined the forces of law and order and, more than any other single cause, are directly responsible for the nation's soaring crime rate. This is a broad statement, to be sure, but it is more than substantiated by a review of the Court's decisions involving confessions, material evidence and police investigative procedures. Space does not permit a detailed analysis of the impact upon law and order of such milestone cases as Mallory, Mapp, Escobedo and Miranda, but they all add up to one incontrovertible fact: *The modern Supreme Court has tipped the scales of justice in favor of the rights of criminals at the expense of the rights of law-abiding citizens who are the victims of those criminals.*[2]

Most Americans are not fooled by the glib communist phrases about "peaceful coexistence." They realize that communists are *not* merely members of some minority political party, but are, just as were members of the Nazi party during World War II, part of an organization whose objectives and activities place them in the position of being enemies of the United States.[3] The American branch of the Communist party is comparable to a commando detachment of enemy troops working on our own soil to create the conditions necessary for the eventual communist conquest of our nation. The only difference is that, unlike our enemies of the past, the communists plan to conquer from the *inside* using such weapons as riots, civil war, political manipulations, brainwashing, blackmail, false leadership, and treason. Whether we like it or not, the in-

---

[2]"The demand of the hour in America is for jurors with conscience, judges with courage, and prisons which are neither country clubs nor health resorts. It is not the criminals, actual or potential, that need a neuropathic hospital; it is the people who slobber over them in an effort to find excuses for their crime." (New York City Judge, Alfred J. Talley, quoted by J. Edgar Hoover, 1966 *FBI Appropriations*, p. 49)

[3]"Communism is not a political party nor a political plan under the Constitution; it is a system of government that is the opposite of our Constitutional government, and it would be necessary to destroy our government before Communism could be set up in the United States." (The First Presidency of The Church of Jesus Christ of Latter-day Saints, 1936; *P.P.N.S.,* p 211. See Appendix II for full text of this statement by The First Presidency.)

ternational communist organization has declared total war against the United States, and *we are fighting for survival.*[4]

Unfortunately, however, the majority members of the modern Supreme Court apparently know nothing about all this, or at least prefer to pretend that it isn't so. *In one decision after another, the Court has closed its eyes to the facts of life regarding the true nature of communism,* and has treated it as a harmless little group of people who are *not* enemies of the United States, but merely loyal Americans who belong to a minority political party and espouse unpopular ideas and theories. How incredibly naive! The result of this mistaken concept of communism has been as follows:

1. Known communist leaders have been returned to their jobs in all walks of life including labor unions, the teaching profession and even to practice law.
2. The states have been denied the right to have their own anti-communist laws. The Court has required them to depend entirely upon the various federal anti-communist laws, such as the Smith Act and the Internal Security Act.
3. Finally, the Court, has, one by one, declared unconstitutional each of the sections of the federal anti-communist laws, or placed such restrictions upon their operation that they cannot realistically be enforced.
4. The Court has thrown so many obstacles in the path of government agencies investigating communism that, at present, we not only have no laws to protect ourselves against the internal menace of communism, but we have all but stopped any effective investigation into the degree to which communism may have penetrated into the nerve-centers of our nation's life.

---

[4]"Survival, however, depends on more than historical knowledge and psychological insight. If a student is interested in freedom for himself, his family, his children and his country, then he had best get off his chair and do something to understand just exactly what freedom is, and to insure the survival of that freedom. . . . If you want to survive, you had better learn how to fight — it's an *a priori* rule in the ghetto — and most of us had better loosen our ties and begin to wade into the struggle." (Phillip Abbott Luce, an ex-communist, *The Intelligent Student's Guide to Survival,* p. xiv)

Are there communists high in government, in the communications media and elsewhere? It is difficult to know who and where they are until investigations are once again made possible by reversing the effects of certain Supreme Court decisions and Executive Orders. It is incredible that the American people should be denied this vitally important information. It all adds up to one inescapable conclusion. *Decisions of the modern Supreme Court have given tremendous aid and comfort to our communist enemy.*

Every child learns that the American form of government is based upon the concept of diffusion of powers. To prevent any one person or group of persons from acquiring tyrannical power over our people, the founding fathers devised a unique system of dividing political power over many governmental units, and then using each unit as a partial check against the other. Sovereignty was separated between the federal government and the states. The federal government was given those aspects of sovereignty which involved relations with the rest of the world, such as military might, tariffs and treaty powers. But those aspects of sovereignty which were primarily local and internal, such as local law-enforcement, civil courts, schools, and, for that matter, anything else not delegated to the federal government or specifically excluded to the states by the Constitution, these were strictly left to the states or the people of those states to handle in whatever way they saw fit. And this included the right *not to handle it at all,* if that was their wish.

In addition to the safeguard against overconcentration of political power that was effected by a division of sovereignty between the states and the federal government, our founding fathers also wisely established three branches of the federal government — the legislative, executive and judicial — as partial checks against each other. Even the legislative branch was further subdivided into two parts — the House and the Senate — each with different modes of election so that one would represent the people directly, and the other would represent the people indirectly through the states. Every conceivable precaution was taken to insure that the government which they had created would not be able to gather total political power into one place and become as venal and oppressive as the one from which they had separated.

If those who so carefully drafted the checks and balances into our Constitution could have looked into the future and seen what the Supreme Court of the United States would do to their masterpiece, they would have been dismayed. Through the process of supposedly "interpreting" the Constitution, the Court has twisted beyond recognition just about every conceivable clause to justify the transfer of *all* sovereignty from the states to the federal government, to broaden the powers of the federal government beyond any definable limit, and then to make it possible for all such powers to fall into the hands of the executive branch of government.[5] We may still give lip service to the checks and balances of our constitutional republic, but the phrase is now quite hollow. The checks and balances are gone. The Constitution has become but a piece of paper that, instead of protecting men's liberties *against* encroaching govment, is now a source of phrases to be "interpreted" in such a way as to grant new and novel powers *to* government. Instead of a true Republic with limited political power, we have been brought to a democratic dictatorship similar to those in Latin America where one man, although he carries the pleasing title of President, and is elected to office by majority vote, nevertheless has almost unlimited political power during his period of office.[6] Some people may feel that this development is both

---

[5]"How can we expect impartial decision between the General government, of which they are themselves so eminent a part, and an individual State, from which they have nothing to fear? We have seen, too, that contrary to all correct example, they are in the habit of going out of the question before them, to throw an anchor ahead, and grapple further hold for future advances of power. They are then, in fact, the corps of sappers and miners, steadily working to undermine the independent rights of the States, and to consolidate all power in the hands of that government in which they have so important a freehold estate. But it is not by the consolidation, or concentration of powers, but by their distribution, that good government is effected." (Thomas Jefferson, *Autobiography; Works* 1:81-2)

[6]"The contest, for ages, has been to rescue Liberty from the grasp of executive power. . . . Through all this history of the contest for liberty, executive power has been regarded as a lion which must be caged. So far from being considered the natural protector of popular right, it has been dreaded, uniformly, always dreaded, as the great source of its danger." (Daniel Webster, Senate Speech, May 7, 1834; *Works* 4:133-4)

healthy and necessary to deal effectively with other dictator-ships around the world; some may feel that it is a betrayal of the American Revolution and a frightful step backward in political development; but no one can deny that *it has happened*.

The record of the modern Supreme Court in the matters just described is sufficiently tainted to justify a thorough airing and investigation to either vindicate the Justices in the eyes of the public or to have them replaced. The Constitution provides a sensible and orderly procedure for accomplishing just such a review. A simple majority vote of Congress would require the Senate to conduct open hearings to determine if any Supreme Court Justice has disqualified himself for continued public trust, which otherwise is in his hands for his entire lifetime. When Congress asks the Senate to conduct such hearings, it is called impeachment. But impeachment does not necessarily mean removal. That is determined by the outcome of the Sen-ate action, and requires at least a two-thirds vote. If the Senate determines, in accordance with Article II, Section 4, that a Justice has committed "Treason, Bribery, or other high Crimes and Misdemeanors," he is automatically removed from office.[7]

Consider for instance charges of High Crimes and Mis-demeanors. It is true that the Constitution nowhere defines what is encompassed by this phrase, but that does not mean that it cannot be understood. If the Senate can demonstrate that a Justice of the Supreme Court, through the decisions in which he has concurred, actually *has* undermined the forces of law and order, or *has* given aid and comfort to the enemy (even unintentionally), or *has* destroyed our Constitutional checks and balances, then, surely, these do constitute High Crimes and Misdemeanors.

---

[7]"I do not charge the Judges with wilful and ill-intentioned error; but honest error must be arrested, where its toleration leads to public ruin. As, for the safety of society, we commit honest maniacs to Bedlam, so *judges should be withdrawn from their bench, whose erroneous biases are leading us to dissolu-tion.* It may, indeed, injure them in fame or in fortune; but it saves the Republic, which is the first and supreme law." (Thomas Jeferson, *Autobiography; Works* 1:82)

As citizens, we, too, have an obligation to uphold and defend the Constitution. If we believe that the Justices of the modern Supreme Court have committed High Crimes and Misdemeanors, then it is not only our right, but our *duty* to call for Congress to institute impeachment proceedings.[8] Article II, Section 4 was written into the Constitution for a very good reason. The time is long overdue for it to be dusted off and put into operation.

It is my conviction that the Constitution of the United States was established by the hands of wise men whom the Lord raised up unto this very purpose.

The Lord expects us to safeguard this sacred and inspired document for the blessing of all of us and our posterity. If we fail so to do we will not only lose our priceless freedom but jeopardize the cause of truth throughout the entire world.[9]

---

[8]"The people — the people — are the rightful masters of both congresses, and courts — not to overthrow the constitution, but to overthrow the *men* who pervert it." (Abraham Lincoln, September 17, 1859; *Collected Works* 3:435)

[9]"Don't interfere with anything in the Constitution. That must be maintained, for it is the only safeguard of our liberties. And not to Democrats alone do I make this appeal, but to all who love these great and true principles. (Abraham Lincoln, August 30, 1856; *Collected Works* 2:366)

Section III

OUR IMMEDIATE RESPONSIBILITY

"The liberties of our country, the freedom of our civil constitution, are worth defending at all hazards; and it is our duty to defend them against all attacks. We have received them as a fair inheritance from our worthy ancestors: they purchased them for us with toil and danger and expense of treasure and blood, and transmitted them to us with care and diligence. It will bring an everlasting mark of infamy on the present generation, enlightened as it is, if we should suffer them to be wrested from us by violence without a struggle, or be cheated out of them by the artifices of false and designing men." (Samuel Adams, 1771; *Great Quotations,* p. 581)

CHAPTER 24

NOT COMMANDED IN ALL THINGS[1]

"Once to every man and nation comes the moment to decide;

In the strife of Truth with Falsehood, for the good or evil
side;

Some great cause, God's new Messiah, offering each the
bloom or blight,

Parts the goats upon the left hand and the sheep upon the
right,

And the choice goes by forever 'twixt that darkness and
that light."

(James Russell Lowell, *The Present Crisis*)

In 1831 the Lord said this to his Church:

For behold, it is not meet that I should command in all things;
for he that is compelled in all things, the same is a slothful and not
a wise servant; wherefore he receiveth no reward.

Verily I say, men should be anxiously engaged in a good
cause, and do many things of their own free will, and bring to pass
much righteousness;

For the power is in them, wherein they are agents unto
themselves. And inasmuch as men do good they shall in nowise
lose their reward.

But he that does not anything until he is commanded, and receiveth a commandment with doubtful heart, and keepeth it with
slothfulness, the same is damned. (D&C 58:26-29)

The purposes of the Lord — the great objectives — continue the same: the salvation and exaltation of his children.

Usually the Lord gives us the overall objectives to be accomplished and some guidelines to follow, but he expects us
to work out most of the details and methods. The methods and

---

[1]Address delivered on April 5, 1965, at the general conference of The Church
of Jesus Christ of Latter-day Saints in the Tabernacle, Salt Lake City, Utah.

procedures are usually developed through study and prayer and by living so that we can obtain and follow the prompting of the Spirit. Less spiritually advanced people, such as those in the days of Moses, had to be commanded in many things. Today those spiritually alert look at the objectives, check the guidelines laid down by the Lord and his prophets, and then prayerfully act — without having to be commanded "in all things." This attitude prepares men for godhood.

The overall objective to be accomplished in missionary work, temple work, providing for the needy, and bringing up our children in righteousness has always been the same; only our methods to accomplish these objectives have varied. Any faithful member in this dispensation, no matter when he lived, could have found righteous methods to have carried out these objectives without having to wait for the latest, specific Church-wide program.

Sometimes the Lord hopefully waits on his children to act on their own, and when they do not, they lose the greater prize, and the Lord will either drop the entire matter and let them suffer the consequences or else he will have to spell it out in greater detail. Usually, I fear, the more he has to spell it out, the smaller is our reward.

Often, because of circumstances, the Lord, through revelation to his prophets or through inspired programs designed by faithful members which later become adopted on a Church-wide basis, will give to all the membership a righteous means to help accomplish the objective; for instance, any member of the Church a century ago who studied Church doctrine would have known that he had the prime responsibility to see that his children had spiritualized family recreation and were taught in the home lessons in character building and gospel principles. But some did not do it.

Then, in 1915 President Joseph F. Smith introduced, Church-wide, "the weekly home evening program" with promised blessings to all who faithfully adopted it. Many refused and lost the promised blessings. (At the October Conference, 1947, I referred to that promise in a talk on the family home evening.) Today we have the home evening manual and other helps. Yet some still refuse to bring up their children in righteousness.

But there are some today who complain that the home evening manual should have been issued years ago. If this is true, then the Lord will hold his servants accountable; but no one can say that from the inception of the Church up to the present day the Lord through his Spirit to the individual members and through his spokesmen, the prophets, has not given us the objectives and plenty of guidelines and counsel. The fact that some of us have not done much about it even when it is spelled out in detail is not the Lord's fault.

For years we have been counseled to have on hand a year's supply of food. Yet there are some today who will not start storing until the Church comes out with a detailed monthly home storage program. Now suppose that never happens. We still cannot say we have not been told.

Should the Lord decide at this time to cleanse the Church —and the need for that cleansing seems to be increasing — a famine in this land of one year's duration could wipe out a large percentage of slothful members, including some ward and stake officers. Yet we cannot say we have not been warned.

Another warning: You and I sustain one man on this earth as God's mouthpiece — President David O. McKay — one of the greatest seers who has ever walked this earth. We do not need a prophet — we have one — what we desperately need is a listening ear.

Should it be of concern to us when the mouthpiece of the Lord keeps constantly and consistently raising his voice of warning about the loss of our freedom as he has over the years? *There are two unrighteous ways to deal with his prophetic words of warning: you can fight them or you can ignore them. Either course will bring you disaster in the long run.*

Hear his words: "No greater immediate responsibility rests upon members of the Church, upon all citizens of this Republic and of neighboring Republics than to protect the

freedom vouchsafed by the Constitution of the United States."
(*P.P.N.S.*, p. 157)   As important as are all other principles of the gospel, it was the freedom issue which determined
whether you received a body. To have been on the wrong side
of the freedom issue during the war in heaven meant eternal
damnation. How then can Latter-day Saints expect to be on
the wrong side in this life and escape the eternal consequences?
The war in heaven is raging on earth today. The issues are the
same: Shall men be compelled to do what others claim is for
their best welfare or will they heed the counsel of the prophet
and preserve their freedom?

Satan argued that men given their freedom would not
choose correctly; therefore he would compel them to do right
and save us all. Today Satan argues that men given their freedom do not choose wisely; therefore a so-called brilliant,
benevolent few must establish the welfare government and
force us into a greater socialistic society. We are assured of
being led into the promised land as long as we let them put a
golden ring in our nose. In the end we lose our freedom and
the promised land also. No matter what you call it — communism, socialism, or the welfare state — our freedom is sacrificed. We believe the gospel is the greatest thing in the
world; why then do we not force people to join the Church if
they are not smart enough to see it on their own? Because this
is Satan's way, not the Lord's plan. The Lord uses persuasion
and love.

Hear again the words of God's mouthpiece:

> Today two mighty forces are battling for the supremacy of
> the world. The destiny of mankind is in the balance. It is a question
> of God and liberty, or atheism and slavery . . .
>
> Those forces are known and have been designated by differ-
> ent terms throughout the ages. "In the beginning" they were known
> as Satan on the one hand, and Christ on the other.
>
> In Joshua's time they were called "gods of the Amorites,"
> on one, and "the Lord" on the other. . . . In these days, they are
> called "domination by the state," on one hand, "personal liberty,"
> on the other hand; communism on one, free agency on the other.
> (*P.P.N.S.*, pp. 215-216)

Now the Lord knew that before the gospel could flourish there must first be an atmosphere of freedom. This is why he first established the Constitution of this land through gentiles whom he raised up before he restored the gospel. In how many communist countries today are we doing missionary work, building chapels, etc.? And yet practically every one of those countries have been pushed into communism and kept under communism with the great assistance of evil forces which have and are operating within our own country and neighboring lands. *Yes, were it not for the tragic policies of governments — including our own — tens of millions of people murdered and hundreds of millions enslaved since World War II would be alive and free today to receive the restored gospel.*

President J. Reuben Clark, Jr., put it clearly and courageously when he said:

> Reduced to its lowest terms, the great struggle which now rocks the whole earth more and more takes on the character of a struggle of the individual versus the state. . . .
>
> This gigantic world-wide struggle, more and more takes on the form of a war to the death. We shall do well and wisely so to face and so to enter it. And we must all take part. Indeed, we all are taking part in that struggle, whether we will or not. Upon its final issue, liberty lives or dies. . . . The plain and simple issue now facing us in America is freedom or slavery. . . . We have largely lost the conflict so far waged. But there is time to win the final victory, if we sense our danger, and fight. (*P.P.N.S.,* pp. 318, 327-328)

Now where do we stand in this struggle, and what are we doing about it?

The devil knows that if the elders of Israel should ever wake up, they could step forth and help preserve freedom and extend the gospel. Therefore the devil has concentrated, and to a large extent successfully, in neutralizing much of the priesthood. He has reduced them to sleeping giants. His arguments are clever. Here are a few samples:

First: "We really haven't received much instruction about freedom," the devil says. This is a lie, for we have been warned time and time again. No prophet of the Lord has ever issued more solemn warning than President David O. McKay. Last conference I spoke of a book embodying much of the prophets' warnings on freedom, from Joseph Smith to David O. McKay, which I commend to you. It is entitled *Prophets, Principles, and National Survival.*

Second: "You're too involved in other Church work," says the devil. But freedom is a weighty matter of the law; the lesser principles of the gospel you should keep but not leave this one undone. We may have to balance and manage our time better. Your other Church work will be limited once you lose your freedom, as our saints have found out in Czechoslovakia, Poland, and many other nations.

Third: "You want to be loved by everyone," says the devil, "and this freedom battle is so controversial you might be accused of engaging in politics." Of course the government has penetrated so much of our lives that one can hardly speak for freedom without being accused of being political. Some might even call the war in heaven a political struggle — certainly it was controversial. Yet the valiant entered it with Michael. Those who support only the popular principles of the gospel have their reward. And those who want to lead the quiet, retiring life but still expect to do their full duty can't have it both ways.

Said Elder John A. Widtsoe:

> The troubles of the world may largely be laid at the doors of those who are neither hot nor cold; who always follow the line of least resistance; whose timid hearts flutter at taking sides for truth. As in the great Council in the heaven, so in the Church of Christ on earth, there can be no neutrality. (*P.P.N.S.,* p. 440)

Fourth: "Wait until it becomes popular to do," says the devil, "or, at least until everybody in the Church agrees on what should be done." But this fight for freedom might never become popular in our day. And if you wait until everybody agrees in this Church, you will be waiting through the second coming of the Lord. Would you have hesitated to follow the inspired counsel of the Prophet Joseph Smith simply because some weak men disagreed with him? God's living mouthpiece has spoken to us — are we for him or against him? In spite of the Prophet's opposition to increased federal aid and compulsory unionism, some Church members still champion these freedom-destroying programs. Where do you stand?

Fifth: "It might hurt your business or your family," says the devil, "and besides why not let the gentiles save the country? They aren't as busy as you are." Well, there were many businessmen who went along with Hitler because it supposedly helped their business. They lost everything. Many of us are here today because our forefathers loved truth enough that they fought at Valley Forge or crossed the plains in spite of the price it cost them or their families. We had better take our small pain now than our greater loss later. There were souls who wished afterwards that they had stood and fought with Washington and the founding fathers, but they waited too long — they passed up eternal glory. *There has never been a greater time than now to stand up against untrenched evil.* And while the gentiles established the Constitution, we have a divine mandate to preserve it. But unfortunately, today in this freedom struggle many gentiles are showing greater wisdom in their generation than the children of light.

Sixth: "Don't worry," says the devil, "the Lord will protect you, and besides, the world is so corrupt and heading toward destruction at such a pace that you can't stop it, so why try." Well, to begin with, the Lord will not protect us unless we do our part. This devilish tactic of persuading people not to get concerned because the Lord will protect them no matter what they do is exposed by the Book of Mormon. Referring to the devil, it says, "And others will he pacify, and lull them away into carnal security, and they will say: All is well in Zion; yea, Zion prospereth, all is well — and thus the devil cheateth their souls, and leadeth them away carefully down to hell." (2 Nephi 28:21)

I like that word "carefully." In other words, don't shake them, you might awake them. But the Book of Mormon warns us that when we should see these murderous conspiracies in our midst that we should awake to our awful situation. Now why should we awake if the Lord is going to take care of us anyway? Now let us suppose that it is too late to save freedom. It is still accounted unto us for righteousness' sake to stand up and fight. Some Book of Mormon prophets knew of the final desolate end of their nations, but they still fought on, and they saved some souls including their own by so doing. For, *after all, the purpose of life is to prove ourselves and the final victory will be for freedom.*

But many of the prophecies referring to America's preservation are conditional. That is, if we do our duty we can be preserved, and if not, then we shall be destroyed. This means that a good deal of the responsibility lies with the Priesthood of this Church as to what happens to America and as to how much tragedy can be avoided if we do act now.

And now as the last neutralizer that the devil uses most effectively — it is simply this: "Don't do anything in the fight for freedom until the Church sets up its own specific program to save the Constitution." This brings us right back to the scripture I opened with today — to those slothful servants who will not do anything until they are "compelled in all things." Maybe the Lord will never set up a specific Church program for the purpose of saving the Constitution. Perhaps if he set up one at this time it might split the Church asunder, and perhaps he does not want that to happen yet, for not all the wheat and tares are fully ripe.

The Prophet Joseph Smith declared it will be the elders of Israel who will step forward to help save the Constitution, not the Church. And have we elders been warned? Yes, we have. And besides, if the Church should ever inaugurate a program, who do you think would be in the forefront to get it moving? It would not be those who were sitting on the sidelines prior to that time or those who were appeasing the enemy. It would be those choice spirits who, not waiting to be "commanded in all things," used their own free will, the counsel of the prophets, and the Spirit of the Lord as guidelines and who entered the battle "in a good cause" and brought to pass much righteousness in freedom's cause.[2]

---

[2]"God grants liberty only to those who love it, and are always ready to guard and defend it." (Daniel Webster, June 3, 1834; *Familiar Quotations,* pp. 340-341)

Years ago Elder Joseph F. Merrill of the Council of the Twelve encouraged the members of the Church to join right-to-work leagues and President Heber J. Grant concurred. For our day President David O. McKay has called communism the greatest threat to the Church, and it is certainly the greatest mortal threat this country has ever faced. What are you doing to fight it?

Brethren, if we had done our homework and were faithful, we could step forward at this time and help save this country. The fact that most of us are unprepared to do it is an indictment we will have to bear. *The longer we wait, the heavier the chains, the deeper the blood,*[3] *the more the persecution, and the less we can carry out our God-given mandate and world-wide mission. The war in heaven is raging on earth today.* Are you being neutralized in the battle?

> Verily I say, men should be anxiously engaged in a good cause, and do many things of their own free will, and bring to pass much righteousness;
>
> For the power is in them, wherein they are agents unto themselves. . . . (D&C 58:27-28)

---

[3]"The tree of liberty must be refreshed from time to time, with the blood of patriots and tyrants. It is its natural manure." (Thomas Jefferson, To Colonel Smith, Nov. 13, 1787; *Works* 2:319)

CHAPTER 25

SAFETY IN THE FACE OF DANGERS[1]

"Let none falter, who thinks he is right, and we may succeed. But, if after all, we shall fail, be it so. We still shall have the proud consolation of saying to our consciences, and to the departed shade of our country's freedom, that the cause approved of our judgment, and adored of our hearts, in disaster, in chains, in torture, in death, we NEVER faltered in defending." (Abraham Lincoln, December 26, 1839; *Collected Works* 1:179)

Humbly and gratefully I approach this sacred assignment — humble in the awesome task of speaking to you, grateful for mortal life, for the gospel, and for a prophet of God to lead us.

As latter-day Saints, members of the true Church of Christ, we live *in* the world but we must not be *of* the world. Our Heavenly Father wants us to be happy; he wants us to be successful in our chosen fields; he wants us to become good citizens in free governments, and he wants us eventually to be exalted in the celestial kingdom of God.

It is my purpose today to try to give you assurance that there can be safety even in the face of danger. This I know. Especially should this be true at Brigham Young University, a God-centered institution of learning with a destiny as a majestic world influence still to be fully realized.

Mormon philosophy, based on the revelations of God, assures us that our Heavenly Father is the supreme scientist of the universe. He is the supreme authority of the humanities. God is the supreme authority on politics, on economics, on sociology. He knows what works best in human relations.

[1]Address given on May 10, 1966, to the student body of Brigham Young University, Provo, Utah.

He is the master teacher with a glorious plan based on freedom of choice, for the building of godlike men and women. He stands today ready to help us reach out and tap that great unseen power as we heed the counsel of his living mouthpiece, a true prophet of God.

Safety in the face of dangers — that is the challenge and promise. You can realize the fulfillment of this promise in your individual lives. This I can promise you as you follow the divine plan of a kind Father in heaven.

Some years ago President Joseph F. Smith, a prophet of the Lord, warned that "There are at least three dangers that threaten the Church within. . . . " (*Gospel Doctrine,* p. 312) He also counseled the authorities of the Church to warn the people unceasingly against them.

These dangers are: Flattery of prominent men in the world, false educational ideas, and sexual impurity.

As a part of this discussion I should like to comment briefly on these three dangers.

First, the flattery of prominent men in the world: The Master warned, "Woe unto you, when all men shall speak well of you! . . . " (Luke 6:26)

As Latter-day Saints, we have been driven, mobbed, misunderstood, and maligned. We have been a peculiar people. Now we are faced with world applause. It has been a welcome change, but can we stand acceptance? Can we meet the danger of applause? In the hour of man's success, applause can be his greatest danger.

There is, of course, nothing wrong with being honored by men, if one is being honored for a good thing, if one comes to these honors through righteous living, and if, while holding these honors, one lives honorably. One should strive to have wide influence for good.

However, virtue is not the only basis for being singled out and promoted. As the world becomes more wicked, a possible way to attain worldly success may be to join the wicked. The time is fast approaching when it will require great courage for

Latter-day Saints to stand up for their peculiar standards and doctrine — all of their doctrine, including the more weighty principles such as the principle of freedom. Opposition to this weighty principle of freedom caused many of our brothers and sisters in the pre-existence to lose their first estate in the war in heaven.

We are far removed from the days of our forefathers who were persecuted for their peculiar beliefs. Some of us seem to want to share their reward, but are ofttimes afraid to stand up for principles that are controversial in our generation. We need not solicit persecution, but neither should we remain silent in the presence of overwhelming evils, for this makes cowards of men. We should not go out of the path of duty to pick up a cross there is no need to bear, but neither should we sidestep a cross that clearly lies within the path of duty.

We are in the world, and I fear some of us are getting too much like the world. Rather than continue a peculiar people, some are priding themselves on how much they are like everybody else, when the world is getting more wicked. The Lord, as he prayed for his apostles, said, " . . . the world hath hated them, because they are not of the world, even as I am not of the world." (John 17:14) As Latter-day Saints, we too have been called out of the world.

Some things are changeless, priceless. We must anchor ourselves to the eternal verities of life, for life is eternal. The honors of men, more often than not, are fleeting. Anxious to run after the honors of office or succumb to the pressures of public glamour and worldly acclaim, some of us are no longer willing to stand up for all the principles of the gospel. We seek to justify our unrighteousness by claiming that, if only we can get title or position, then think of the good we can do. Hence we lose our salvation en route to those honors. We sometimes look among our numbers to find one to whom we can point who agrees with us, so we can have company to justify our apostasy. We rationalize by saying that some day the Church doctrine will catch up with our way of thinking. *Truth is not established by Gallup polls.*

Seeking the applause of the world, we like to be honored by the men the world honors. But therein lies real danger, for ofttimes in order to receive these honors, we must join forces with and follow those same devilish influences and policies which brought some of those men to positions of prominence.

More and more the honors of this world are being promoted by the wicked for the wicked. We see this in publicity and awards that are given to movies, literature, art, journalism, etc. We see in our own newspapers widely-read columnists carried who advocate one-world socialism, who have been consistently caught in falsehoods, and who continually parrot the communist line. Less and less we see the virtuous rewarded by the world, and when they are, ofttimes it almost seems to be done insidiously in order to get us to swallow the many evils for which the wicked are even more profusely honored.[2]

Second, false educational ideas: During the past several years many of our institutions of learning have been turning out an increasing number of students schooled in amorality, relativity, and atheism — students divested of a belief in God, without fixed moral principles or an understanding of our constitutional republic and our capitalistic, free enterprise economic system. This follows a pattern which was established years ago at some of our key colleges that produced many of the teachers and leaders in the educational field across the country today.

The fruits of this kind of teaching have been tragic, not only to the souls of the individuals involved, but also to the parents, and even to our country. We saw these tragic fruits with some of our boys in Korea.

---

[2]"We ought to beware of the passion for glory, for it robs us of liberty, which brave men should pursue with all their might, and we should not seek command or rather upon occasion decline it or lay it down. . . .

"Nothing is worthy of the admiration, the desire, or the effort of man except what is honourable and decorous and . . . he must surrender neither to his fellow-men, to passion, or to fortune. . . .

"It is a mark of moral courage to make light of those objects which dazzle the world, and steadily to despise them on fixed and settled principles. . . . "
(*Cicero, On Moral Duties*, I, 20)

When a survey was recently made among students asking which they would prefer, nuclear war or surrender to the communists, those campuses scored highest for surrender who had been most permeated by these cowardly teachings of false economic principles, atheism, and amorality. On one very liberal college campus over 90 percent favored surrender. Other surveys on moral standards are equally alarming. More disturbing is the fact that the more college courses the students take on these campuses, the worse their thinking seems to become. Freshmen who have just left home or work do not seem as fully permeated with the brainwashing as the seniors.

Some alumni of various schools have expressed concern. One alumnus from Yale wrote a book a few years ago entitled *God and Man at Yale*. Another group (which includes Teddy Roosevelt's hero son Archibald) from Harvard University established the Veritas Foundation and wrote a book, *Keynes at Harvard,* explaining the degree to which the destructive Fabian economic philosophy has permeated educational institutions and government. Concerned educators have begun to write books. Professor E. Merrill Root authorized *Collectivism on the Campus* and *Brainwashing in the High Schools.* Dr. Max Rafferty, now state superintendent of schools in California, wrote *Suffer Little Children* and *What Are They Doing to Your Children.*

In the school history textbooks of recent years, some of the greatest phrases in American history have been dropped. *This Week* magazine recently surveyed history books issued before 1920 and since 1920. Patrick Henry's famous words, "Give me liberty or give me death," appeared in 12 out of 14 earlier texts, but in only 2 out of 45 recent texts. Perhaps this might help explain the percentage of students who are willing to surrender to communism.

The whole process can be quite insidious. Young people know that the best jobs are available to college graduates. They want to do well at school. When exam time comes, they must give back to the teacher what the teacher wants. Under the guise of academic freedom — which some apparently feel is freedom to destroy freedom — some teachers reserve to themselves the privilege of teaching error, destroying faith in God, debunking morality, and depreciating our free economic system. If questions reflecting the teacher's false teachings appear on the exam, how will the student answer who believes in God and morality and our Constitution? One student put on his exam paper what he knew the professor wanted to see, but then the student added a little p.s., which said, "Dear Professor So-and-So: I just want you to know I don't believe one word of what I just wrote above."

These kinds of professors — and I hope there are none on this campus, and if there are such here they should be dismissed — are not concerned about the truth, or even giving both sides of a question that only has one right answer. They weight the scales on the side of falsehood. If they can see there is another side, it usually gets but passing and belittling reference. To give the impression they are objective, these professors often invite someone to present a different point of view in one lecture, while the professor spends the whole semester pointing out the other side.

Now *truth, if given as much time and emphasis as error, will invariably prove itself.* And if our young students could have as much time studying the truth as they and some of their professors have had studying error, then there would be no question of the outcome.

The problem arises when under the pressure of a heavy course of study and the necessity of parroting back what certain professors have said, the student does not have the time or take the time to learn the truth. If he does not learn the truth, some day he will suffer the consequences. Many an honest student, after graduation, has had to do some unlearning and then fresh learning of basic principles which never change and which he should have been taught initially.

No doubt this is one of the reasons why the president of this institution spoke out so vigorously April 21, 1966, in warning of our drift toward the soul-destroying welfare state. I urge all of you to obtain a personal copy of that address for your prayerful study.

These false educational ideas — set forth in many textbooks today — are prevalent in the world, and we have not entirely escaped them among teachers in our own system. There are a few teachers within the Church who, while courting apostasy, still want to remain members of the Church, for being members makes them more effective in misleading the saints. But their day of judgment is coming, and when it does come, for some of them it would have been better, as the Savior said, that a millstone had been put around their necks and they had been drowned in the depths of the sea than to have led away any of the youth of the Church.

The Lord has stated that his Church will never again be taken from the earth because of apostasy. But he has also stated that some members of his Church will fall away. There has been individual apostasy in the past; it is going on now, and there will be an ever-increasing amount in the future. While we cannot save all the flock from being deceived, we should, without compromising our doctrine, strive to save as many as we can. For, as President J. Reuben Clark said, "We are in the midst of the greatest exhibition of propaganda that the world has ever seen." Do not believe all you hear.

Students, study the writings of the prophets. Fortunately the consistent position taken over the years by the prophets of the Church on vital issues facing this nation have recently been published in an excellent book entitled *Prophets, Principles and National Survival,* compiled by Jerreld L. Newquist.

Students, pray for inspiration and knowledge. Counsel with your parents. Let Sunday be the day to fill up your spiritual batteries for the week by reading good Church books, particularly the Book of Mormon. Take time to meditate. Don't let the philosophies and falsehoods of men throw you. Hold on to the iron rod. Learn to sift. Learn to discern error through the promptings of the Spirit and your study of the truth.

Yes, false educational ideas are a serious threat today.

Third, sexual immorality: Sexual immorality is a viper that is striking not only in the world, but also in the Church today. Not to admit it is to be dangerously complacent or is like putting one's head in the sand. In the category of crimes, only murder and denying the Holy Ghost come ahead of illicit sexual relations, which we call fornication when it involves an unmarried person, or the graver sin of adultery when it involves one who is married.

I know the laws of the land do not consider unchastity as serious as God does, nor punish as severely as God does, but that does not change its abominableness. In the eyes of God there is but one moral standard for men and women. In the eyes of God chastity will never be out of date.

The natural desire for men and women to be together is from God. But such association is bounded by his laws. Those things properly taken within the bonds of marriage are right and pleasing before God and fulfill the commandment to multiply and replenish the earth. But those same things when taken outside the bonds of marriage are a curse.

No sin is causing the loss of the Spirit of the Lord among our people today more than sexual promiscuity. It is causing our people to stumble, damning their growth, darkening their spiritual powers, and making them subject to other sins.

Recently a young man commented that if he quit reading books, watching TV, seeing movies, reading newspapers and magazines, and going to school, there was a chance he might live a clean life.

This explains, in large part, the extent to which this insidious evil has spread, for the world treats this sin flippantly. These evil forces build up your lust and then fail to tell the tragic consequences. In so many movies the hero is permitted to get away with crime so long as he can joke about it, or explain he was powerless to do anything, or else at the close of the movie show forth one minimal virtue that is supposed to cover the grossest sin. Many of our prominent national magazines pander to the baser side, but then try to cover for themselves by including other articles too.

So garbled in values have our morals become that some youth would not dare touch a cigarette, but freely engage in petting. Both are wrong, but one is infinitely more serious than the other.

Years ago President David O. McKay, God bless him, read a statement written by Mrs. Wesley to her famous son John. I commend it to you as a basis for judgment pertaining to the matter of chastity.

> Would you judge of the lawfulness or unlawfulness of pleasure? Take this rule: Now note, whatever weakens your reason, impairs the tenderness of your conscience, obscures your sense of God, takes off your relish for spiritual things, whatever increases the authority of the body over the mind, that thing is sin to you, however innocent it may seem in itself.

May I suggest some steps to avoid the pitfalls of immorality:

(1) *Avoid late hours and weariness.* The Lord said, "Retire to thy bed early" (D&C 88:124), and there are good reasons for that. Some of the worst sins are committed after midnight by tired heads. Officers in the wards and stakes, branches and missions should not keep our people, especially our youth, up late at night even for wholesome recreation.

(2) *Keep your dress modest.* Short skirts are not pleasing to the Lord, but modesty is. Girls, do not be an enticement for your downfall because of your immodest and tightfitting clothes.

(3) *Have good associates or don't associate at all.* Be careful in the selection of your friends. If in the presence of certain persons you are lifted to nobler heights, you are in good company. But if your friends or associates encourage base thoughts, then you had best leave them.

(4) *Avoid necking and petting like a plague,* for necking and petting are the concessions which precede the complete loss of virtue.

(5) *Have a good physical outlet of some sport or exercise.* Overcome evil with good. You can overcome many evil inclinations through good physical exertion and healthful activities. A healthy soul, free of the body-and spirit-dulling in-

fluences of alcohol and tobacco, is in better condition to overthrow the devil.

(6) *Think clean thoughts.* Those who think clean thoughts do not do dirty deeds. You are not only responsible before God for your acts, but also for controlling your thoughts. So live that you would not blush with shame if your thoughts and acts could be flashed on a screen in your own ward meetings. The old adage is still true that you sow thoughts and reap acts; you sow acts and reap habits; you sow habits and you reap a character; and your character determines your eternal destiny. "As a man thinketh, so is he." (See Proverbs 23:7)

(7) *Pray.* There is no temptation placed before you which you cannot shun. Do not allow yourself to get in positions where it is easy to fall. Listen to the promptings of the Spirit. If you are engaged in things where you do not feel you can pray and ask the Lord's blessings on what you are doing, then you are engaged in the wrong kind of activity.

Yes, avoid late hours; dress modestly; seek good associates; avoid necking and petting; have a good physical outlet; think good thoughts; pray.

May the Lord bless us as a people. We have taken upon us sacred covenants. We must be faithful. We are in the world, it is true, but we must not partake of the evils of the world. Let us be ever on guard against the flattery of prominent men of the world, false educational ideas, and sexual impurity.

God grant that in all the days to come we will so live that we will not be deceived, that we will be able to discern the truth which will keep us free.

Years ago my great-grandfather, while an investigator, attended a Mormon meeting during which a member had a quarrel over the sacrament table with the branch president. When the service was over, Mrs. Benson turned to Ezra T. and asked him what he thought of the Mormons now. I'll always be grateful for his answer. He said he thought the actions of its members in no way altered the truth of Mormonism. That conviction saved him from many a tragedy.

Before joining the Church, Grandfather was moved by a marvelous prayer by Apostle John E. Page. But later the young convert was greatly shocked by the same man, whose actions reflected his gradual apostasy. Ironically, when Elder Page eventually was excommunicated, Brigham Young selected the young convert to fill his place in the Quorum of the Twelve.

Six of the original twelve apostles selected by Joseph Smith were excommunicated. The three witnesses to the Book of Mormon left the Church. Three of Joseph Smith's counselors fell — one even helped plot his death.

A natural question that might arise would be that if the Lord knew in advance that these men would fall, as he undoubtedly did, why did he have his prophet call them to such high office? The answer is, to fill the Lord's purposes. For even the Master followed the will of the Father by selecting Judas. President George Q. Cannon suggested an explanation, too, when he stated, "Perhaps it is his own design that faults and weaknesses should appear in high places in order that his saints may learn to trust in him and not in any man or men." (*Millennial Star* 53:658, February 15, 1891) And this would parallel Nephi's warning, put not your "trust in the arm of flesh." (2 Nephi 4:34)

"The Church," says President McKay, "is little, if at all, injured by persecutions and calumnies from ignorant, misinformed, or malicious enemies." (*The Instructor,* Feb. 1956, p. 33) It is from within the Church that the greatest hindrance comes. And so, it seems, it has been. Now the question arises, will we stick with the kingdom and can we avoid being deceived? Certainly this is an important question, for the Lord has said that in the last days the devil will "rage in the hearts of the children of men" (2 Nephi 28:20), and if it were possible, "[he] shall deceive the very elect." (*Joseph Smith* 1:22)

Brigham Young said:

> The adversary presents his principle and arguments in the most approved style, and in the most winning tone, attended with the most graceful attitudes; and he is very careful to ingratiate

himself into the favor of the powerful and influential of mankind, uniting himself with popular parties, floating into offices of trust and emolument by pandering to popular feeling, though it should seriously wrong and oppress the innocent. Such characters put on the manners of an angel, appearing as nigh like angels of light as they possibly can, to deceive the innocent and the unwary. The good which they do, they do to bring to pass an evil purpose upon the good and honest followers of Jesus Christ. (*Journal of Discourses* 11:238-239)

Those of us who think "all is well in Zion" (2 Nephi 28:21), in spite of the Book of Mormon warning, might ponder the words of Heber C. Kimball, wherein he said,

> Yes, we think we are secure here in the chambers of these everlasting hills . . . but I want to say to you, my brethren, the time is coming when we will be mixed up in these now peaceful valleys to that extent that it will be difficult to tell the face of a Saint from the face of an enemy against the people of God. Then is the time to look out for the great sieve, for there will be a great sifting time, and many will fall. For I say unto you there is a test, a Test, a TEST coming. (Heber C. Kimball, 1856. Quoted by J. Golden Kimball, *Conference Report,* October 1930, pp. 59-60.)

There is no guarantee that the devil will not deceive a lot of men who hold the priesthood.

> Free agency is the principle against which Satan waged his war in heaven. It is still the front on which he makes his most furious, devious, and persistent attacks. That this would be the case was foreshadowed by the Lord.
>
> [When Satan] was cast out of heaven, his objective was (and still is) "to deceive and to blind men, and to lead them captive at his will." This he effectively does to as many as will not hearken unto the voice of God. His main attack is still on free agency. When he can get men to yield their agency, he has them well on the way to captivity.
>
> We who hold the priesthood must beware concerning ourselves, that we do not fall in the traps he lays to rob us of our freedom. We must be careful that we are not led to accept or support in any way any organization, cause or measure which in its remotest effort, would jeopardize free agency, whether it be in politics, government, religion, employment, education, or in any other field. It is not enough for us to be sincere in what we support. We must be right! (Elder Marion G. Romney, *Conference Report,* October 1960, pp. 73-75)

Now this is crucial for us to know, for as President John Taylor said, "Besides the preaching of the Gospel, we have another mission, namely, the perpetuation of the free agency of man and maintenance of liberty, freedom and the rights of man." (*Journal of Discourses* 23:63)

It was the struggle over free agency that divided us before we came here. It may well be the struggle over the same principle which will deceive and divide us again.

May I suggest three short tests to avoid being deceived, both pertaining to this freedom struggle and all other matters:

(1) *What do the standard works have to say about it?*

Isaiah said,

> To the law and to the testimony: if they speak not according to this word, it is because there is no light in them. (Isaiah 8:20)

And Hosea, "My people are destroyed for lack of knowledge. . . . " (Hosea 4:6)

We must diligently study the scriptures. Of special importance to us are the Book of Mormon and the Doctrine and Covenants. Joseph Smith said,

> . . . that the Book of Mormon was the most correct of any book on earth, and the keystone of our religion, and a man would get nearer to God by abiding its precepts, than by any other book. (*History of the Church* 1:461)

The Book of Mormon, Brigham Young said, was written on the tablets of his heart and no doubt helped save him from being deceived. The Book of Mormon has a lot to say about America, freedom and secret combinations.

The Doctrine and Covenants is important because it contains the revelations which helped lay the foundation of this great latter-day work. It speaks of many things. In Section 134:2, it states that government should hold inviolate the right and control of property. This makes important reading in a day when government controls are increasing and people are losing the right to control their own property.

(2) The second guide is: *What do the latter-day Presidents of the Church have to say on the subject — particularly the living President?*

President Wilford Woodruff related an incident in Church history when Brigham Young was addressing a congregation in the presence of the Prophet Joseph Smith:

> Brother Brigham took the stand, and he took the Bible and laid it down; he took the Book of Mormon and laid it down; and he took the Book of Doctrine and Covenants and laid it down before him, and he said: "There is the written word of God for us, concerning the work of God from the beginning of the world, almost, to our day. And now," said he, "when compared with the living oracles, those books are nothing to me; those books do not convey the word of God direct to us now, as do the words of a Prophet or a man bearing the Holy Priesthood in our day and generation. I would rather have the living oracles than all the writing in the books." That was the course he pursued.
>
> When he was through, Brother Joseph said to the congregation: "Brother Brigham has told you the word of the Lord, and he has told you the truth." (*Conference Report,* October 1897, pp. 18-19)

There is only one man on the earth today who speaks for the Church. (See D&C 132:7; 21:4) That man is President David O. McKay. Because he gives the word of the Lord for us today, his words have an even more immediate importance than those of the dead prophets. When speaking under the influence of the Holy Ghost, his words are scripture. (See D&C 68:4) I commend also for your reading the masterful discourse of President J. Reuben Clark, Jr., in the "Church News" section of the *Deseret News,* July 31, 1954, entitled: "When Are Church Leader's Words Entitled to Claim of Scripture?"

The President can speak on any subject he feels is needful for the Saints. As Brigham Young stated:

> I defy any man on earth to point out the path a Prophet of God should walk in, or point out his duty, and just how far he must go, in dictating temporal or spiritual things. Temporal and spiritual things are inseparably connected, and ever will be. (*Journal of Discourses* 10:364)

Other officers in the kingdom have fallen, but never the presidents. "Keep your eye on the Captain" is still good counsel. The words of a living prophet must and ever will take precedence.

President McKay has said a lot about our tragic trends toward socialism and communism and the responsibilities liberty-loving people have in defending and preserving our Constitution. Have we read these words from God's mouthpiece and pondered on them?

(3) *The third and final test is the Holy Ghost — the test of the Spirit.* By the Spirit we "may know the truth of all things." (Moroni 10:5) This test can only be fully effective if one's channels of communication with God are clean and virtuous and uncluttered with sin.

Said Brigham Young:

> You may know whether you are led right or wrong, as well as you know the way home; for every principle God has revealed carries its own convictions of its truth to the human mind. . . . Let every man and woman know, by the whispering of the Spirit of God to themselves, whether their leaders are walking in the path the Lord dictates or not. This has been my exhortation continually. What a pity it would be if we were led by one man to utter destruction! Are you afraid of this? I am more afraid that this people have so much confidence in their leaders that they will not inquire for themselves of God whether they are led by Him. I am fearful they settle down in a state of blind self-security, trusting with a reckless confidence that in itself would thwart the purposes of God in their salvation, and weaken that influence they could give to their leaders, did they know for themselves, by the revelations of Jesus, that they are being led in the right way. (*Journal of Discourses* 9:149-150)

Heber C. Kimball stated: "The time will come when no man or woman will be able to endure on borrowed light." (Orson F. Whitney, *Life of Heber C. Kimball*, 1888 Edition, p. 461)

How, then, can we know if a man is speaking by the Spirit? The Bible, the Book of Mormon and the Doctrine and Covenants give us the key. (See D&C 50:17-23; 100:5-8; I Corinthians 2:10-11)

President Clark summarized them well when he said:

> We can tell when the speakers are moved upon by the Holy Ghost only when we, ourselves, are moved upon by the Holy Ghost. In a way, this completely shifts the responsibility from them to us to determine when they so speak. . . .
>
> The Church will know by the testimony of the Holy Ghost in the body of the members whether the brethren in voicing their views are moved upon by the Holy Ghost; and in due time that knowledge will be made manifest. (*Church News,* July 31, 1954)

Will this Spirit be needed to check actions in other situations? Yes, and it could be used as a guide and a protector for the faithful in many situations.

These, then, are the three tests: the standard works; the inspired words of the Presidents of the Church, particularly the living President; and the promptings of the Holy Ghost.

Now, in this great struggle for free agency, just think what a power for good we could be in this world if we were united. Remember how President Clark used to reiterate in the general priesthood meeting of the Church that there was not a righteous thing in this world that we couldn't accomplish if we were only united.

President McKay has reiterated it again and again when he stated:

> Next to being one in worshiping God, there is nothing in this world upon which this Church should be more united than in upholding and defending the Constitution of the United States!
>
> May the appeal of our Lord in his intercessory prayer for unity be realized in our homes, our wards, our stakes, and in our support of the basic principles of our Republic. (*The Instructor,* February 1956, p. 34)

President McKay speaks of *a unity on principles.*

President Clark said:

> God provided that in this land of liberty our political allegiance shall run not to individuals, that is, to government officials, no matter how great or how small they may be. Under His plan our allegiance and the only allegiance we owe as citizens or denizens of the United States, runs to our inspired Constitution which

God himself set up. So runs the oath of office of those who participate in government. A certain loyalty we do owe to the office which a man holds, but even here we owe, just by reason of our citizenship, no loyalty to the man himself. In other countries it is to the individual that allegiance runs. This principle of allegiance to the Constitution is basic to our freedom. It is one of the great principles that distinguishes this "land of liberty" from other countries.

Thus God added to his priceless blessings to us.

I wish to say with all the earnestness I possess that when the youth and maidens see any curtailment of these liberties I have named, when you see government invading any of these realms of freedom which we have under our Constitution, you will know that they are putting shackles on your liberty, and that tyranny is creeping upon you, no matter who curtails these liberties or who invades these realms, and no matter what the reason and excuse therefore may be. (*The Improvement Era,* July 1940, p. 444)

Again I say heed the counsel of President Ernest L. Wilkinson, who by appointment represents the President of the Church on this campus.

We all should know by now what President McKay has said about liberty-loving people's greatest responsibility. We know of his feelings regarding recent tragic decisions of the Supreme Court. We know the Church position supporting "right-to-work" laws[3] and the Church opposition to programs of federal aid to education.[4] These and many more things has President McKay told us that involve this great struggle against state slavery and the anti-Christ.

Now, inasmuch as all these warnings have come through the only mouthpiece of the Lord on the earth today, there is

---

[3]"We believe it is fundamental that the right to voluntary unionism should once again be reestablished in this nation and that State right-to-work laws should be maintained inviolate. At the very basis of all of our doctrine stands the right to the free agency of man. We are in favor of maintaining this free agency to the greatest extent possible. We look adversely upon any infringement thereof not essential to the proper exercise of police power of the state." (President David O. McKay, *Church News,* June 26, 1965; *P.P.N.S.,* p. 415)

[4]"As a matter of general policy, the BYU Board of Trustees has long adhered to a position opposed to general federal aid to education. We have always objected to the Church or any of its branches or agencies receiving any subsidy or 'gift' from the government. . . . We have steadfastly refused to participate in any federal educational program which is based upon the subsidy principle." (President David O. McKay, *Deseret News,* Nov. 2, 1964; *P.P.N.S.,* p. 378)

one major question we should ask ourselves: Assuming we are living a life so we can know, then what does the Holy Spirit have to say about it?

We are under obligation to answer this question. God will hold us responsible. Let us not be deceived in the sifting days ahead. Let us rally together on principle behind the Prophet as guided by the promptings of the Spirit.

Now may I call your attention to the historic priesthood session of the 1966 April General Conference of the Church. Two very significant things occurred:

(1) A talk previously given at Brigham Young University was repeated for the general priesthood membership of the Church, at the request of President David O. McKay, entitled "Socialism and the United Order Compared."

(2) Secondly, and of even more significance, a powerful statement prepared by President David O. McKay for the priesthood of the Church was read. I quote briefly from this important message:

> The position of this Church on the subject of communism has never changed. We consider it the greatest Satanical threat to peace, prosperity, and the spread of God's work among men that exists on the face of the earth. . . .
>
> We, therefore, commend and encourage every person and every group who are sincerely seeking to study Constitutional principles and awaken a sleeping and apathetic people to the alarming conditions which are rapidly advancing about us. We wish all of our citizens throughout the land were participating in some type of organized self-education in order that they could better appreciate what is happening and know what they can do about it. . . .[5]
>
> No member of the Church can be true to his faith, nor can any American be loyal to his trust, while lending aid, encouragement, or sympathy to any of these false philosophies; for if he does, they will prove snares to his feet. (*Conference Report,* April 1966, pp. 109-110)

I commend to you the reading and study of the entire statement.

---

[5]"The tyranny of a prince in an oligarchy is not so dangerous to the public welfare as the apathy of a citizen in a democracy." (Montesquieu, *Great Quotations,* p. 38)

There you have the timely, inspired words of our Prophet-leader David O. McKay,[6] which I hope we will all recall as we sing, "We Thank Thee, O God, for a Prophet."

We should continue to speak out for freedom and against socialism and communism, as President McKay has consistently admonished us. We should continue to come to the aid of patriots, programs, and organizations which are trying to save our Constitution through every legal and moral means possible.

God has not left us in darkness regarding these matters. We have the scriptures — ancient and modern. We have a living Prophet, and we may obtain the Spirit.

Yes, my beloved brothers and sisters, we have the truth. Joseph Smith did see the Father and the Son. This I know. The kingdom established through the Prophet's instrumentality will roll forth. We can move forward with it in safety, even in the face of dangers. That we may all do so and be not deceived is my humble prayer.

---

[6]See Appendix III for the full text of this historic statement by President David O. McKay.

CHAPTER 26

THE GREATEST WORK IN THE WORLD[1]

"I am not bound to win, but I am bound to be true. I am not bound to succeed, but I am bound to live up to what light I have. I must stand with anybody that stands right; stand with him while he stands right, and part company with him when he goes wrong." (Abraham Lincoln, Stevenson's *Home Book of Quotations*)

The greatest work in all the world is the building of men and women of character. Without character there is not much that's worthwhile, because character is the one thing we take with us from this world into the next. The greatest activity of our Heavenly Father is the saving and exaltation of all his children. I have visited in forty-five nations and have come away knowing that most of our Father's children essentially are good. Many of them live under bad and atheistic leadership. But they want to live in peace and to be good neighbors. They love their homes; they want to raise their standard of living, to do what's right. I know our Father loves them.

I am convinced, as was President Wilford Woodruff, that the Lord held in the spirit world for six thousand years some of the choicest spirits of all times, that they might come forth in this day when the gospel is upon the earth and when the Church has been restored, that they might help to build up the kingdom in preparation for the second coming of the Messiah. Many of these choicest spirits are young people born under the covenant, into Latter-day Saint homes.

---

[1]Address delivered in June 1966 at the Mutual Improvement Association Conference in the Tabernacle, Salt Lake City, Utah.

But *the adversary has never been so well organized and has never had so many emissaries and representatives as he has today.* The enemy of righteousness is supported by millions of people, and he has a most powerful and effective program to lead our youth astray. The big question of our time is, who reaches youth today? Who communicates with them? Parents? Schoolteachers? Civil officials? Community leaders? Any adults? In too many cases, these people are having trouble talking to — as well as listening to — young people. Into this void steps the Mutual Improvement Associations, recognizing teens for what they are: growing individuals seeking to establish their identity, find themselves, and build upon sound intellectual and spiritual foundations. We have a program that should reach them. Yet the enemy is insidious. He uses devious methods and is clear and persistent.

Recently, while browsing through several newly published books, I read one titled *The Great Deceit,* a study of America's foundation, by a group of prominent Harvard University graduates. It opens with this shocking statement:

> We are living in a most perplexing period of human history. Moral, legal, and social attitudes seem to have undergone a drastic change. Human values that have developed over thousands of years have been discarded or drastically altered. Attitudes as to what is right or wrong have become uncertain. Individual initiative and personal ability are labeled as anti-social acts. The building up of private enterprise is pictured as exploitation and economic piracy. Our founding fathers are smeared. Fabian Socialists have twisted American history and are carrying on a successful war against human liberty. We are faced with political wolves in sheep's clothing.

In a recent article entitled "Turbulence on the Campus," J. Edgar Hoover says:

> According to the latest statistics there are 34,500,000 full-time students enrolled in more than 2,000 institutions of higher learning. A high percentage of these young people are serious and concerned. They know they live in a world of change, challenge, and conflict, where their very best will be required. There is in today's campus turbulence a new style in conspiracy, a conspiracy that is extremely subtle and devious and hence difficult to

understand. It is a conspiracy reflected by questionable moods and attitudes.

Often called the new leftist conspiracy, it has utter disrespect for law, contempt for institutions of free government, and disdain for spiritual and moral values.

As parents and teachers, you should know more about this new-style perversion that is erupting in civil disobedience and encouraging young people to mock the law. Every town and every teacher must recognize the absolute need of instructing and guiding our young people to respect the law and to realize that freedom does not mean license, that with citizen's rights go corresponding duties. We want our young people to be good citizens, able to think for themselves, to have personal convictions, but we want them to be loyal to our constitutional principles and the democratic traditions that have molded this country.

I recently received a letter from a bishop who is a father, a farmer and rancher, and a former state official. He writes,

I am shocked at the brainwashing our own Latter-day Saint children seem to be getting from our teachers. This is my second experience this month in which conservative speakers have been heckled by high school students, coached by teachers who have given them loaded questions to ask. Karl Prussian, a former counterspy for the FBI for fourteen years, was given a bad time by these high school teenagers.

The bishop reports that these young people made the following statements in a discussion: Communism is an improvement over capitalism. The U.S. Constitution is archaic; it's out of date. A one-world setup governed by the United Nations would be a step forward. When the question of religious freedom came up, one student asked, "Who is God? Did you ever see him?"

The bishop continues:

These are a few of the questions and statements and attitudes that appear to be from nice, clean-cut young Americans in a small town rural high school. Can there be any doubt as to the source of this philosophy? Yet if you label it part of the so-called communist conspiracy, you are regarded as a wild-eyed fanatic who sees a communist behind every door. These teachers invite communist speakers, encourage the study of communist authors, and are exposing the students to communist culture and doctrine as they extol it under the guise of social progress and reform.

From the fifth grade through the fourth year of college, our young people are being indoctrinated with a Marxist philosophy, and I am fearful of the harvest. The younger generation is further to the left than most adults realize. The old concepts of our founding fathers are scoffed and jeered at by young moderns whose goals appear to be the destruction of integrity and virtue, and the glorification of pleasure, thrills, and self-indulgence.

America is asleep. So are its churches and its patriotic organizations, for the most part. It's already too late, I am afraid, to stem the fearsome, awesome power of Marx and Lenin now so apparent in our government, our schools, the United Nations, many Protestant churches, the press, radio, TV, and other news media.

The president of one of our great independent educational institutions sent me an article, "Today's Three Horsemen," which says:

Certain soldiers of public opinion in America who call themselves liberal in politics and economics and religion have virtually canonized and glorified three men who have lived within the hundred years since 1866. All three wrote books. One, Charles Darwin, with his origin of the species, gained a world-wide attention in 1850's. This was the period also in which another of the three, Karl Marx, published the Communist Manifesto and *Das Kapital*. The third, Maynard Keynes, entered the liberal throne room years later with his book *The General Theory on Economics*.

The growing influence of these three men is visible in all segments of American life today. The influence is not all powerful, but it has penetrated some of the vital centers of our government, educational system, and church life. If the doctrines of these three men were to become the basic philosophy of our way of life, we as a people would fail as has no other generation before us since the days of Noah.

Another item that has come to my attention is the narrative part of the filmstrip on the Berkeley revolution, which says,

While most Americans have been watching television, others have been busy implementing plans to use America's most priceless natural resource, its youth, to knowingly or unknowingly become the tools for fermenting the destruction of the American way of life. Successful Communist exploitation and manipulation of youth and student groups throughout the world today are a major challenge that free world forces must meet and defeat. Recent world events clearly reveal that world Communism has launched a massive campaign to capture and maneuver youth and student groups.

Young people are the key to success in any movement, good or bad, for they are idealistic, bold, and vigorous. The author of the script quotes from the early leaders of the communist movement to show that books have even been published on how to get control of the young people in the world.

This is just some of the evidence indicating that our young people and leaders of youth today face challenges the likes of which they have never before had.

Now, what will we do about it? Most importantly, we have this great Church, the one church that stands up in support of the inspired Constitution of America and the basic concepts embodied in that document. Our church has not in any way lowered its standards.

First, let's set our homes and our lives in order. Let us as leaders be what we want our youth to be. They need fewer critics and more models. They should know what the prophets have said. They should know that all is not well in Zion. They should not become lulled away into a false security. They should become alerted and informed about the greatest evil in this world, the greatest threat to the Church and to youth: the godless socialist-communist conspiracy.

I appeal to our young people to keep their eye on the Prophet, to heed his counsel, to read what he says, to read his messages in *The Improvement Era,* to read his most recent statement on communism.[2]

Leaders of youth, teach our young people to love freedom, to know that it is God-given. Teach them that the greatest evil in this world is to destroy the Church of God. Teach them that truth is eternal, that time is on the side of truth, and that they should not be afraid to stand up for truth. Teach them to love their country, to know that it has a spiritual foun-

---

[2]See Appendix III for text of full statement.

dation, that it has a prophetic history, that it is the Lord's base of operation.

Teach them that the Constitution of the United States was established by men whom God raised up for that very purpose, that it is not outmoded, that it is not an old-fashioned agrarian document, as some men in high places are calling it today.[3] Teach them to love the scriptures, especially the Book of Mormon.

Teach them to form an acquaintance with Nephi, Alma, and General Moroni. Teach them to know the power of prayer, that they can reach out and tap that unseen power, without which help no man can do his best. Teach them the need for spirituality, whether they are in the classroom or employed.

But above all, teach them to know that God lives, that Jesus is the Christ, the Savior and Redeemer of the world, that these two heavenly beings, our Father and our Savior Jesus Christ, did in very deed appear to the boy Prophet in the Sacred Grove. Teach them to know this, and it will be an anchor to them in all the days to come.

---

[3]In this day when the principles and traditions of our founding fathers have largely been forgotten or cast aside and the Constitution is literally "hanging by a thread," these words of Cicero, written a half-century before the birth of Christ, merit our reading and thinking about: "Thus, before our own time, the customs of our ancestors produced excellent men, and eminent men preserved our ancient customs and the institutions of their fore-fathers. But though the republic, when it came to us, was like a beautiful painting, whose colours, however, were already fading with age, our own time not only neglected to freshen it by renewing the original colours, but has not even taken the trouble to preserve its configuration and, so to speak, its general outlines. For what is now left of the 'ancient customs' on which . . . 'the commonwealth of Rome' was 'founded firm'? They have been, as we see, so completely buried in oblivion that they are not only no longer practised, but are already unknown. And what shall I say of the men? For the loss of our customs is due to our lack of men, and for this great evil we must not only give an account, but must even defend ourselves in every way possible, as if we were accused of capital crime. For it is through our own faults, not by any accident, that we retain only the form of the commonwealth, but have long since lost its substance. . . . " (Cicero, The Republic, V, 1-2)

CHAPTER 27

OUR IMMEDIATE RESPONSIBILITY [1]

"Be it remembered that liberty must at all hazards be supported. We have a right to it, derived from our Maker. But if we had not, our fathers have earned and bought it for us at the expense of their ease, their estates, their pleasure, and their blood. And liberty cannot be preserved without a general knowledge among the people, who have a right, from the frame of their nature, to knowledge, as their great Creator, who does nothing in vain, has given them understandings and a desire to know; but besides this, they have a right, an indisputable, unalienable, indefeasible, divine right to that most dreaded and envied kind of knowledge — I mean, of the characters and conduct of their rulers." (John Adams, 1765, *A Dissertation on the Canon and Feudal Law*)

President Wilkinson, distinguished members of the faculty, members and friends of this great student body, my brethren and sisters. This is a signal honor, a very great pleasure and a challenging responsibility. Humbly and gratefully I stand before you this morning. . . .

The message I bring is not a happy one, but it is the truth — and time is always on the side of truth. I take as my theme the words of President David O. McKay, God's mouthpiece on the earth today, a prophet of God:

> The position of this Church on the subject of Communism has never changed. We consider it the greatest Satanical threat to peace, prosperity and the spread of God's work among men that exists on the face of the earth. (*Conference Report*, April, 1966, p. 109.)

> No greater immediate responsibility rests upon members of the Church, upon all citizens of this Republic and of neighboring Republics than to protect the freedom vouchsafed by the Constitution of the United States. (*The Instructor*, August, 1953)

---

[1] An address delivered on October 25, 1966, to the student body of Brigham Young University, Provo, Utah.

In the days of the prophet Noah, men had no greater immediate responsibility than to repent and board the ark. Now in our day, the day of the Prophet David O. McKay, he has said that we have no greater immediate responsibility than to protect the freedom vouchsafed by the Constitution of the United States.

At the last general conference of the Church (October 1966), President McKay, in his opening address, said,

> Efforts are being made to deprive man of his free agency — to steal from the individual his liberty. . . . There has been an alarming increase in the abandoning of the ideals that constitute the foundation of the Constitution of the United States. (*Conference Report,* pp. 5-6.)

Toward the close of his talk, our Prophet, quoting Paul's letter to Timothy regarding the preaching of the word, said,

> There should be no question in the mind of any true Latter-day Saint as to what we shall preach . . . the gospel plan of salvation. (*Ibid.,* p. 6)

Then President McKay lists the areas our preaching should cover and admonishes us to include in our preaching what governments should or should not do in the interest of the preservation of our freedom.

Do we preach what governments should or should not do as a part of the gospel plan, as President McKay has urged, or do we refuse to follow the Prophet by preaching a limited gospel plan of salvation? *The fight for freedom cannot be divorced from the gospel — the plan of salvation.*

We sing that we are thankful to "God for a prophet to guide us in these latter days." By commandment of the Lord we assemble in general conference twice a year to get that guidance from the Lord's representative. Do we realize that in the last five years prior to October Conference, the Prophet has keynoted three of these conferences with an opening discourse on freedom and given nine other addresses in the conferences that touched on freedom?

Do we see any pattern here? Can we name any other gospel theme that has received as much emphasis from the man who holds the keys, as has the theme of freedom?

We do not need a prophet — we have one. What we need is a listening ear, a humble heart, and a soul that is pure enough to follow his inspired guidance.

Now why this consistent voice of warning from the Prophet?

Consider the following: Since World War II the communists have brought under bondage — enslaved — on the average approximately 6,000 persons per hour, 144,000 per day, 52,000,000 per year — every hour of every day of every year since 1945.

Since 1945 the communists have murdered in one country alone enough people to wipe out the entire population of over fifteen of our states.

The communist threat from without may be serious, but it is the enemy within, warns President McKay, that is most menacing.[2] (*P.P.N.S.*, p. 229)

President McKay has said that he would not deal with a nation that treats another as Russia has treated America. (*P.P.N.S.*, p. 235) Yet the tragedy is that one of the major reasons for the rapid growth of communism is because of the help — yes, the increasing help — which they are receiving from right within our own government.

Today our boys are dying in a war with the communists, a war which our government has not declared — the largest undeclared war in the history of the world — and one which it is alleged our government has no intention of winning. Yet

[2]"Timely references and appropriate warnings have been given from time to time on the danger and evils of war. There is another danger even more menacing than the threat of invasion of a foreign foe of any peace-loving nation. It is the unpatriotic activities and underhanded scheming of disloyal groups and organizations within any nation, bringing disintegration, that are often more dangerous and more fatal than outward oppostion. . . . It is the enemy from within that is most menacing, especially when it threatens to disintegrate established forms of good government." (President David O. McKay, *Conference Report*, Sept. 29, 1967, p. 9)

our government encourages us to buy communist goods and our government continues to give aid to the enemy.

One of the tragic results of prolonging the war in Vietnam is that it weakens our economy and gives excuses for more socialistic controls over our people. Of course, within the next few days there may be some dramatic moves made to placate and deceive the electorate as there was during the so-called Cuban missile crisis. But do not be misled.

President McKay has said that the Supreme Court is leading this nation down the road to atheism. (*P.P.N.S.,* p. 187) Not only is the court leading this nation down the road to atheism, but in one tragic decision after another they are leading us down the road to communism. One such decision caused Dorothy Healey, communist spokesman for the West Coast, to rejoice in these words, "This is the greatest victory the Communist Party ever had." The communists have held victory rallies to honor the Supreme Court and its decisions. The Book of Mormon tells us what corrupt judges can do to freedom.[3]

Communists dedicated to the destruction of our government are allowed to teach in our schools, to hold offices in labor unions, to run for public office. Recently an open and avowed leader of the Communist party in one of our states ran for a county office and received over 87,000 votes.

J. Edgar Hoover, the best-informed man in government on the socialist-communist conspiracy, stated:

> We must now face the harsh truth that the objectives of communism are being steadily advanced because many of us do not readily recognize the means used to advance them. . . . No one who truly understands what it really is can be taken in by it. Yet the individual is handicapped by coming face to face with a conspiracy so monstrous he cannot believe it exists. The American mind simply has not come to a realization of the evil which has been introduced into our midst. (J. Edgar Hoover, *The Elks Magazine,* August 1956; *P.P.N.S.,* p. 273)

---

[3]"And now behold, I say unto you, that the foundation of the destruction of this people is beginning to be laid by the unrighteousness of your lawyers and your judges." (Alma 10:27)

President McKay has said that this nation has "traveled far into the soul-destroying land of socialism." (*Church News,* October 18, 1952, p. 2) Now if we understand what socialism embraces, then we will realize that this present Congress has passed more socialistic legislation recommended by a president than probably any other Congress in the history of our Republic.

At this particular moment in history the United States is definitely threatened and every citizen should know about it. *The warning of this hour should resound through the corridors of every American institution — schools, churches, the halls of Congress, press, radio, and television, and so far as I am concerned, it will resound — with God's help.*[4]

One regrettable development is the increasing number of government programs embracing our youth. President J. Reuben Clark, Jr., former Under-secretary of State, foreign ambassador, a great constitutional statesman, and counselor to three Presidents of the Church, put it well when he said,

> Our government with its liberty and free institutions will not long survive a government trained and supervised youth. . . . Such a youth can be a revolutionary machine. (*Church News,* June 15, 1940; *P.P.N.S.,* p. 367)

And let me warn you, if these programs are fully introduced here in our midst, we will suffer the tragic consequences.

Some of these things strike pretty close to home. Communists or communist-fronters have appeared on our three major university campuses in this state. An identified communist performed in our Mormon Tabernacle. Some of our newspapers have carried columns with communist-front records in this state and in our country that should alarm us.

---

[4]"Let the pulpit resound with the doctrines and sentiments of religious liberty. Let us hear the danger of thraldom to our consciences from ignorance, extreme poverty, and dependence, in short, from civil and political slavery. Let us see delineated before us the true map of man. Let us hear the dignity of his nature, and the noble rank he holds among the works of God — that consenting to slavery is a sacrilegious breach of trust, as offensive in the sight of God as it is derogatory from our own honor or interest or happiness — and that God Almighty has promulgated from heaven, liberty, peace and goodwill to man!" (John Adams, 1765, *A Dissertation on the Canon and Feudal Law*)

One of the main thrusts of the communist drive in America today is through the so-called civil rights movement. Now there is nothing wrong with civil rights — it's what is being done in the name of civil rights that is shocking.

The man who is generally recognized as the leader of the so-called civil rights movement today in America is a man who has lectured at a communist training school, who has solicited funds through communist sources, who hired a communist as a top-level aide, who has affiliated with communist fronts, who is often praised in the communist press, and who unquestionably parallels the communist line. This same man advocates the breaking of the law and has been described by J. Edgar Hoover as "the most notorious liar in the country." (*U.S. News and World Report,* November 30, 1964.)

I warn you, *unless we wake up soon and do something about the conspiracy, the communist-inspired civil rights riots of the past will pale into insignificance compared to the bloodshed and destruction that lie ahead in the near future.*

Do not think the members of the Church shall escape. The Lord has assured us that the Church will still be here when he comes again. But has the Lord assured us that we can avoid fighting for freedom and still escape unscathed both temporally and spiritually? We could not escape the eternal consequences of our pre-existent position on freedom. What makes us think we can escape it here?

Listen to President Clark's grave warning:

> I say unto you with all the soberness I can, that we stand in danger of losing our liberties, and that once lost, only blood will bring them back; and once lost, we of this Church will, in order to keep the Church going forward, have more sacrifices to make and more persecutions to endure than we have yet known, heavy as our sacrifices and grievous as our persecutions of the past have been. (J. Reuben Clark, Jr., *Conference Report,* April 1944, pp. 115-116; *P.P.N.S.,* p. 89)

Now that is the price we are going to have to pay unless we can help to reverse the course our country is taking. The Lord does not want us to have to pay that price, but we will pay it in full if we fail to fight to preserve our freedom. Often the Lord has to send persecutions in order to rebuke and try to purge the unfaithful. He has done it in the past and he can do it again. If we deserve it, we will get it.

"Next to being one in worshiping God," says President McKay, "there is nothing in this world upon which this Church should be more united than in upholding and defending the Constitution of the United States!" (President David O. McKay, 1956, *The Instructor* 91:34; *P.P.N.S.,* p. 101)

There are some who would have us believe that the final test of the rightness of a course is whether everyone is united on it. But the Church does not seek unity simply for unity's sake. The unity for which the Lord prayed and of which President McKay speaks is the only unity which God honors — that is, "unity in righteousness," unity in principle.

We cannot compromise good with evil in an attempt to have peace and unity in the Church, any more than the Lord could have compromised with Satan in order to avoid the war in heaven.

Think of the impact for good we could have if we all united behind the Prophet in preserving our Constitution. Yet witness the sorry spectacle of those presently of our number who have repudiated the inspired counsel of our Prophet when he has opposed federal aid to education and asked support for the right-to-work laws. (*P.P.N.S.,* pp. 192, 415; *Church News,* June 26, 1965.)

It is too much to suppose that all the priesthood at this juncture will unite behind the Prophet in the fight for freedom. Yet we can pray for that day and in the meantime the faithful should strive to be in harmony with the inspired counsel given by the Lord's mouthpiece — the Prophet — and thus in unity with the Lord — and hence receive peace to their souls.

The more who are united with the Lord and his Prophet, the greater will be our chances to preserve our families and to live in freedom.

President Clark knew how righteous unity could stop the communists when he said:

> Now, what has business and industry done about all this revolutionary activity? . . . Business and industry neither planned nor did anything effective. There was no concerted effort. . . .
>
> A common cause with a united front would have worked salvation for us. But business officials were afraid of their stockholders and their outcry against loss of dividends; the lawyers were afraid of getting whipped in courts, businessmen felt strong vigorous action might further disturb business; bankers (I am a bank director) shivered at their own shadows.
>
> So one constitutional right after another yielded without any real contest, our backs getting nearer to the wall with each retreat. It is now proposed we retreat still further. Is not this suicide? Is there anyone so naive as to think that things will right themselves without a fight? There has been no more fight in us than there is in a bunch of sheep, and we have been much like sheep. Freedom was never brought to people on a silver platter, nor maintained with whisk brooms and lavender sprays.
>
> And do not think that all these usurpations, intimidations, and impositions are being done to us through inadvertence or mistake; the whole course is deliberately planned and carried out; its purpose is to destroy the Constitution and our constitutional government; then to bring chaos, out of which the new Statism with its slavery, is to arise, with a cruel, relentless, selfish, ambitious crew in the saddle, riding hard with whip and spur, a red-shrouded band of night riders for despotism. . . .
>
> If we do not vigorously fight for our liberties, we shall go clear through to the end of the road and become another Russia, or worse. . . . (J. Reuben Clark, Jr., *Church News,* Sept. 25, 1949; *P.P.N.S.,* pp. 327-328)

According to Norman Vincent Peale, "There was a time when the American people roared like lions for liberty; now they bleat like sheep for security."

"But," some say, "shouldn't we have confidence in our government officials — don't we owe them our allegiance?" To which we respond in the words of President Clark,

> God provided that in this land of liberty, our political allegiance shall run not to individuals, that is, to government officials . . . the only allegiance we owe as citizens or denizens of the United States, runs to our inspired Constitution which God Him-

self set up. (J. Reuben Clark, Jr., *The Improvement Era,* 1940, 43:444; *P.P.N.S.,* p. 198)

Jefferson warned that we should not talk about confidence in men but that we should inhibit their power through the Constitution.[5] In the meantime, we pray for our leaders as we have always been counseled to do.

It is the devil's desire that the Lord's priesthood stay asleep while the strings of tyranny gradually and quietly entangle us until, like Gulliver, we awake too late and find that while we could have broken each string separately as it was put upon us, our sleepiness permitted enough strings to bind us to make a rope that enslaves us.

For years we have heard of the role the elders could play in saving the Constitution from total destruction.[6] But how can the elders be expected to save it if they have not studied it and are not sure if it is being destroyed or what is destroying it?

An informed patriotic gentile was dumbfounded when he heard of Joseph Smith's reported prophecy regarding the mission our elders could perform in saving the Constitution.[7] He lived in a Mormon community with nice people who were busily engaged in other activities but who had little concern in preserving their freedom. He wondered if maybe a letter

---

[5]"It would be a dangerous delusion were a confidence in the men of our choice to silence our fears for the safety of our rights. . . . confidence is everywhere the parent of despotism — free government is founded in jealousy, and not in confidence; it is jealousy and not confidence which prescribes limited constitutions, to bind down those whom we are obliged to trust with power. . . . our Constitution has accordingly fixed the limits to which, and no further, our confidence may go. . . . In questions of power, then, let no more be heard of confidence in man, but bind him down from mischief by the chains of the Constitution." (Thomas Jefferson, Draft of Kentucky Resolutions of 1798; *Works* 9:470-471)

[6]"Our friends wish to know our feelings towards the Government. I answer, they are first-rate, and we will prove it too, as you will see if you only live long enough, for that we shall live to prove it is certain; and when the Constitution of the United States hangs, as it were, upon a single thread, they will have to call for the 'Mormon' Elders to save it from utter destruction; and they will step forth and do it." (President Brigham Young, 1855; *Journal of Discourses* 2:182)

[7]"Will the Constitution be destroyed? No; it will be held inviolate by this people; and, as Joseph Smith said, 'the time will come when the destiny of the nation will hang upon a single thread. At this critical juncture, this people will step forth and save it from the threatened destruction!" (President Brigham Young, 1854; *Journal of Discourses* 7:15)

should not be sent to President McKay, urging him to release some of the elders from their present Church activities so there would be a few who could help step foward to save the Constitution.

Now it is not so much a case of a man giving up all his other duties to fight for freedom as it is a case of a man getting his life in balance so he can discharge all of his God-given responsibilities. And of all these responsibilities, President Mc-Kay has said that we have "no greater immediate responsibility" than "to protect the freedom vouchsafed by the Constitution of the United States."

There is no excuse that can compensate for the loss of liberty.

Satan is anxious to neutralize the inspired counsel of the Prophet and hence keep the priesthood off balance, ineffective and inert in the fight for freedom. He does this through diverse means, including the use of perverse reasoning.

For example, he will argue, "There is no need to get involved in the fight for freedom — all you need to do is live the gospel." Of course this is a contradiction, because we cannot fully live the gospel and not be involved in the fight for freedom.

We would not say to someone, "There is no need to be baptized — all you need to do is live the gospel." That would be ridiculous because baptism is a part of the gospel.

How would you have reacted if during the war in heaven someone had said to you, "Look, just do what's right, there is no need to get involved in the fight for free agency." It is obvious what the devil is trying to do, but it is sad to see many of us fall for his destructive line.

The cause of freedom is a most basic part of our religion. Our position on freedom helped get us to this earth and it can make the difference as to whether we get back home or not.

General Moroni, one of the great men of the Book of Mormon, raised the "title of liberty" and on it he inscribed these words:

> In memory of our God, our religion, and freedom, and our peace, our wives, and our children. . . . (Alma 46:12)

Why didn't he write upon it "Just live your religion, there is no need to concern yourselves about your freedom, your peace, your wives or your children?" The reason he didn't was because all of these things were a part of his religion, as they are of ours.

Listen to what the Book of Mormon has to say of the man who raised the "title of liberty":

> And Moroni was a strong and a mighty man; he was a man of a perfect understanding; yea, a man that did not delight in bloodshed; a man whose soul did joy in the liberty and the freedom of his country, and his brethren from bondage and slavery;
>
> Yea, and he was a man who was firm in the faith of Christ, and he had sworn with an oath to defend his people, his rights, and his country, and his religion, even to the loss of his blood. (Alma 48:11, 13)
>
> Yea, verily, verily I say unto you, if all men had been, and were, and ever would be, like unto Moroni, behold, the very powers of hell would have shaken forever; yea, the devil would never have power over the hearts of the children of men. (Alma 48:17)

Now part of the reason why we do not have sufficient priesthood bearers to save the Constitution, let alone to shake the powers of hell, is, I fear, because unlike Moroni, our souls do not joy in keeping our country free and we are not firm in the faith of Christ, nor have we sworn with an oath to defend our rights.

The Book of Mormon also tells us of some of the perverse reasoning the devil will use in our day to keep the saints ignorant, complacent and asleep.

> And others will he pacify, and lull them away into carnal security, that they will say: All is well in Zion; yea, Zion prospereth; all is well — and thus the devil cheateth their souls, and leadeth them away carefully down to hell. (2 Nephi 28:21)

Now this reasoning takes several forms. For instance, "Don't worry," say some, "the Lord will take care of us." This is the usual theme of those who believe in faith without works.

Brigham Young said:

> Some may say, "I have faith the Lord will turn them away."
> What ground have we to hope this? Have I any good reason to say
> to my Father in Heaven, "Fight my battles," when He has given
> me the sword to wield, the arm and the brain that I can fight for
> myself? Can I ask Him to fight my battles and sit quietly down
> waiting for Him to do so? I cannot. I can pray the people to
> hearken to wisdom, to listen to counsel; but to ask God to do for
> me that which I can do for myself is preposterous to my mind.
> (*Journal of Discourses* 12:241)

"Don't you have faith in America?" say others. But
America is made up of people — and only righteous, patriotic
people work to preserve their freedom. The American people's
blessings are conditioned on righteousness and nothing else.
We have faith in a faithful citizenry.

"There is no need to learn about communism in order to
avoid it," some argue. But this counsel can help keep our
people in ignorance and apparently flies in the face of the
inspired counsel of President McKay who said: "I believe that
only through a truly educated citizenry can the ideals that
inspired the Founding Fathers of our nation be preserved and
perpetuated." (*Church News,* March 13, 1954; *P.P.N.S.,*
p. 178)

And then President McKay said that one of the "four
fundamental elements in such an education" was the "open
and forcible teaching of facts regarding communism as an
enemy to God and to individual freedom." (*P.P.N.S.,* p. 181)

Do we teach people to avoid alcohol and tobacco by
pointing out its evil effects? Of course we do. Should we then
avoid telling people about the evil nature and devious designs
of communism — the greatest satanical threat to the spread
of God's work?

"Just preach the gospel — that will stop communism,"
is another neutralizing argument used by some. Did teaching
the truth stop the war in heaven or convert Satan and his
hosts? Satan himself, through his earthly followers, is directing
the communist conspiracy and as President Clark said, "You

cannot mollify an unconvertible." (J. Reuben Clark, *Conference Report*, October 1959, p. 46; *P.P.N.S.*, p. 232)

As members of the Church, we have some close quarters to pass through if we are to save our souls. As the Church gets larger, some men have increasing responsibility and more and more duties must be delegated. We all have stewardships for which we must account to the Lord.

Unfortunately some men who do not honor their stewardship may have an adverse effect on many people. Often the greater the man's responsibility the more good or evil he can accomplish. The Lord usually gives a man a long enough rope and sufficient time to determine whether that man wants to pull himself into the presence of God or drop off somewhere below.

There are some regrettable things being said and done by some people in the Church today. As President Clark so well warned, "The ravening wolves are amongst us, from our own membership, and they, more than any others, are clothed in sheep's clothing because they wear the habiliments of the priesthood. . . . We should be careful of them." (*Conference Report*, April 1949, p. 163)

Sometimes from behind the pulpit, in our classrooms, in our council meetings, and in our Church publications, we hear, read or witness things that do not square with the truth. This is especially true where freedom is involved. Now do not let this serve as an excuse for your own wrongdoing. *The Lord is letting the wheat and the tares mature before he fully purges the Church. He is also testing you to see if you will be misled. The devil is trying to deceive the very elect.*

Let me give you a crucial key to help you avoid being deceived. It is this — learn to keep your eye on the Prophet. He is the Lord's mouthpiece and the only man who can speak for the Lord today. Let his inspired counsel take precedence. Let his inspired words be a basis for evaluating the counsel of all lesser authorities. Then live close to the Spirit so you may know the truth of all things.

All men are entitled to inspiration, but only one man is the Lord's mouthpiece. Some lesser men have in the past, and will in the future, use their office unrighteously. Some will use it to lead the unwary astray; some will use it to persuade us that all is well in Zion; some will use it to cover and excuse their ignorance. Keep your eye on the Prophet — for the Lord will never permit his Prophet to lead this Church astray.

This is the word of the Lord to us today regarding the president of the Church.

> Wherefore, meaning the church, thou shalt give heed unto all his words and commandments which he shall give unto you as he receiveth them, walking in all holiness before me;
>
> For his word ye shall receive, as if from mine own mouth, in all patience and faith. (D&C 21:4-5)

At our last annual conference in April, President McKay issued a statement on communism. It was printed on the editorial page of the June *Improvement Era* and has recently been reprinted by the Deseret Book Company in an attractive folder entitled "Communism: A statement of the position of The Church of Jesus Christ of Latter-day Saints." Every student and every family in America should have a copy. The cost is five cents in lots of 100, or three for 25 cents.

Let me quote a few excerpts from that inspired statement — and you who have been misled into believing that you can somehow righteously avoid standing up for freedom, heed his counsel:

> In order that there may be no misunderstanding by bishops, stake presidents, and others regarding members of the Church participating in nonchurch meetings to study and become informed on the Constitution of the United States, Communism, etc., I wish [said President McKay] to make the following statements that I have been sending out from my office for some time and that have come under question by some stake authorities, bishoprics, and others.
>
> Church members are at perfect liberty to act according to their own conscience in the matter of safeguarding our way of life. They are, of course, encouraged to honor the highest standards of the gospel and to work to preserve their own freedoms. They are free to participate in nonchurch meetings that are held to warn

people of the threat of Communism or any other theory or principle that will deprive us of our free agency or individual liberties vouchsafed by the Constitution of the United States.

The position of this Church on the subject of Communism has never changed. We consider it the greatest satanical threat to peace, prosperity, and the spread of God's work among men that exists on the face of the earth.

In this connection [President McKay continues], we are continually being asked to give our opinion concerning various patriotic groups or individuals who are fighting Communism and speaking up for freedom. Our immediate concern, however, is not with parties, groups, or persons, but with principles. We therefore commend and encourage every person and every group who is sincerely seeking to study Constitutional principles and awaken a sleeping and apathetic people to the alarming conditions that are rapidly advancing about us. We wish all of our citizens throughout the land were participating in some type of organized self-education in order that they could better appreciate what is happening and know what they can do about it.

Supporting the FBI, the police, the congressional committees investigating Communism, and various organizations that are attempting to awaken the people through educational means is a policy we warmly endorse for all our people. . . . (President David O. McKay, *The Improvement Era*, June 1966, p. 477; *Conference Report,* April 1966, p. 109)

I bear witness that this Church position given by our inspired leader — our Prophet-leader — is sound, timely and clear. The need for such counsel has never been greater.

Brethren and sisters, I have talked straight to you, today. I know I will be abused by some for what I have said, but I want my skirts to be clean.

"Watchman, what of the night?" (Isaiah 21:11) is the cry of the faithful. I have tried to warn you of the darkness that is moving over us and what we can do about it if we will only follow the Prophet.

Have you counted the cost if our countrymen, and especially the body of the priesthood, continue to remain complacent, misled through some of our news media, deceived by some of our officials, and perverted by some of our educators?

Are you prepared to see some of your loved ones murdered, your remaining liberties abridged, the Church persecuted, and your eternal reward jeopardized?

I have personally witnessed the heart-rending results of the loss of freedom. I have seen it with my own eyes. I have been close to the godless evil of the socialist-communist conspiracy on both sides of the iron curtain, particularly during my years as European Mission President at the close of the war, and today and also during my eight years in the cabinet.
. . .

I have talked face-to-face with the godless communist leaders. It may surprise you to learn that I was host to Mr. Khrushchev for a half day when he visited the United States. Not that I'm proud of it — I opposed his coming then and I still feel it was a mistake to welcome this atheistic murderer as a state visitor. But according to President Eisenhower, Khrushchev had expressed a desire to learn something of American agriculture, and after seeing Russian agriculture I can understand why.

As we talked face-to-face, he indicated that my grandchildren would live under communism. After assuring him that I expected to do all in my power to assure that his and all other grandchildren will live under freedom, he arrogantly declared in substance:

> You Americans are so gullible. No, you won't accept communism outright, but we'll keep feeding you small doses of socialism until you'll finally wake up and find you already have communism. We won't have to fight you. We'll so weaken your economy until you'll fall like over-ripe fruit into our hands.

And they are ahead of schedule in their devilish scheme.

I stood in Czechoslovakia in 1946 — two citizens of that country came up to me before this meeting — I stood in Czechoslovakia in 1946 and witnessed the ebbing away of freedom resulting in the total loss of liberty to a wonderful people. I visited among the liberty-loving Polish people and talked with their leaders as the insidious freedom-destroying conspiracy moved in, imposing the chains of bondage on a Christian nation.

In both of these freedom-loving nations were members of the Church, striving, as we are, to live the gospel. But did they stop the communists? Although their numbers were relatively few, the danger to freedom seemed to be far away. Now there are, no doubt, Mormons in communist slave-labor camps.

But here in America, the Lord's base of operations — so designated by the Lord himself through his holy prophets — we of the priesthood, members of his restored Church, might well provide the balance of power to save our freedom. Indeed we might, if we go forward as General Moroni of old, and raise the standard of liberty throughout the land.

My brethren, we CAN do the job that must be done. We can, as a priesthood, provide the balance of power to preserve our freedom and save this nation from bondage.

The Prophet Joseph Smith is reported to have prophesied the role the priesthood might play to save our inspired Constitution. Now is the time to move forward courageously — to become alerted, informed and active. We are not just ordinary men. We bear the priesthood and authority of God. We understand the world and God's divine purpose as no other men.

The gospel and its preaching can prosper only in an atmosphere of freedom. And now, in this critical period when many pulpits are being turned into pipelines of collectivist propaganda — preaching the social gospel and denying basic principles of salvation — is the time for action.

We know, as do no other people, that the Constitution of the United States is inspired — established by men whom the Lord raised up for that very purpose. We cannot — we must not — shirk our sacred responsibility to rise up in defense of our God-given freedom.[8]

___
[8]"It is your business to rise up and preserve the Union and liberty, for yourselves, and not for me. . . . I appeal to you again to constantly bear in mind that with you, and not with politicians, not with Presidents, not with office-seekers, but with you, is the question, 'Shall the Union and shall the liberties of this country be preserved to the latest generation?' " (Abraham Lincoln, Feb. 11, 1861; *Collected Works* 4:194)

In our day the Lord has declared to his Church:

> Verily I say unto you all: Arise and shine forth, that thy light may be a standard for the nations;
>
> And that the gathering together upon the land of Zion, and upon her stakes, may be for a defense, and for a refuge from the storm, and from wrath when it shall be poured out without mixture upon the whole earth. (D&C 115:5-6)

Will we of the priesthood "arise and shine"? Will we provide the "defense" and "refuge"? Now is our time and season for corrective and courageous action.

We have been warned again and again and again. The Lord's spokesman has consistently raised his voice of warning about the loss of our freedom. He that has ears, let him hear, and you who praise the Lord, learn to also follow his spokesman.

I know not what course others may take, but as for me and my house, we will strive to walk with the Prophet. And the Prophet has said that:

> No greater immediate responsibility rests upon members of the Church, upon all citizens of this Republic and of neighboring Republics than to protect the freedom vouchsafed by the Constitution of the United States. (*The Instructor,* August 1953)

In this mighty struggle each of you has a part. Be on the right side. Stand up and be counted. If you get discouraged, remember the words of Edward Everett Hale, when he said:

> I am only one, but I am one.
> I can't do everything, but I can do something.
> What I can do, that I ought to do,
> And what I ought to do,
> By the grace of God, I shall do!

God bless us to heed the oft-repeated counsel of our Prophet-leader.

CHAPTER 28

PROTECTING FREEDOM — AN URGENT DUTY[1]

"The first object of a free people is the preservation of their liberty. . . . The spirit of liberty is, indeed, a bold and fearless spirit; but it is also a sharp-sighted spirit; it is a cautious, sagacious, discriminating, far-seeing intelligence; it is jealous of encroachment, jealous of power, jealous of men. It demands checks; it seeks for guards; it insists on securities; it intrenches itself behind strong defences, and fortifies itself with all possible care against the assaults of ambition and passion. It does not trust the amiable weaknesses of human nature, and therefore it will not permit power to overstep its prescribed limits, though benevolence, good intent, and patriotic purpose come along with it." (Daniel Webster, May 7, 1834; *Works* 4:122)

Humbly and gratefully I take as my theme for these brief remarks the following words from the inspiring opening address by President David O. McKay at the Friday morning session of this great conference.

Efforts are being made to deprive man of his free agency, to steal from the individual his liberty. . . . There has been an alarming increase in the abandoning of the ideals that constitute the foundation of the Constitution of the United States. . . .

I therefore speak on the subject: "Protecting Freedom — An Urgent Duty."

The Church of Jesus Christ of Latter-day Saints proclaims that life is eternal, that it has purpose. We believe we lived as intelligent beings in a world of progress before this mortal life. Our life on this earth is a probation, a testing per-

---

[1]Address delivered on October 2, 1966, at the general conference of The Church of Jesus Christ of Latter-day Saints, Salt Lake City, Utah.

iod, an opportunity for growth and experience in a physical world. It is all part of the plan of our Heavenly Father for the benefit and blessing of us, his children.

This is to be done through a great and all-wise plan — the gospel of Jesus Christ. This master plan, if lived, will build men of character, men of strength, men of deep spirituality, godlike men.

Basic to this all-important plan is our free agency, the right of choice. Free agency is an eternal principle. We enjoyed freedom of choice in the spirit world as spirit children. In fact, a counterplan to the gospel of our Lord was presented by Lucifer, a plan of force that would have robbed man of his freedom of choice. Lucifer's plan was rejected, and the scriptures tell us that he, with one-third of the hosts of heaven, was cast out; and they continue their opposition to God's plan, which is based on the freedom of the individual.

The scriptures make clear that there was a great war in heaven, a struggle over the principle of freedom, the right of choice. (See Moses 5:1-4; D&C 29:36-38; 76:25-27; Rev. 12:7-9)

History, both sacred and secular, clearly records that the struggle to preserve freedom has been a continuous one. Prophets of God, as watchmen on the towers, have proclaimed liberty. Holy men of God have led the fight against anarchy and tyranny. Moses was commanded to "proclaim liberty throughout all the land unto all the inhabitants thereof." (Lev. 25:10)

Why have prophets of God been commanded to proclaim liberty and lead the battle to preserve freedom? Because freedom is basic to the great plan of the Lord. The gospel can prosper only in an atmosphere of freedom. This fact is confirmed by history, as well as by sacred scriptures. The right of choice — free agency — runs like a golden thread throughout the gospel plan of the Lord for the blessing of his children.

To a modern-day prophet the Lord declared that "it is not right that any man should be in bondage one to another."

In a revelation to the restored Church in 1833 the Lord declared:

> . . . That law of the land which is constitutional, supporting that principle of freedom in maintaining rights and privileges, belongs to all mankind, and is justifiable before me.
>
> I, the Lord God, make you free, therefore ye are free indeed; and the law also maketh you free.
>
> Nevertheless, when the wicked rule the people mourn.
>
> Wherefore, honest men and wise men should be sought for diligently, and good men and wise men ye should observe to uphold; otherwise whatsoever is less than these cometh of evil. (D&C 98:5, 8-10)

A year ago in a great general conference address on freedom and how it is threatened today, our beloved President warned us, saying,

> I do not know that there was ever a time in the history of mankind when the Evil One seemed so determined to take from man his freedom.

He went on to explain that "pernicious efforts and sinister schemes are cunningly and stealthily being fostered to deprive man of his individual freedom and have him revert to the life of the jungle." (*Conference Report,* October 1965, pp. 7, 11)

Still earlier the First Presidency warned the saints that

> Satan is making war against all the wisdom that has come to men through their ages of experience. He is seeking to overturn and destroy the very foundations upon which society, government, and religion rest. He aims to have men adopt theories and practices which he induced their forefathers, over the ages, to adopt and try, only to be discarded by them when found unsound, impractical and ruinous. He plans to destroy liberty and freedom — economic, political, and religious, and to set up in place thereof the greatest, most widespread, and most complete tyranny that has ever oppressed man. He is working under such perfect disguise that many do not recognize either him or his methods. . . . Without their knowing it, the people are being urged down paths that lead only to destruction. Satan never before had so firm a grip on this generation as he has now. ("Message of the First Presidency," *Conference Report,* October 1942, p. 13)

In spite of the scriptural evidence and the counsel of modern-day prophets during the past more than a hundred years, there are still some who seem to feel we have no responsibility to safeguard and strengthen our precious God-given freedom. There are some who apparently feel that the fight for freedom is separate from the gospel. They express it in several ways, but it generally boils down to this: Just live the gospel; there's no need to get involved in trying to save freedom and the Constitution or to stop communism.

Of course, this is dangerous reasoning, because in reality you cannot fully live the gospel without working to save freedom and the Constitution, and to stop communism. . . .

Should we counsel people, "Just live your religion — there's no need to get involved in the fight for freedom"? No, we should not, because our stand for freedom is a most basic part of our religion; this stand helped get us to this earth, and our reaction to freedom in this life will have eternal consequences. Man has many duties, but he has no excuse that can compensate for his loss of liberty.[2]

As members of the Church we have some close quarters to pass through if we are going to get home safely. We will be given a chance to choose between conflicting counsel given by some. That's why we must learn — and the sooner we learn, the better — to keep our eye on the Prophet, the President of the Church. And that Prophet today is President David O. McKay.

On the day the Church was organized, the Lord gave a revelation, too often overlooked, that he expects members of the Church to "give heed unto all his words and commandments which [the Prophet and President] shall give unto you

---

[2]"What constitutes the bulwark of our own liberty and independence? It is not our frowning battlements, our bristling sea coasts, the guns of our war steamers, or the strength of our gallant and disciplined army. These are not our reliance against a resumption of tyranny in our fair land. All of them may be turned against our liberties, without making us stronger or weaker for the struggle. Our reliance is in the *love of liberty* which God has planted in our bosoms. Our defense is in the preservation of the spirit which prizes liberty as the heritage of all men, in all lands, everywhere. Destroy this spirit, and you have planted the seeds of despotism around your own doors." (Abraham Lincoln, Sept. 11, 1858; *Collected Works* 3:95)

as he receiveth them, walking in all holiness before me; For his word ye shall receive, as if from mine own mouth, in all patience and faith." (D&C 21:4-5)

All men are entitled to inspiration, especially men who bear the priesthood, but only one man is the Lord's mouthpiece. Some lesser men have used in the past, and will use in the future, their offices unrighteously. Some will, ignorantly or otherwise, use their office to promote false counsel; some will use it to lead the unwary astray; some will use it to persuade us that all is well in Zion; some will use it to cover and excuse their ignorance. Keep your eye on the Prophet, for the Lord will never permit his Prophet to lead this Church astray. Let us live close to the Spirit, so we can test all counsel. . . .

Today our Prophet and President has said: "No greater immediate responsibility rests upon members of the Church, upon all citizens of this Republic and of neighboring Republics than to protect the freedom vouchsafed by the Constitution of the United States."[3] Is this plain enough? In view of this solemn warning, how can any member of the Church fail to act to help save our freedom? We must not be lulled away into a false security.

We have a Prophet today. What we need is a listening ear. Let us live the gospel in its fulness, and by so doing we will work unceasingly to preserve and strengthen our God-given freedom.[4]

I bear witness that David O. McKay is a prophet of God —I know it as I know that I live — and that through him the Lord reveals his will for each of us, our families and the kingdom of God on earth. God grant we may heed his inspired counsel, I humbly pray.

---

[3]"The citizens of the United States have peculiar motives to support the energy of their constitutional charters. . . . Being republicans, they must be anxious to establish the efficacy of popular charters in defending liberty against power, and power against licentiousness, and in keeping every portion of power within its proper limits. . . . " (James Madison, 1792; *Works* 4:468)

[4]"The last hope of human liberty in this world rests on us. We ought, for so dear a state, to sacrifice every attachment and every enmity." (Thomas Jefferson, To Colonel William Duane, March 28, 1811; *Works* 5:577)

CHAPTER 29

THE BOOK OF MORMON WARNS AMERICA[1]

". . . there were exceeding many prophets among us.
And the people were a stiffnecked people, hard to understand. And there was nothing save it was exceeding harsh-
ness, preaching and prophesying of wars, and contentions,
and destructions, and continually reminding them of death,
and the duration of eternity, and the judgments and the
power of God, and all these things —- stirring them up continually to keep them in the fear of the Lord. I say *there was
nothing short of these things, and exceeding great plainness
of speech, would keep them from going down speedily to
destruction.*" (The Book of Enos in the Book of Mormon,
verses 22-23)

The Eighth Article of Faith of The Church of Jesus
Christ of Latter-day Saints reads as follows: "We believe the
Bible to be the word of God as far as it is translated correctly;
we also believe the Book of Mormon to be the word of God."

It is because of our belief in the Book of Mormon, along
with the Bible, that we were nicknamed "Mormons."

On a spring day in the year 1820 in the State of New
York a young boy by the name of Joseph Smith went into a
grove of trees on his father's farm to pray. He needed help.
He wanted to join a church but he was confused as to which
one. Seeking an answer he read one day these words from the
Bible: "If any of you lack wisdom, let him ask of God that
giveth to all men liberally, and upbraideth not; and it shall
be given him." (James 1:5)

This Joseph Smith did. In response to his prayer our
Heavenly Father and his Son Jesus Christ appeared to him.
Joseph was told to join none of the churches.

---

[1]Address delivered on May 21, 1968, to the student body of Brigham Young
University, Provo, Utah.

Joseph was to learn that Christ established the Church in former days when he was here on earth. Its members were called saints, but because of the wickedness of men the prophets were taken away from the people and so revelation ceased, the scripture ended and the doctrines and creeds of uninspired men prevailed. As predicted in the scriptures, there was an apostasy.

But, as had also been predicted, the Lord was planning to restore his Church in these latter days prior to his second coming, and like the former-day Church, his restored Church was to have apostles and prophets and have new revelation and added scripture. And so through Joseph Smith the Lord established The Church of Jesus Christ of Latter-day Saints.

On the evening of September 21, 1823, an angel appeared to the Prophet Joseph Smith. The angel's name was Moroni. He was the last of a long line of ancient prophets of two great civilizations who lived here on the American continent centuries ago. The angel told Joseph Smith that a history of these early inhabitants of America was written on metallic plates and lay buried in a hill nearby.

These records covered a period of American history from the time of the Tower of Babel until about A.D. 421. Part of these cumulative records engraved and handed down from generation to generation were abridged by Moroni's father, Mormon. Moroni added some additional writings and then laid the records in the earth where they remained until he delivered them to Joseph Smith. Under the inspiration of God, Joseph Smith translated part of these records and this is known today as the Book of Mormon.

Besides Joseph Smith there were other witnesses who saw the angel and the plates and whose written testimony you will find printed in the front of each copy of the Book of Mormon.

As the Bible is a scriptural account of God's dealings with his children in the Old World, so also is the Book of Mormon a scriptural account of God's dealings with his children in the Americas.

The Book of Mormon is a second witness along with the Bible that Jesus is the Christ. It testifies of Christ's appearance to the American inhabitants shortly after his resurrection in Jerusalem. It makes plain many of the precious truths of the Gospel.

The Prophet Joseph Smith said that "the Book of Mormon was the most correct of any book on earth, and the keystone of our religion, and a man would get nearer to God by abiding by its precepts than by any other book." (*Teachings of the Prophet Joseph Smith*, p. 194)

The last chapter of the Book of Mormon contains the promise that if a person will read the book he may then ask God, the Eternal Father, in the name of Christ if the book is not true, and if he will ask with a sincere heart, with real intent, having faith in Christ, God will manifest the truth of it unto him by the power of the Holy Ghost. (Moroni 10:3-7) (We invite all men to make this test.)

One of the great themes of the Book of Mormon is that America is a land of promise — a chosen land. "Behold, this is a choice land, and whatsoever nation shall possess it shall be free from bondage, and from captivity, and from all other nations under heaven, if they will but serve the God of the land, who is Jesus Christ. . . ." (Ether 2:12)

The Book of Mormon records the rise and fall of two great civilizations. They fell because they failed to serve the God of the land, Jesus Christ. The American Indians are the descendants of that last great civilization.

Fortunately, under the inspiration of the Lord, many of the Book of Mormon prophets realized that the historical account which they were making of their people would eventually come forth in this day and age while our own great civilization was flourishing here in America.

These prophets were anxious to see that the tragedies that befell their ancient American civilizations would not happen to us. It would be well for us to seriously consider their warnings.

They record that both of their great civilizations were destroyed through the insidious work of a murderous, secret conspiracy whose designs were to get power and gain and to overthrow the freedom of all lands. And then, realizing that in our time we would be threatened with a similar conspiracy, the Book of Mormon warns as follows:

> Wherefore . . . it is wisdom in God that these things should be shown unto you, that thereby ye may repent of your sins, and suffer not that these murderous combinations shall get above you, which are built up to get power and gain — and the work, yea, even the work of destruction come upon you, yea, even the sword of the justice of the Eternal God shall fall upon you, to your overthrow and destruction if ye shall suffer these things to be.
>
> Wherefore, the Lord commandeth you, when ye shall see these things come among you that ye shall awake to a sense of your awful situation, because of this secret combination which shall be among you. . . .
>
> For it cometh to pass that whoso buildeth it up seeketh to overthrow the freedom of all lands, nations, and countries; . . . for it is built up by the devil; . . . (Ether 8:23-25)[2]

Today, the international, criminal, communist conspiracy fits this Book of Mormon description perfectly, for there is a combination of gangsters who lust for power, who have liquidated some 70 million people, brought one-third of the world's population under bondage and who seek to overthrow the freedom of all nations.[3] I have talked face to face to some of these godless leaders, on both sides of the iron curtain.

---

[2]"For behind the concrete forces of revolution . . . beyond that invisible secret circle which perhaps directs them all, is there not yet another force, still more potent, that must be taken into account? In looking back over the centuries at the dark episodes that have marked the history of the human race from its earliest origins — strange and horrible cults, waves of witchcraft, blasphemies, and desecrations — how is it possible to ignore the existence of an Occult Power at work in the world? Individuals, sects, or races bred with the desire of world-domination, have provided the fighting forces of destruction, but behind them are the veritable powers of darkness in eternal conflict with the powers of light." (Nesta H. Webster, 1924, *Secret Societies and Subversive Movements*, pp. 405-406)

[3]"It is the common fate of the indolent, to see their rights made a prey by the active. The condition upon which God has given liberty to man is eternal vigilance; which condition if he break, servitude is at once the consequence of his crime, and the punishment of his guilt." (John Philpot Curran, July 10, 1790; *Great Quotations*, p. 586)

President David O. McKay, whom we sustain as a latter-day Prophet and as President of The Church of Jesus Christ of Latter-day Saints, has said: "The position of this Church on the subject of communism has never changed. We consider it the greatest satanical threat to peace, prosperity, and the spread of God's work among men that exists on the face of the earth."[4]

And then, as the Lord commands us in the Book of Mormon to awake to a sense of our awful situation, so President McKay commends and encourages those who are seeking to "awaken a sleeping and apathetic people to the alarming conditions that are rapidly advancing about us." Then President McKay adds: "We wish all of our citizens throughout the land were participating in some type of organized self-education in order that they could better appreciate what is happening and know what they can do about it." (Talk by President David O. McKay, general priesthood session of conference, April, 1966)

The Book of Mormon points out how these ancient conspirators were able to fill the judgment seats, usurp power, destroy justice, condemn the righteous and let the guilty and the wicked go unpunished. Do you see any parallel between this and the present-day decisions of our Supreme Court?

President McKay has stated that the Supreme Court is leading this Christian nation down the road to atheism. *I believe the Court is also leading us down the road to anarchy and atheistic communism.* Here is the net effect of a few of their decisions:

Communists can work in our defense plants.
Communists can teach in our schools.
Communists can hold offices in labor unions.
Communists can run for public offices.
Communists can serve in the merchant marines.[5]

---

[4]"The advice nearest to my heart and deepest in my convictions is, that the Union of the States be cherished and perpetuated. Let the open enemy to it be regarded as a Pandora with her box opened, and the disguised one as the serpent creeping with his deadly wiles into Paradise." (James Madison, "Advice to My Country"; *Works* 4:439)

[5]See *A Memorandum On Supreme Court Decisions* by G. Edward Griffin. (Published by American Opinion, Belmont, Massachusetts, 02178)

Today by court edict a person is allowed to advocate and convince others of the duty and necessity to overthrow the government by force and violence.

The Supreme Court justices would probably have been accused of treason if they had dealt in this manner with the Nazis during World War II. Yet how does one explain the court's attitude towards the communist conspiracy which is a much greater threat than the Nazis ever were. Perhaps you can understand why the communists have held victory rallies to honor the Supreme Court and its decisions.

I have not even covered the areas of how the court is hamstringing the police, destroying property rights, encouraging civil disobedience, undermining state sovereignty, etc.[6]

And now I come to a passage in the Book of Mormon which gives me great concern about the future of our country because of the way we are helping the communists. The passage reads as follows:

> And whatsoever nation shall uphold such secret combinations, to get power and gain, until they shall spread over the nation, behold, they shall be destroyed. . . . (Ether 8:22)

And so the crucial question is, "Has our nation upheld communism so that it could get power and gain?" And the tragic answer is, "Yes." And so, *unless we as a people can soon stop and reverse the disastrous course we are taking, then our nation shall be destroyed. For the sad truth is that communism would be insignificant in our country and the world today were it not for the consistent and persistent help which it is continuing to receive from right within our own government.*

Returning a few days ago from a month in Europe and the Middle East I found in my accumulated mail an advance

---

[6]"This member of the government [Supreme Court] was at first considered as the most harmless and helpless of all its organs. But it has proved that the power of declaring what the law is, ad libitum, by sapping and mining, slily, and without alarm, the foundations of the constitution, can do what open force would not dare to attempt. . . . Experience has proved that impeachment in our forms is completely inefficient." (Thomas Jefferson, To Edward Livingston, March 25, 1825; *Works* 7:404)

copy of a courageous, hard-hitting, truthful magazine — a rare thing today — and one not carried by the liberal news agencies on our newsstands. On the title page the fearless young managing editor, Scott Stanley, Jr., had this in his letter to the readers:

> Dear Reader:
>
> We write in the wake of burning and looting in 168 American cities, at a time when we are at war in Vietnam and our own government is sending raw materials to the arsenal of an enemy killing our soldiers in the field. We write in the midst of an economic crisis described by the Chairman of the Federal Reserve Board as the most serious since the Depression year of 1931. And, as we write, a leading candidate for the Presidency of the United States has called for openly paying blackmail to the Communists, and for the resignation of J. Edgar Hoover, the anti-Communist Director of the F.B.I.
>
> It is a time when black Marxists call for burning down America, and make a good try at it, and every Presidential candidate — save one — recommends buying off those burning our cities with more of the federal subsidies which are enlarging the inflationary debt about to destroy our entire economy. It is a day in which men who have been chairmen of officially cited Communist Fronts sit even in the Cabinet of the President of the United States and protect the revolutionaries, promote Marxist schemes, and drive America's back ever closer to the wall. (*American Opinion Magazine,* June 1968)

From his letter transmitting the June Issue I read the last paragraph:

> The Constitution surely hangs by a thread. Without God's help this republic will fall as certain as it was with His help that it was born.[7]

From the lead article, which I recommend to all, entitled "Insurrection — Is America Sleeping Through Civil War?", I quote from the first page:

---

[7]"Just as a builder must have a plan on his paper in order to build wisely and well, so must a people have a Constitution in order to guide them. But we have abandoned our plan and our map so painfully wrought by our fathers. Hence, we have dictators, men who lust for centralized power in order to oppress us." (Cicero, quoted in *A Pillar of Iron,* p. 338)

America has just endured the most widespread civil uprising in a hundred years — except for the Civil War, the largest in American history. . . .

Arrests totaled well over twenty thousand. Washington, D.C., reported more than a thousand fires set by arsonists. Baltimore between seven and eight hundred, Pittsburgh five hundred, two hundred in Chicago and so on. . . .

The federal government was itself effectively shut down on Friday afternoon, April fourth, as word of unchecked, marauding mobs ranging freely in the downtown. . . .

All over the world, sophisticated people must have laughed at us uproariously, and a hundred million no doubt lost any faith they ever had in us.

The author, Dr. Susan L. M. Huck, concludes the 25-page article with these words:

Okay, let's take the gloves off. This insurrection didn't just happen. It was set up — just as the assassination of Martin Luther King was a set-up. The Communists and their Black Power fanatics have been working to create just such a situation for years. They even *told* us what they were planning to do, again and again, as they did it.

This is only the beginning! And, this time the Administration used only seventy thousand troops to stop them. This time our politicians who have tied the hands of our police officers put only ten million or so good citizens under house arrest — employing curfews enforced by federal soldiers. This time the insurrectionists hit only 168 towns and cities; they killed only forty-three people; and, they set only three thousand or so major fires.

And remember, the Reds and their Black Power troops have promised us that this is only the beginning! Stokely has said that his forces plan to burn down America.

They're sure going to try.

How do you stop it? It's very simple. You stop Communist racial agitation; you arrest the leaders for conspiracy to commit murder, arson, and burglary, prove their guilt in a court of law, and lock them up; and, you free the hands of our police so that they can *prevent* rioting and looting and arson by those citizens now convinced by the actions of our "Liberals" that theft, incendiarism, and assault will be tolerated.

Don't kid yourself. The people who are behind all of this mean to have a civil war. We either stop them now or they will escalate this thing. (*American Opinion Magazine,* June 1968)

Also on my desk as I returned from abroad was the new volume entitled *The Law Breakers — America's Number One Domestic Problem,* by the brilliant young editor of the *Indianapolis News,* Mr. Stanton Evans. I give you the opening paragraphs:

> Americans in this second half of the twentieth century have been told, with some justice, that they never had it so good. By every material standard, ours is the richest society on earth. We have higher personal incomes, more consumer goods, less poverty, and more leisure than any other nation known to history. And our government has set about, through a variety of programs in every field of human effort, to supply deficiencies in the web of comfort.

> Yet if in that sense we never had it so good, in another sense we never had it so bad. Or so scared. Precisely as we have achieved our present affluence, precisely as our government has proclaimed its readiness to spread the good things more widely still, the nation is clawed by nameless apprehensions. Richer than any other generation of Americans, we are also more frightened. Blessed with better food, finer clothes, and more expensive cars, we are also haunted by the fear that the enjoyment of these things might be taken from us by mirauders who stalk our streets and attack our homes.

> The paradox is of the sort suggested by the Pennsylvania Dutch saying, "The faster I run, the behinder I get." The faster we multiply our material comforts, the greater seems the likelihood of losing them through hoodlum terror. The more our government suggests we are advancing toward utopia, the more we stumble backward toward the jungle. We are a people for whom anything seems possible — except to defend ourselves against primitive evils which the rudest of societies can control. . . .

> The people of the United States are fast losing one of their most precious rights — the simple right to move as they please, to go to church meetings at night, to shop where and when they would like, to take walks near their homes. . . .

> A survey conducted by the Crime Commission found that one-third of a representative sample of all Americans say it is unsafe to walk alone at night in their neighborhoods. Slightly more than one-third say they keep firearms in the house for protection against criminals. Twenty-eight per cent say they keep watchdogs for the same reason. (*The Law Breakers,* Evans, Stanton M. & Moore, Margaret, Arlington House, New Rochelle, N.Y.)

There is not time for a full outline of this treacherous development. We have mentioned briefly the help which the communists have received from our Supreme Court. Suffice it to say that they have penetrated every major segment of our society, as J. Edgar Hoover has testified — the news media, the schools, the churches, the unions, etc. But their greatest desire and most successful drive has come from their effective penetration of government.[8]

They knew the power, prestige, influence and finances that would be theirs once they got the machinery of the United States government headed in their direction. And they were right. For let the government of the United States stop helping communism and communists all over the world, and in a short period of time the conspiracy would be in retreat and in due time would collapse.

But we extend the advantage of diplomatic recognition to their puppets when they come to power. We send them billions in foreign aid. We've trained their pilots. We ship them wheat. Through cultural and other exchanges their spies come to America. We supply them know-how. We extend them credit. We buy their goods. Their propaganda goes through our mails at our expense. We've helped them in their conquests through secret agreements. Our government does all it can to keep the anti-communists from coming to power in any country.

And once we've helped the communists to take over a nation such as China and Cuba, we do all in our power to keep the anti-communists from freeing their land. We even negotiate with these butchers and sign treaties with these criminals who have no respect for treaties. Said President McKay:

---

[8]"It is sometimes said that the Communist penetration of the United States Government, while sensational, was after all comparatively small. The comparison is with the thousands of loyal Government employes. I think this is a poor yardstick. Effectiveness, not numbers, is a more accurate measure of the infiltration. But even if numbers are the yardstick, I am inclined to believe, from what I saw of the operation through my relatively small peephole, that the Communist penetration was numerically great." (Whittaker Chambers, former Communist; *Witness,* p. 32)

"I would not deal with a nation which treats another as Russia has treated America. It is a condition which cannot be permitted to exist." (President David O. McKay, *Statements on Communism and the Constitution,* p. 18) But it does exist and every day brings in new evidence of the increasing help which our government extends the communists.

The vast majority of American citizens and federal employees are loyal to our republic. But there are a few traitors whose numbers are growing and who are in key positions to influence and help shape government policy. *In fact, it is becoming increasingly apparent that appointment to high government office is not hampered by one's past affiliations with communist fronts or one's ability to follow the communist line. You don't need to look further than the President's cabinet and recent appointments to the Supreme Court to find ample evidence of this fact.* Parrot the communist line and you can expect to be glamorized by the liberal news media and pushed to the front. But take a strong anti-communist position and you can expect to be passed over, smeared and silenced. And this has happened and is happening to too many great and distinguished Americans to be accidental.

Now mind you, the communists could not do this all by themselves. They knew that communism would also have to be built by non-communist hands. So, as in the past, they use, to suit their purpose, the misguided idealist, the political opportunists, the dupes and fellow travelers, and the ignorant and apathetic Americans.

Nor does the communist always deal in totally black instrumentalities — especially when he is trying to come to power. He must deceive. He must produce counterfeits. He must be willing at times to take one step backward, especially when it pacifies people about his past advances and makes it easier for him to take his next two steps forward.

---

⁹See: *The Unelected,* by Gary Allen (American Opinion, June 1968, p. 81), *The Usurpers,* by Dr. Medford Evans (Western Islands, Boston & Los Angeles), *Congressional Record,* July 15, 1965, pp. 16466-7, and *Congressional Record,* August 9, 1965, p. 18995.

He knows that some of his greatest successes have come with programs which have been sold to the American public as ways to fight the communists but which in reality had the net effect of promoting communism. This has been true of our foreign aid program. Designed, supposedly, to help nations, its overall effect has been to keep socialist governments in business, enhance the communists, discourage free enterprise, and demoralize the anti-communists.

Another illustration is the war in Vietnam. We're supposed to be fighting the communists in Vietnam, yet we're helping them everywhere else. Why do we trade with communist countries and supply them the means with which to kill our sons? Why do we build plants for them? We ship them machinery, metals, chemicals, rubber, airborne equipment, and many other things for their war machine. In return we get back coffins — hundreds of them per week.

We cancelled a seventeen million dollar debt which the Polish Communist Government owed us on the very day a Polish ship pulled into Haiphong Harbor with war materials to kill our men. On one side of Stettin Harbor in Poland they unload the wheat we send them and on the other side of the harbor they load their ships with equipment to kill our men in Vietnam.

Why not let our men win in Vietnam? Why handcuff them? In war there is no substitute for victory. We've been pouring tens of billions into defense for years. Is it possible that we cannot win a war against a third rate country of 17 million people smaller than the State of Missouri? Honest and competent military men have stated that we could win the war in six weeks or less.

What can you do, you ask? Listen to the conclusion of a shocking article every American should read, by Wallis W. Wood, Coordinator for TRAIN Committees (To Restore American Independence Now):

> What can one person do? You can try to match the determination of Lieutenant Colonel Wilbur Outlaw of North Carolina. He is a twenty-five-year veteran of the U.S. Air Force. His oldest

son, Bill, is now a helicopter pilot in South Vietnam, and in the past nine months has been shot down once and strafed several times. In a recent letter to his family from Vietnam, he urged:

> "Tell those . . . fools back home that there is a war going on over here and they'd better start doing something about it, either by signing those petitions or by getting the powers that be (which is probably impossible) to start fighting a war instead of playing Mickey Mouse games. I feel sure that every one else over here is as tired as I am of being shot at and knowing they can't do anything about it most of the time."

As Bill's father told me: "I spent twenty-five years trying to defend my country; now I'm going to spend the rest of my life trying to save it."

What can you do? You can help protect the lives of your fellow Americans — the 500,000 super-patriots fighting Communism in Vietnam. You can get to work with TRAIN, or on your own, to help stop this treasonous aid and trade with the enemy — and insist on the removal of the restrictions on our military. If not? Well, if not mister, go back to sleep. But don't call yourself an American. (*American Opinion Magazine,* May)

What can you do? Hear the pleading warning and counsel of a Mormon elder, an Air Force Captain, in the following letter:

APO San Francisco
26 March 1968

Elder Ezra Taft Benson
of the Council of the Twelve

Dear Sir:

I am an Air Force Captain serving in (..........................) Republic of Vietnam. I have a wife and three young sons living in (.....................) whom I love very deeply and for whom I want to secure the freedom that I have thus far enjoyed. In discussions with members and non-members alike who are caught up in this war, I've found a unifying fear concerning the destiny of our country, a fear which I feel confident that you and many church leaders share. Since this is an election year, and a very crucial year for the future of our nation, I'd like to do more than I am presently doing to further the cause of freedom.

I've attached a letter which I've prepared intending to express thoughts which our elders must employ with their own members if we're to survive the present challenge to our nation. Certainly I'd like to go into greater detail with them about the communist threat . . . but what I've written may be useful.

As a member of the Armed Forces I cannot actively participate in the political destiny of my country; but as an elder in The Church of Jesus Christ of Latter-day Saints, I am obligated to watch over the Church and to do what I can to protect the liberty that God has given us. Therefore, I write the accompanying letter, hoping that it might have some use in convincing the priesthood of their pressing obligation to the cause of freedom.

Then he signed his name and attached this letter, which is addressed to the priesthood of The Church of Jesus Christ of Latter-day Saints:

Dear Brethren:

We in Vietnam, who are struggling and dying that men and women, you and your loved ones, might maintain the free agency which thousands before us have died to protect; are deeply concerned with the state of our beloved nation. . . .

The news that comes to us from home is disheartening. While we endeavor to assist in securing freedom for a weak and tottering nation, but a nation filled with people desirous of freedom, the greatest nation of all, our homeland, now overflowing with selfish and materialistic millions, is staggering clumsily but steadily toward the clutches of self-imposed slavery. How sincerely we cry to our countrymen in words similar to those of our Master who cried,

"O Jerusalem, Jerusalem, . . . how often would I have gathered thy children together, even as a hen gathereth her chickens under her wings, and ye would not! Behold, your house is left unto you desolate." (Matthew 23:37-38)
Dear Brethren, we stand upon the very threshold of calamity . . .

Brethren, truly our freedom hangs by a thread, and if we wish to keep it then we, the elders of Israel, must now step forward to preserve it.

I am a soldier. I am doing what I can to help. You are free and educated citizens capable of guiding our country's destiny. How can you do it? Your local political organizations need your support and your participation. Your newspapers need your opinions. Your representatives in your state and national legislatures need your continuing support, interest, and advice. . . . We know only too well the consequences if we fail to meet the challenge before us. It is time to act, to be doers and not hearers only. We plead with you from this the dark side of the earth. Put your shoulders to the wheel and push with your might. . . .

Are there advantages to the communists of our being involved in a long no-win war? Can it eventually be converted into World War III? Can it be used to create bitterness, confusion and a breakdown in American morale? Can it be used as an excuse to institute greater socialistic controls over the people — to weaken our economy? Can it be used to get the American people to accept peace on almost any terms?

If we really mean to oppose communist aggression, why did we pick distant Vietnam instead of Cuba? We had the Monroe Doctrine before there ever was a U.N. or a SEATO. If our government leaders are really opposed to communism, why don't they start cleaning them out at home?

Why do they allow the Office of Economic Opportunity to be the means of providing finances and programs for the communist revolutionaries and their allies who plan to ravish and burn down America.

Yes, communism is tightening its stranglehold on America and the world because of the help it is receiving increasingly from right within our own government. Americans are destroying America.

And so I return to the grave warning of the inspired Book of Mormon:

> And whatsoever nation shall uphold such secret combinations, to get power and gain, until they shall spread over the nation, behold they shall be destroyed.

God grant that we may repent prayerfully, study the Book of Mormon, follow the Prophet, do our homework, and wake up in time to reverse the tragic course we are following, I humbly pray.[10]

---

[10]"Let me say that it is with you, the people to advance the great cause of the Union and the constitution, and not with any one man. It rests with you alone. . . . If all do not join now and save the good old ship of the Union [on] this voyage nobody will have a chance to pilot her on another voyage." (Abraham Lincoln, Feb. 15, 1861; *Collected Works* 4:215-6)

APPENDIXES

Appendix I

THE CREED OF OUR POLITICAL FAITH [1]

Thomas Jefferson

About to enter, fellow citizens, on the exercise of duties which comprehend everything dear and valuable to you, it is proper that you should understand what I deem *the essential principles of our government,* and consequently those which ought to shape its administration. I will compress them within the narrowest compass they will bear, stating the general principle, but not all its limitations. Equal and exact justice to all men, of whatever state or persuasion, religious or political; peace, commerce, and honest friendship, with all nations — entangling alliances with none; the support of the state governments in all their rights, as the most competent administrations for our domestic concerns and the surest bulwarks against anti-republican tendencies; the preservation of the general government in its whole constitutional vigor, as the sheet anchor of our peace at home and safety abroad; a jealous care of the right of election by the people — a mild and safe corrective of abuses which are lopped by the sword of the revolution where peaceable remedies are unprovided; absolute acquiescence in the decisions of the majority — the vital principle of republics, from which there is no appeal but to force, the vital principle and immediate parent of despotism; a well-disciplined militia — our best reliance in peace and for the first moments of war, till regulars may relieve them; the supremacy of the civil over the military authority; economy in the public expense, that labor may be lightly burdened; the honest payment of our debts and sacred preservation of the public faith; encouragement of agriculture, and of commerce

[1]*"The principles of Jefferson are the definitions and axioms of free society. And yet they are denied, and evaded, with no small show of success. . . . Soberly, it is now no child's play to save the principles of Jefferson from total overthrow in this nation." (Abraham Lincoln, April 6, 1859; Collected Works 3:375)

as its handmaiden; the diffusion of information and the arraignment of all abuses at the bar of public reason; freedom of religion; freedom of the press; freedom of person under the protection of the *habeas corpus;* and trial by juries impartially selected — these principles form the bright constellation which has gone before us, and guided our steps through an age of revolution and reformation. The wisdom of our sages and the blood of our heroes have been devoted to their attainment. They should be *the creed of our political faith — the text of civil instruction — the touchstone by which to try the services of those we trust;* and should we wander from them in moments of error or alarm, let us hasten to retrace our steps and to regain the road which alone leads to peace, liberty, and safety.   (First Inaugural Address, March 4, 1801; *Works* 8:4-5)

Appendix II

WARNING TO CHURCH MEMBERS [1]

The First Presidency

With great regret we learn from credible sources, governmental and others, that a few Church members are joining directly or indirectly, the communists and are taking part in their activities.

The Church does not interfere, and has no intention of trying to interfere with the fullest and freest exercise of the political franchise of its members, under and within our Constitution which the Lord declared: "I established . . . by the hands of wise men whom I raised up unto this very purpose," and which, as to the principles thereof, the Prophet, dedicating the Kirtland Temple, prayed should be "established forever."

But *Communism is not a political party nor a political plan under the Constitution; it is a system of government that is the opposite of our Constitutional government,* and it would be necessary to destroy our government before Communism could be set up in the United States.

Since Communism, established, would destroy our American Constitutional government, *to support Communism is treasonable* to our free institutions, and no patriotic American citizen may become either a Communist or supporter of Communism.

To our Church members we say: Communism is not the United Order, and bears only the most superficial resemblance thereto; Communism is based upon intolerance and force, the United Order upon love and freedom of conscience and action;

---

[1]This warning was published as an editorial in the August 1936 issue of *The Improvement Era.*

Communism involves forceful despoliation of confiscation, the United Order voluntary consecration and sacrifice.

Communists cannot establish the United Order, nor will Communism bring it about. The United Order will be established by the Lord in His own due time and in accordance with the regular prescribed order of the Church.

Furthermore, it is charged by universal report, which is not successfully contradicted or disproved, that Communism undertakes to control, if not indeed to prescribe the religious life of the people living within its jurisdiction, and that it even reaches into the sanctity of the family circle itself, disrupting the normal relationship of parent and child, all in a manner unknown and unsanctioned under the Constitutional guarantees under which we in America live. Such interference would be contrary to the fundamental precepts of the Gospel and to the teachings and order of the Church.

Communism being thus hostile to loyal American citizenship and incompatible with true Church membership, of necessity no loyal American citizen and no faithful Church member can be a Communist.

We call upon all Church members completely to eschew Communism. The safety of our divinely inspired Constitutional government and the welfare of our Church imperatively demand that Communism shall have no place in America.

Signed: Heber J. Grant

Signed: J. Reuben Clark, Jr.

Signed: David O. McKay

Appendix III

STATEMENT CONCERNING THE POSITION
OF THE CHURCH ON COMMUNISM [1]

President David O. McKay

In order that there may be no misunderstanding by bishops, stake presidents, and others regarding members of the Church participating in non-church meetings to study and become informed on the Constitution of the United States, Communism, etc., I wish to make the following statements that I have been sending out from my office for some time and that have come under question by some stake authorities, bishoprics, and others.

Church members are at perfect liberty to act according to their own consciences in the matter of safeguarding our way of life. They are, of course, encouraged to honor the highest standards of the gospel and to work to preserve their own freedoms. They are free to participate in nonchurch meetings that are held to warn people of the threat of Communism or any other theory or principle that will deprive us of our free agency or individual liberties vouchsafed by the Constitution of the United States.

The Church, out of respect for the rights of all its members to have their political views and loyalties, *must maintain the strictest possible neutrality.* We have no intention of trying to interfere with the fullest and freest exercise of the political franchise of our members under and within our Constitution, which the Lord declared he established "by the hands of wise men whom [he] raised up unto this very purpose" (D&C 101:80) and which, as to the principles thereof, the Prophet Joseph Smith, dedicating the Kirtland Temple, prayed should

[1]Statement read at the general priesthood session of the annual general conference of The Church of Jesus Christ of Latter-day Saints, April 9, 1966)

be "established forever." (D&C 109:54) The Church does not yield any of its devotion to or convictions about safeguarding the American principles and the establishments of government under federal and state constitutions and the civil rights of men safeguarded by these.

The position of this Church on the subject of Communism has never changed. We consider it the greatest satanical threat to peace, prosperity, and the spread of God's work among men that exists on the face of the earth.

In this connection, we are continually being asked to give our opinion concerning various patriotic groups or individuals who are fighting Communism and speaking up for freedom. Our immediate concern, however, is not with parties, groups, or persons, but with principles. *We therefore commend and encourage every person and every group who is sincerely seeking to study Constitutional principles and awaken a sleeping and apathetic people to the alarming conditions that are rapidly advancing about us. We wish all of our citizens throughout the land were participating in some type of organized self-education in order that they could better appreciate what is happening and know what they can do about it.*

Supporting the FBI, the police, the congressional committee investigating Communism, and various organizations that are attempting to awaken the people through educational means is a policy we warmly endorse for all our people.

The entire concept and philosophy of Communism is diametrically opposed to everything for which the Church stands — *belief in Deity, belief in the dignity and eternal nature of man, and the application of the gospel to efforts for peace in the world.* Communism is militantly atheistic and is committed to the destruction of faith wherever it may be found.

The Russian Commissioner of Education wrote: "We must hate Christians and Christianity. Even the best of them must be considered our worst enemies. Christian love is an obstacle to the development of the revolution. Down with love for one's neighbor. What we want is hate. Only then shall we conquer the universe."

On the other hand, the gospel teaches the existence of God as our Eternal and Heavenly Father and declares: " . . . him only shalt thou serve." (Matt. 4:10)

Communism debases the individual and makes him the enslaved tool of the state, to which he must look for sustenance and religion. Communism destroys man's God-given free agency.

No member of this Church can be true to his faith, nor can any American be loyal to his trust, while lending aid, encouragement, or sympathy to any of these false philosophies; for if he does, they will prove snares to his feet.

INDEX

Monroe, James, 241; proclaims Monroe Doctrine, 242.
Monroe Doctrine, 241-5; basic principles of, 242; development of, 241; ignored today, 51, 96, 244; new application of needed, 245; policy of self-defense, 243-5; proclaiming of, 242; when to be applied, 245.
Montesquieu, abuse of power, 178; danger of apathy, 297.
Moral erosion, evidences of, 7.
Moral law, applies to all, 144; basis of free governments, x, 4, 143; unchangeable, x.
Morality, America's security depends on, vii; disintegration of, 50; lack of destroys nations, ix; lack of greatest problem, 6, 120; return to vital, 13.
Moreell, Admiral Ben, spiritual rebirth needed, 122.
Mormon, 329.
Mormon Tabernacle, communist performs in, 309.
Moroni, 304; a mighty man, 315; America a choice land, 330; America to serve God or perish, 118; raises title of liberty, 314-5, 321; test of Holy Ghost, 294; secret combinations, 333; warning to America, 118, 331.
Moses, commanded to proclaim liberty, 324.
Mullendore, W. C., quotes Supreme Court decision, 228.
Mussolini, referred to, 68.

- N -

Naked Communist, The, recommended by President McKay, 44; quoted from, 166.
Narcotics, America biggest market for, 7.
National Committee For Economic Freedom, address of, 225.
National leaders, responsible for America's problems, 9.
National police force, opposed, 199; tool of despotism, 199.
National Program Letter, referred to, 209, 211.
National Strategy Committee, members of, 165; quoted, 165.
Nationalism, current derision of, 156; meaning of, 155-6.
Nationhood, end of recommended, 175-6.
Navigation, thrives when free, 255.
Nazism, communism similar to, 67; totalitarian, 67.
Necking, to be avoided, 288.
Negroes, not to be blamed, 197; priesthood withheld from, 190.
Negroes in a Soviet America, referred to, 192.

Neither Liberty Nor Safety, quoted from, 98, 174, 175.
Nephi, all is well in Zion, 277, 315; devil rages in hearts, 290; precepts of men, 189; referred to, 304; trust not arm of flesh, 189.
Nestorenko, Aleskie, 180.
Neutrality, Church maintains, 349; none in heaven or earth, 276.
Neutralizers, examples of, 314-6.
New Role of National Legislative Bodies in the Communist Conspiracy, referred to, 195.
New York Times, The, quoted from, 168, 169.
Newquist, Jerreld L., book compiled by, 286; Preface written by, xi-xv.
News-Advertiser, quoted from, 47.
Ninth Amendment, quoted, 204.
No Substitute for Victory, quoted from, 167.
No-win policy, briefly stated, 181; cleverly coordinated, 64; increases chances for war, 182; increases losses, 182.
Noah, days of, 306.
North Vietnam, free world aid to, 76.
Nuclear blackmail, cannot be disregarded, 206.
Nuclear war, reality of threat, 206.

- O -

Obedience, brings blessings, 55.
Office of Economic Opportunity, finance revolutionaries, 342.
On Moral Duties, quoted from, 58, 126, 137, 227, 283.
Oppenheimer, Dr. Julius, contributes to Communist Party, 69.
Opportunity, America a land of, 26.
Oppression, example of, 132.
Optimism, needed by all patriots, 59.
Organizations, Church's support of, 350; come to aid of, 298; more effective, 44; need for joining of, 111; type to support, 291.
Oswald, Lee Harvey, communist affiliations of, 32; assassinates Kennedy, 67; requested John Abt, 65.
Otepka, Otto, sacrifice of, 103.

- P -

Paarlberg, Dr. Don, agreed with, 249.
Page, Apostle John E., 290.
Paine, Thomas, origin of rights, 128; times that try men's souls, 12-13, 147.
Paper money, redeemable, 220; irredeemable, 145; to become worthless, 217.
Parable of Virgins, referred to, 59.
Passman, Representative Otto E., 210.
Paternalism, increase of, 8; lessons of to be unlearned, 250.

Statesmen, advice to, 126; all people should be, 147; stand for principles, 126.

Statism, increase of, 8.

Steinbeck, John, how to destroy a nation, 120.

Stevenson, Adlai, quoted, 176.

Straight Talk, quoted from, 120.

Strength, not from irresolution, 87.

Strikes, at missile bases, 7.

Study groups, needed, 44.

Subsidies, refusal of, 250.

Success, greatest danger in, 281; none compensates for failure in home, 57.

Success, quoted from, 146.

Suffer Little Children, referred to, 284.

Suicide, civilizations die by, 51.

Suitcases, bombs brought in, 206-7.

Summit Conferences, 105.

Supply and demand, natural laws of, 235.

Supreme Court, 262-8; quoted, 24, 228; communist threat ignored by, 264; congressional protest to, 31; decisions aid communism, 264; decisions destroy Constitution, 262; effect of decisions, 262, 332, 333; grapple for power, 266; honored by communists, 68, 104, 308, 333; hostile attitude toward police, 5; impeachment of, 31, 267; interpreting the Constitution, 266; leading nation to atheism, 104, 308; Lincoln on decisions of, 262; people master of, 268; punches holes in Constitution, 104; result of decisions, 264; soft-on-crime decisions, 198; undermining Constitution, 333; undermines rights of states, 266.

Surrender, blueprint for, 174-180; favored by students, 284.

Survey, results of, 10.

Survival, action needed for, 264; design for, 171; fighting for, 264; issue of, 91; requirements for, 11; suggestions for, 197.

Suslov, Vladimir, 180.

- T -

Taft, Senator Robert A., other policies depend on foreign policy, 149-150; policy of free hand, 155; purpose of foreign policy, 150-1, 164.

Talley, Judge Alfred J., the demand of the hour, 263.

Taylor, General Maxwell D., opposes unlimited bombing, 183.

Taylor, Henry J., 222.

Taylor, John, a mission to preserve freedom, 292.

Taxation, 222-5; freedom diminished by, 255; increase of, 8, 21; justification for, 145; light when government honest, 222; power over man's will, 224; power to destroy, 225; progressive, 224; reduction of, 225; robbery of, 228; ruthless extortion, 146; socialism measured by, 255-6; unwillingness to pay, 222.

Tchernychev, Ilya, 179.

Teachings of the Prophet Joseph Smith, The, quoted from, 330.

Teheran Conference, 94.

Tenth Amendment, quoted, 204, 231.

Test, coming, 291.

Test-Ban Treaty, foolishness of, 79.

Theodore Roosevelt Cyclopedia, quoted from, 187.

This Week, referred to, 284.

Thoreau, Henry D., government hinders progress, 138.

Thoughts, clean, 289.

Three Witnesses, left Church, 290.

Thucydides, quotes Pericles, 116.

Thurmond, Senator Strom, praises capitalism, 20; quotes Walt Rostow, 38.

Time, balancing of, 276.

Tito, loyal to Moscow, 75; U. S. aid to, 68.

Titusville Herald, quoted from, 84.

Timothy, quoted from, 308.

Totalitarianism, examples of, 67; true meaning of, 67; U. S. on road to, 101.

Tower of Babel, 329.

Trade, Lenin's prediction on, 71; examples of, 72; treason and, 63; with communism, 69.

TRAIN Committees, 339-340.

Traitors, actions of, 63.

Treason, defined, 81, 145; nation cannot survive, 63; trade and, 63.

Treaties, legitimate objects of, 146; made to be broken, 79.

True, bound to be, 299.

Trust, liberty and, 204.

Truth, arrived at by free debate, 37; contrasted with repose, 15; feared by communists, 111; ignored, 66; most effective weapon, 111; must be repeated, 15; not established by Gallup polls, 282; people entitled to, 52; proves itself, 285; self-evident, 129; strife with falsehood, 271; though unpleasant must be told, 63; time on side of, 15, 60, 61; will prevail, 15; will someday be in majority, 60.

Twining, General Nathan F., accommodation policy, 98; disarmament won't eliminate war, 175; major crisis coming, 177; views on security planning, 174.

Two contending forces, battling for supremacy, 274; eternal struggle between, 66; individual versus state, 275; a world-wide battle, 112.